Foster Family Care for Persons With Mental Retardation

Monographs of the American Association On Mental Retardation, 17

Michael J. Begab, Series Editor

Foster Family Care for Persons With Mental Retardation

by

Sharon A. Borthwick-Duffy

Keith F. Widaman

Todd D. Little

Richard K. Eyman

University of California at Riverside

Published by
American Association On Mental Retardation
1719 Kalorama Road, NW
Washington, DC 20009-2683

The points of view expressed herein are those of the authors and do not necessarily represent the official policy or opinion of the American Association On Mental Retardation. Publication does not imply endorsement by the Editor, the Association, or its individual members.

Authors' Note: The first two authors shared equally in their contribution to the writing of this monograph and have therefore been listed in alphabetical order.

This study was supported by grants HD72847, HD14688, and HD22953 from the National Institute of Child Health and Human Development.

No. 17, Monographs of the American Association On Mental Retardation (ISSN 0895-8009)

Library of Congress Cataloging-in-Publication Data
Borthwick-Duffy, Sharon A., 1950–
  Foster family care for persons with mental retardation / Sharon A. Borthwick-Duffy and Keith F. Widaman, with Todd D. Little, Richard K. Eyman
    p.   cm. — (Monographs of the American Association On Mental Retardation, ISSN 0895-8009 ; 17)
  Includes bibliographical references.
  ISBN 0-940898-27-6 : $24.95
  1. Mentally handicapped—Home care—California, Southern—Case studies. 2. Foster home care—California, Southern—Case studies. I. Widaman, Keith F. II. Title. III. Series.
HV3006.C2B67 1992
362.3'8—dc20

91-47961
CIP

Table of Contents

Foreword

If you could read only one book on "Foster Family Care" for persons with mental retardation, I would recommend that it be this book. Why? Because the authors have a reputation for being meticulous researchers who have an uncanny ability to conduct complex analyses of a given topic and then report their findings in a practical manner that allows for systematic application. That is, these authors have accomplished a formidable task in the writing of this monograph, as fellow researchers in this area of study will readily recognize.

Very few books are as thoroughly referenced as this one. These authors validate their findings and recommendations via a thorough review of the literature. In addition, the Appendix presents and summarizes the technical material required to examine their statistical analyses in detail. However, placing this information in an Appendix enables the authors to maintain a fluid writing style in the body of the monograph, assisting the reader to focus on the key issues.

We are given few things in life that are of greater responsibility (or joy) than the raising of our children. Because of this, we need answers—what to do, how to do it, and why. What is provided best in this book is the identification of factors associated with optimal development and improved quality of life for children with developmental disabilities in the foster family care setting. The objective of this three-year study was to isolate characteristics of individuals and foster home environments that are likely to affect the persons' development and quality of life. At least some of the answers we seek are provided in this monograph.

As we continue to emphasize community residential placement of persons with mental retardation, our focus must be on what are the best, most appropriate settings for these individuals. Certainly, foster family care homes can closely approximate environments found in natural homes, allowing an excellent mode of conducting research in this area. In addition, such research also has implications for model development involving children who do not have developmental disabilities. The reading of this monograph is particularly useful as it provides an excellent example of conducting research on foster family care via the presentation of a family care design, research samples, and survey instruments used in the evaluation and analysis process itself. As we continue to place individuals in the community and our population ages, we will experience a rapidly growing need for careproviders as more families choose to utilize the foster care system. Indeed, in major geographic areas, foster care homes are in such great demand that decisions to place clients are often made on a space available basis rather than by selecting providers who have adaptable characteristics. However, in situations where the selection of caregivers and homes is possible, the results of this monograph provide useful criteria for placement that will optimize the development and quality of life of people living in foster family care homes.

The concept of "quality of life" for persons with mental retardation has virtually exploded upon the research scene during the last five years. Quality of life is moving from being a "buzz word" and popular concept to being a solid, researched-based outcome in its own right. The attention to this topic in the monograph is perhaps its strongest contribution. The general issues and research findings on quality of life for all levels and ages of persons with mental retardation are thoroughly reviewed. Then, a comprehensive quality of life model is presented and validated based on the data obtained in the Family Care Study. Unique to this study, dimensions of quality of life are viewed both as outcomes and as potential influences on the development of adaptive behavior.

This scientific analysis of foster family care should serve as a seminal work, providing a solid foundation for future research.

Jack A. Stark, President
American Association On Mental Retardation

_____ Acknowledgments

The Foster Family Care Study was conceptualized and conducted with the help of a number of people who were not involved in the writing of this monograph. Without their contribution and insights, we would not be as confident that our findings represent a well-designed and carefully executed research investigation. As project coordinator, Dr. Jennie Lei was responsible for managing the complexities of following a large sample over a two-year period. Dr. Lyly Nihira was instrumental in all issues related to careproviders; she developed the _Careprovider Preference Survey_, and has played an important role in the interpretation of findings. Dr. C. E. Meyers was also a key investigator in the study. His contribution focused on the measurement of the home environment, but his wisdom and expertise were appreciated in all areas of the study. Nancy Sheehy, Greg Legutki, Sue Wilson, and Stephanie LaBarr comprised the core team of research associates whose dedication and professional commitment to the field of mental retardation added significantly to the quality of the Foster Family Care Study.

We are grateful to Dr. Michael Begab for his support of a study such as the one reported here, and especially for his patience and guidance throughout the writing of the monograph. We also gratefully acknowledge the work of Karen Fleck, Justina Powers, and Fran Tepper throughout the writing and editing process.

We extend our sincere appreciation to the staff of the Inland Regional Center, and to the careproviders and parents of the individuals whose lives were the focus of this study. It is our hope that this monograph will lead to an improved quality of life for individuals with mental retardation, regardless of where they live.

Chapter 1

The Study Setting: Foster Family Care

The study reported in this monograph focused on factors that influence the development and quality of life of people with mental retardation. The objective of the three-year Family Care Study was to isolate characteristics of the individual and home environment that were likely to affect development and quality of life and yet were unaffected by differences in licensing or other system-related standards associated with a particular type of setting.

One residence type, foster family care, was the setting for all individuals studied. There were several reasons for this. First, among the community residential alternatives, family care homes are the most similar to natural homes, and yet, like other placement alternatives, they have the challenges of being an out-of-home placement. A second benefit of studying people in foster family care is that these individuals represent a relatively heterogeneous group of people who have mental retardation, spanning all levels of retardation, ages, abilities, and handicaps (Borthwick, Meyers, & Eyman, 1981; Borthwick-Duffy, Eyman, & White, 1987; Eyman & Borthwick, 1980). Family foster care was selected also because of its historical background and parallel model within child welfare programs for children who do not have mental retardation.

Finally, an important methodological advantage of limiting the study to just one residence type is that the unique characteristics of each home are emphasized and the findings are not confounded by differences in the basic philosophies and administrative structures of various setting types. This design avoids problems associated with placement selection bias. The literature stresses that without random assignment to residence types, it is impossible to evaluate the effects of different program models on individual outcomes (Butterfield, 1985; Conroy, Efthimiau, & Lemanowicz, 1982; Heal, Sigelman, & Switzky, 1978). Butterfield (1985) identified the placement process as being the chief source of bias in studies of special living arrangements, observing that:

> Differences between persons assigned non-randomly to different arrangements are at least as likely to be the reasons why they were assigned as they are to be the results of the living environment or of an interaction between the environment and their pre-existing characteristics. The lack

of random assignment always defeats the scientific purpose of comparing people in differing living environments (p. 3).

Given the presence of constraints that precluded non-random assignment, individuals residing in one residence type, foster family care, were examined and the unique characteristics of each home, i.e., characteristics that were not associated with the family care program model, were described as carefully as possible.

The variability within broad classifications of residences has been documented throughout the literature. Landesman-Dwyer (1985) reported that simply knowing an individual lives in a particular setting conveys very little about the physical or functional qualities of the environment. She further noted that across different states the same terms are used to identify very different types of programs and cited foster care as an example. In some states, foster care refers to natural families, usually with two parents, that have one or two individuals with mental retardation who become additional family members. In other states, such as California where the study took place, foster family care homes differ slightly from that model in that single adults are allowed to provide care for as many as six individuals with mental retardation, as their primary means of income.

Although Landesman-Dwyer's comments regarding differences in foster care models across states are well taken, the basic philosophy behind foster family care and the reasons for current trends toward using this kind of placement are similar, even across states, i.e., foster family care is viewed as the most reasonable substitute for the natural home because it is most like it.

The study was not an investigation of the foster care model per se; rather, it was a study of the influences of various environmental characteristics and caregiving styles on a heterogeneous group of children and adolescents who lived in small family-like settings. However, since residential care models differ according to philosophy, purpose, and general administrative structure, and since the foster family care system for individuals with mental retardation has a unique history that has shaped current programs, an historical overview is presented in the remainder of this chapter.

HISTORY OF AND RATIONALE FOR FOSTER FAMILY CARE PROGRAMS

Family foster care programs date back to the middle ages, when the citizens of Gheel, Belgium utilized community residential care for people with mental retardation and mental illness. For the most part, this residential placement resembled the family care programs of today, with the individuals with mental retardation being involved in family life and community activity. However, despite its continued success, the program was not widely accepted because of difficulties that resulted from the inappropriate placements of some individuals who had mental retardation in addition to severe emotional and health disorders (Scheerenberger, 1983).

Several European countries incorporated family care programs into their mental retardation residential service systems in the late 19th century. At about the same time, the United States was experimenting with family care for non-handicapped children, but was not ready to extend this option to people with mental retardation.

Foster Family Care for Non-retarded Children

Use of the foster family care model in the United States grew from a need for substitute parental care for non-retarded children who came from chronically deprived, lower class families who were living in substandard conditions (*Encyclopedia of Social Work*, 1987). Charles Loring Brace and the New York Children's Aid Society pioneered efforts in the 1850s to provide rural foster home care for children with normal intelligence who lived in impoverished areas of New York City. Following the Civil War, a similar, yet more professional approach to indenturing was established under the leadership of Samuel Gridley Howe, who arranged for inmates of state operated almshouses to live with and work for families in nearby communities. Thus, the concept of foster family care grew from the need for residential placement alternatives for individuals with a variety of problems, although initially the problems did not include mental retardation.

Residential Schools for Retarded Children

Family care placement was used occasionally in the United States in the 19th century for people with mental retardation, however, the American public was generally unwilling to accept this kind of model for children with mental retardation or mental illness (*Encyclopedia of Social Work*, 1977). In fact, it was Samuel Gridley Howe, who, while establishing family care programs for poor non-retarded children, had other plans for children with mental retardation. Focusing on education and training for this group, Howe labored to establish residential training schools for children who had mental retardation. The purpose of these training institutions was to educate and stimulate "idiotic children" in a humane environment so that they would learn to be more acceptable to society when they completed their schooling and rejoined their families. The idealistic notion that all of these children could be helped and returned home was behind the development of these residential schools (Heal, et al., 1978; Lazerson, 1975; Meyers & Blacher, 1987). Many of the higher functioning individuals who entered institutions for the feebleminded left after a short time, however, it soon became evident that large numbers of people with more serious levels of retardation would not be "cured" by the programs offered and would remain in the institutions indefinitely (Kanner, 1964).

Improvements in Foster Care Programs for Non-retarded People

Foster family care programs for non-handicapped children eventually became the responsibility of child welfare agencies in the community. Child welfare programs were based on the concept of *parens patriae*, which suggests that society has the ultimate parental responsibility for all children in its community (*Encyclopedia of Social Work*, 1977). Therefore, when a child cannot be adequately cared for at home, society will provide adequate, alternate care. In accordance with this concept, formal standards and procedures were adopted to protect all parties involved in family care programs. These programs were a significant improvement over the early indenturing programs.

Early Differences Between Programs for People With and Without Mental Retardation

The child welfare programs emphasized the non-retarded child's need for a family-like home atmosphere, while residential programs for children with mental retardation focused on education and training, with the setting being less important. (Howe did, however, ensure that the children would live in small living units and eat family-style in small groups). It is not surprising, then, that the paths of the two service systems became separated in the earliest stages of foster family care and became even more pronounced as different bureaucratic structures assumed responsibility for the care and residential placement of the two groups (Adams, 1975).

The first White House Conference on the Care of Dependent Children (1909) emphasized the importance of children remaining with their natural families (Adams, 1975). At the conference, child welfare foster family care programs were identified as viable residential alternatives when it was no longer possible for children to remain in their natural homes. Adams (1975) noted, however, that the needs of children with mental retardation were not considered at this time.

Societal Attitudes Toward People with Mental Retardation

Residential placement practices have historically been influenced by the vacillating attitudes of society toward people with mental retardation (Heal et al., 1978). A number of writers (e.g. Heal et al., 1978; Lazerson, 1975) have spoken of what Mercer and Richardson (1975) called a "Public Menace Cycle" from about 1850 to 1930 that was characterized by the intentional segregation of people with mental retardation in state operated homes and by public pressure to prevent re-entry into the community. As a result, Howe's training schools and other residential facilities that had initially been established in order to educate children with mental retardation in small groups were subsequently pressured to expand and provide permanent custodial care for many of the residents. An unfortunate dehumanization of institutions also occurred during this period, based on the notion that institutions existed primarily to protect society from the deviant mentally retarded (Lazerson, 1975; Mercer & Richardson, 1975). Institutions were transformed from residential schools into asylums with a custodial ideology, in response to the perception of mental retardation as a social problem.

Lazerson (1975) argues that history must be understood within the social and institutional contexts in which change occurs. Thus, negative societal attitudes as well as the generally agreed upon poor prognosis of people with mental retardation probably had something to do with the needs of these children being overlooked in the early welfare family care programs. The potential for foster family care programs for children with mental retardation was largely ignored by national planning groups. By the time attitudes toward people with mental retardation had shifted to an Education-Welfare emphasis in the 1930s (Mercer & Richardson, 1975) and consideration was given to the re-entry of many of these people into the community, foster family care programs for non-retarded children were already well established.

Introduction of Family Care for People with Mental Retardation: 1920-1940

With decreasing societal fear regarding the re-integration of institutionalized people with mental retardation into the community, a parole plan was established in the United States in the 1920s. Individuals were released from institutions and placed in the community but remained the responsibility of the institutional staff for a period of time after release. These procedural shifts were motivated by a new awareness that people with mental retardation were not a homogeneous population and, therefore, would be served best by different residential services, including foster family care (Fernald, 1919; Scheerenberger, 1983). In the 1930s the first alternate care programs (family care) were established with the state paying for care outside the natural home or institution (Vaux, 1935).

Charles Vaux, superintendent of an institution for people with mental retardation in New Jersey, followed European examples in his attempt to establish a family care program for hospital residents who were selected for placement in a small village of low income families. In 1933, Vaux placed 32 adults of varying intelligence levels with 14 families who received reimbursement for their care. An attractive aspect of the program was the relatively low cost of care compared to institutional costs. By 1936, the family care program initiated by Vaux had tripled in size, and had been expanded to include school-age children as young as five (Scheerenberger, 1983).

Since the initiative for family care placement of people with mental retardation came from the institutions with more progressive-minded directors, this program was established as an offshoot of the institutional model, and was financed by funds from the mental health system, rather than the child welfare bureaucracy. Hence, the expertise and experience of caring for children with mental retardation continued to be the responsibility of social workers in the institutions (Adams, 1975; Bishop, 1959; Vaux, 1935).

Slow Growth of Family Care Model for Mental Retardation: 1940-1960

The initial momentum of foster family care programs for people with mental retardation was not sustained in the 1940s and 1950s for a number of reasons. Potential foster parents became more selective about the people they would accept into their homes and often requested more money for the care they provided. Moreover, while the people being released from institutions were becoming an older, more severely retarded group with multiple disabilities, family care parents wanted younger children with few or no additional handicaps, thus limiting the number of placement options for the majority of these people. Additional problems resulted from the hesitancy of society to welcome these individuals back into the community, e.g., local communities became outspoken about not wanting individuals with mental retardation to live in their neighborhoods. Institutional releases were also resisted by natural families because they believed that the larger state-operated facilities provided a safer, more understanding environment in which their children were protected from ridicule and harm (Scheerenberger, 1983). Similarly, many professionals felt that communities were unprepared to provide adequate facilities, supervision, and programs for people with mental retardation, and that placement outside the institution was not in the best interest of the individual (Intagliata, Crosby, & Neider, 1981).

Adams (1975) outlined five additional theoretical arguments and practical obstacles that may have served as barriers to the utilization of the family care system. While Adams challenged the logic in most of these claims, it is likely that these beliefs were held by some families, service system staff, and potential caregivers:

1. The management of a child with an intellectual handicap requires special skills and expert knowledge that are unlikely to be found in ordinary run-of-the-mill foster families.
2. The supposedly static nature of this disability makes the task of raising a retarded child unrewarding at best and exceedingly frustrating at worst.
3. The behavior problems and lack of social skills that may be mani-

fested by retarded children, who cannot be managed in their own homes or have been institutionalized, would mitigate against their successful assimilation into the nuclear unit of the foster family and the broader network of the community and school system, which supports the family.

4. Given the limited supply of foster homes available and the inverse ratio of supply and demand it is not politic to waste them on children whose placement success is in doubt and whose long term future social adjustment and productivity do not warrant the utilization of this scarce resource . . . the normalizing experience of foster home care is less necessary as a preparation for adult life than it is for children of normal social and intellectual potential whose future role is not theoretically in doubt.

5. Families of the more conspicuously handicapped children may have many misconceptions about foster care, associate it with social pathology and a negative social image, and are often resistant to accepting this form of care, much preferring the traditional socially affirmed option of institutional placement (p. 273).

Research findings, along with increased knowledge and experience in the field of mental retardation suggest that the above obstacles should not have affected the acceptance and development of foster care programs. However, there were few research findings at the time (Adams, 1975), and the knowledge of mental retardation professionals and policy makers was limited. As a result, institutions grew in number and size, and community alternatives became less available than in earlier years.

Reporting on the status of family care programs for people with mental retardation, Morrisey (1966) found that despite evidence supporting the efficacy of the model, development and expansion were slow until the mid-1960s. Based on Morrisey's nationwide survey of family care programs for people with mental retardation, favorable candidates for this kind of placement were described as: a) in stable physical condition; b) capable of relative self-care; c) possessing a degree of emotional stability and ability to communicate, socialize and adjust to others; d) having received maximum benefit from hospitalization; e) not severely retarded; f) not having a natural home to return to, and; g) having rehabilitation potential to benefit from the therapeutic value of family care (Morrisey, 1966). Younger people were also to be given priority, as they were thought to have a better family care prognosis (Brown, Windle, & Stewart, 1959). In other words, foster family care programs in the 1960s were thought to be most appropriate for relatively high-functioning, young children whose needs required a minimum of specialized skills. Not surprisingly, this profile was more similar to that of most *non-retarded* children who were candidates for child welfare family care homes, than to the retarded children who were currently candidates for family care placement. Thus the foster family care model for children and adults with mental retardation was not widely used until recent years when it was finally utilized in response to the emphasis placed on normalization principles and the process of deinstitutionalization.

As the number of people with mental retardation leaving institutions continued to increase during the 1970s, the use of family care homes was accelerated (Intagliata, Crosby, & Neider, 1981). The idea of placing individuals with families in the community was consistent with efforts to move them out of restrictive institutional settings and provide care that was the closest substitute to living with the person's own family.

Current Foster Care Programs for People with Mental Retardation

Despite its slow beginning, foster family care is now recognized as a viable and cost-efficient approach to the residential care of people with mental retardation (Best-Sigford, Bruininks, Lakin, Hill, & Heal, 1982). Intagliata et al. (1981) define foster family care as a program administered by a state's department of mental hygiene, mental retardation, health, or other department involved in the placement of people with mental retardation into specifically licensed or approved private homes. Homes average two to three residents with mental retardation and usually do not exceed six. Small family homes typically offer care in a relatively unrestricted environment. They are usually family-owned and operated, and provide training in self-help skills and community living skills. The primary purpose of family care is to "employ the physical and social environment of the home, and the psychosocial structure of the family to enhance interpersonal and group living skills" (Janicki, Jacobson, Zigman, & Lubin, 1987).

Intagliata, Crosby, and Neider (1981) described family care as a community residential model in transition. The shift from institutional to community-based supervision of family care homes carries with it new priorities and increased availability of community services. Moreover, the trend toward community agencies assuming responsibility for placement decisions has resulted in notable changes in the characteristics of people with mental retardation who are now living in family care settings, many of whom come directly from parental homes and have never been institutionalized. Another indication that family care is changing is reflected by the characteristics of the people who provide the care. In addition to differences in education, age, and motivation, people who are family care parents today will have begun their involvement in the program over a 50-year period, and thus represent a wide variety of philosophies and styles of providing care (Intagliata et al., 1981; Saetermoe, Widaman, & Borthwick-Duffy, 1991). Finally, as discussed earlier in this chapter, family care homes differ in the number of people with mental retardation who live with the family and in the degree to which the care provided is viewed as a primary sourc income. For instance, a home whose careprovider relies on the presence five or six residents as a sole source of income might fit the description or what some states refer to as a small group home, rather than to the more traditional description of foster care.

COMPARISON OF FAMILY CARE PROGRAMS FOR PEOPLE WITH AND WITHOUT MENTAL RETARDATION

The historical review presented in the first part of this chapter high-lighted the very different origins of family care programs for individuals with and without mental retardation. Whereas family care programs for people who have mental retardation began in the United States as a parole system for adults who were re-entering the community after institutional placement, young people were the focus of the first child welfare family care programs established for poor, non-handicapped children whose families could not provide adequate care. These differences in purpose were reflected in the types of agencies that assumed primary responsibility for the programs, i.e., family care for people with mental retardation was supervised by large institutions, and family care for non-retarded children became part of the social service or child welfare system. As a result, the generic term "family care" has come to represent two different systems of care. Although the overall objective of providing a substitute family for individuals who cannot live at home is shared by both systems, there are a number of differences that distinguish family care for people with mental retardation from family care for non-retarded individuals.

The majority of people with mental retardation who live in family care settings today represent a different profile from the young mildly retarded, emotionally stable individuals with no physical or behavior problems who were thought at one time to hold the future of foster family care for people with mental retardation. Indeed, the first people to have been released from institutions were higher functioning, but later cohorts consisted of individuals with fewer skills and abilities and more handicapping conditions and behavior problems (Lazerson, 1975). This trend has been even more evident in recent years (Eyman, Borthwick, & Tarjan, 1984) as family care has been utilized to prevent or postpone institutionalization. The early differences between the child welfare and mental health family care programs have been accentuated by this shift in the differences among the types of individuals served by each program. Some of the major differences between family care programs for retarded and non-retarded people are discussed in the following sections.

ls of People with Mental Retardation

;tics of people with and without mental retardation affect
... us placed upon their caregivers. Individuals with mental retardation who are placed in family care today represent a wide range and
combination of characteristics and handicapping conditions, including lack
of self-help skills, presence of behavior problems and health problems
including seizures and sensory deficits, lack of communication skills, etc.
These conditions often require special skills outside the scope of normal
parenting roles, hence the caregiver in a family care program for individuals
with mental retardation is more likely to be viewed as a professional or
colleague than is a foster care parent who cares for non-handicapped
children (Adams, 1975; Bauer & Heinke, 1976; Craig & McCarver, 1984).
Caregivers for emotionally disturbed children within the normal range of
intelligence have also been placed in this category of "co-professional"
(Bauer & Heinke, 1976). Yet the personalities and skills that are most
effective with this group are likely to differ from those required of people
who care for children and adults with mental retardation.

Motivational Differences for Becoming a Caregiver

Although the reasons reported by most people for becoming caregivers
could be considered altruistic, regardless of the type of foster care involvement (*Encyclopedia of Social Work*, 1987; Intagliata, Crosby, & Neider, 1981),
the specific motivation for becoming (and remaining) a family care parent
for people with mental retardation is likely to be different than it is for
regular foster care. Reduced levels of reinforcement resulting from the
retarded individual's slower developmental progress, possible lack of affective feedback from the person, expectations of additional work around the
house, and the need to meet self-care requirements can affect decisions by
potential caregivers to become involved in family care programs for people
with mental retardation (Adams, 1975). Whether the individuals who do
choose to enter and remain in the residential care system for people with
mental retardation do so because of financial advantages, professional
satisfaction, altruism, relationships and interactions with retarded children
in the home, or any combination of the above, has not been systematically
examined.

Residential Placement for Entire Life-span

Whereas the majority of non-retarded children will eventually become
independent and no longer require residential services (Rothschild, 1974),
foster family care is likely to become a residential placement that extends
into adulthood for many individuals with mental retardation. The belief that

foster family care provides temporary substitute parental care, even for non-retarded children, has not been supported by longitudinal examinations of family care placements (*Encyclopedia of Social Work*, 1987; Lei, Nihira, Sheehy, & Meyers, 1981; Maas, 1969).

In a study of child welfare supported foster care, Maas (1969) found that children who remained in foster care for more than 10 years were primarily distinguished by below-average intelligence and physical disabilities. Not only are children with mental retardation more likely to remain in foster care for longer periods, they are often likely to spend their adult lives there. In fact, it has already been noted that the first family care programs for people with mental retardation were *established* for adults rather than children. A significant number of adults and even elderly individuals with mental retardation live in foster family care homes where the residents' average age is 28 (Borthwick, Meyers, & Eyman, 1981; Eyman & Borthwick, 1980). Because of this expanded age range, family care for people with mental retardation is not viewed as a children's model, and the entire life-span of retarded individuals is considered in placement decisions and in the development of family care programs. Conversely, residential planning for non-retarded children typically assumes that the need for placement will be eliminated when the child finishes school and becomes independent, if not sooner. Accordingly, these family care programs must only address issues related to the needs of young children and adolescents.

Parent and Caregiver Concerns

Parents of children with mental retardation are confronted with a number of issues that families of non-retarded children may never have to face. For example, parents of children with severe or profound mental retardation, in particular, have expressed fears about what will happen to their offspring once they, as parents, have died or are no longer able to take care of or oversee services for their children (Seligman, 1983). These concerns may also be shared by older foster family caregivers who are committed to the long-term care of the people with mental retardation in their homes.

Parents and caregivers of children with mental retardation must also deal with the fact that their parental roles will not normally evolve and change over the lifespan of the individual with mental retardation, who is likely to remain dependent regardless of his age. Parent and caregiver "burnout" are not uncommon, as the responsibilities and concerns for the individual continue throughout his or her life. Conversely, parents of non-retarded children can expect that under most circumstances the relationships they have with their children will reflect the growing maturity and independence that develops in them over time.

Continuum of Residential Options

Regardless of a child's intellectual level, placement decisions include a complex set of factors. For children with and without mental retardation, foster family homes are considered to be the least restrictive and most normal type of substitute care (Willer & Intagliata, 1984). However, for people with mental retardation, family care is only one alternative among a wide array of residential placement options that have evolved out of the deinstitutionalization and community placement movements (Bruininks, Kudla, Hauber, Hill, & Wieck, 1981). Decisions to place the child with mental retardation outside the natural home are made in the context of a comprehensive service system that includes foster family care, group homes of different sizes and age ranges, intermediate care facilities with varying specialties of care, skilled nursing facilities, institutions, semi-independent and independent living arrangements, and homes of relatives or friends (Borthwick-Duffy et al., 1981; Borthwick-Duffy et al., 1987). Depending on the person's primary needs (e.g., medical, behavioral, social, self-help, vocational) and the availability of placement alternatives at the time of the decision, residential placement could be recommended for any one of these setting types. This range of alternatives further complicates placement decisions, and emphasizes the need to identify the characteristics of individuals with mental retardation who will be best suited for foster care placement, difficult as that may be.

Variation Among Settings and Residents

The heterogeneity of individual characteristics, as well as natural differences in family lifestyles and parenting practices, has resulted in a family care system for people with mental retardation that is complex and difficult to evaluate. For example, homes that care for adults with mild retardation differ significantly from homes that care for children with profound retardation and multiple handicaps. These differences were observed by Bjaanes and Butler (1974), who found as much variation within family care and group home settings as they found across the two residence types. For example, in California in 1989, approximately one-third of individuals in small family homes had mild mental retardation, one-third had moderate retardation, and one-third had severe or profound retardation. Seventeen percent had cerebral palsy, and of those, the cerebral palsy was moderate or severe for 60 percent. No doubt there are notable differences among the residents of regular foster family care homes as well. However, the wide range of ages and disabilities among people with mental retardation in foster care exaggerate naturally occurring individual differences.

Dependence on Community

The special needs of people with mental retardation result in a greater dependence on community services and support than might be necessary for careproviders of non-handicapped children (Browder, Ellis, & Neal, 1974). Early evaluations of family care programs for people with mental retardation cited lack of community support as being a major barrier to successful service provision (Windle, 1962). Later studies have also noted difficulties in obtaining needed services outside the mental health system for individuals with mental retardation residing in community settings (O'Connor, 1976; Browder et al., 1974; Sutton, Sutter, Long, & Kelley, 1983). Not all communities have educational, recreational, medical or therapeutic resources available for people with mental retardation, particularly those with severe disabilities. Foster home caregivers have also cited inadequate funding, lack of community support, and negative community attitudes toward people with mental retardation as barriers to effective care. These limitations emphasize the fact that decisions to place individuals in family care settings may depend not only on the characteristics of the person and caregiver, but also on the surrounding community. Furthermore, it suggests that caregivers of people with mental retardation may have to spend increased time and emotional energy on the provision of care compared to caregivers of non-retarded children, because of their intellectual and physical handicaps.

Placement Histories

Many of the people with mental retardation coming into family care settings will have had unusual placement histories that may not even include other family care or parental homes. Moreover, given the institutional origins of foster family care for people with mental retardation, it follows that a significant portion of people in family care today will have lived in institutions or other more restrictive settings at some point in their lives. Others may have lived in less restrictive settings, and still others may represent the "revolving door" clients who go back and forth between the institution and different community placements (Keys, Boroskin, & Ross, 1973). The effects of institutional placement have been associated with wariness of adults and unusually great needs for social interaction and reinforcement (Zigler & Balla, 1976, 1977). These findings suggest that a history of institutional placement might affect adjustment later in family care homes or other community settings.

On the contrary, non-retarded people living in family care homes are less likely to have lived in institutions or other more restrictive settings. Like those with mental retardation, these children might have complex histories of living arrangements. However, since non-retarded children are very often placed outside the home by court-initiated procedures as a temporary solution, and since the placement of children with mental retardation is often initiated by parents with a permanent arrangement in mind, both the purpose and the history of residential placements are likely to be different for these two groups.

Education and Training Focus

Whereas the focal point of educational activities for non-retarded children is most often the classroom, a considerable emphasis is placed on education and training of people with mental retardation within the foster family care home environment. The educational aspects of residential placement for people with mental retardation that were emphasized in the first training schools are still visible in current family programs. Definitions of community adaptation often emphasize improvements in performance of self-help, community living skills, and reduction of behavior problems (Seltzer, Sherwood, Seltzer, & Sherwood, 1981), all of which are promoted by education and training that takes place in the home. Moreover, recent legislative decisions regarding students with handicaps (e.g. PL 94-142, Individualized Education Plans) require the involvement of family care parents in the educational programming of their clients, and emphasize the integration of home and school learning environments. With regard to this issue, Intagliata et al. (1981) concluded from their review of the literature that the focus of family care had definitely shifted in recent years from custodial to habilitative programs.

Interpretation of Failure

"Failure" in family care for non-retarded children generally results in movement to a new family care setting. Of the 624 non-retarded foster care children followed by Fanschel (1976), only three percent were discharged to a more restrictive setting during the first five years; 56 percent of the children were discharged altogether; and only 36 percent were still in foster family care placement after five years. Conversely, failure in family care for an individual with mental retardation historically meant that the person could not adapt to the demands of the community, i.e., family care, and would have to return to the institution or another more restrictive placement (Pagel & Whitling, 1978; Eyman et al., 1984). In recent years the "blame" for the failure in placement has shifted from problems within the individual (e.g. behavior or health problems) to the inability of the service system to select the appropriate placement for the individual or to provide the necessary support services. However, the selection of a new placement is made in the context of the entire continuum of setting types. The individual still might be moved to a more restrictive living arrangement where his/her needs can be better met.

Effort to Normalize

A conscious effort is made in family care homes for people with mental retardation to achieve as normal an environment as possible. Such an emphasis is not evident in discussions of family care for non-retarded children. Homes that care for individuals with mental retardation may need to give special attention to this issue because of the professional and business-like arrangement that caregivers have entered into, or because of the characteristics of children with mental retardation who may not naturally contribute to the normalized aspects of the home. As a result, family care environments for people with mental retardation are frequently evaluated in terms of the degree to which they meet standards of normalization (Eyman, Demaine, & Lei, 1979; Scheerenberger & Felsenthal, 1977).

Although efforts are made to provide a warm and homelike environment in foster family care homes for non-retarded children, the concept of making them "normal" is unique to considerations of living arrangements for people with mental retardation and is sometimes thought to be the most important indicator of home quality.

EVALUATION OF FAMILY CARE PROGRAMS

The need for evaluative studies on the relative benefits of foster family care was first documented at the Conference on Research in the Children's Field in 1956. The conference, which largely ignored the potential application of family care programs for children with mental retardation, emphasized the importance of obtaining empirical evidence to support policy and other decisions related to the quality of care (Adams, 1975). In subsequent years, considerable attention was directed toward the identification of predictors of success in family care for non-retarded children, as well as studies on family care parents and the impact of placement on biological families (Adams, 1975).

Research on family care programs designed specifically for children with mental retardation had a slower start, hence early program development occurred without the benefit of evaluation studies. When data became available, Morrisey (1966) found that professional judgments regarding the prognosis of retarded children with certain characteristics for successful family care placement were not supported by the results of the first research studies on this topic (Windle, 1962; Windle, Sabagh, Brown, & Dingman, 1961; Windle, Stewart, & Brown, 1961). These discrepancies highlighted the need for further systematic research on the characteristics of family care parents and children with mental retardation who would be the most likely candidates for a favorable placement (Morrisey, 1966).

Nearly a decade later, family care programs for people with mental retardation continued to be criticized for the lack of definitive evidence predicting the sort of child that would succeed in this setting, and for the inability of researchers to determine the conditions that make family care the best choice for some children (Adams, 1975). A review of the recent literature in this area would probably lead to similar disappointing results, though not for lack of research efforts (see Craig & McCarver, 1984; Heal, Sigelman, & Switzky, 1978; McCarver & Craig, 1974). While the questions appear to be straightforward, they are extremely difficult to answer for a number of reasons, including non-random assignment, limited relevance of early studies, heterogeneity of family care environments, and the many definitions of success or adjustment used in research studies.

Limited Relevance of Early Studies

Research done prior to the deinstitutionalization thrust of the 1970s has limited relevance to examinations of the family care programs of today. Characteristics of the physical environment, caregivers, and people with mental retardation who are placed in family care homes have changed considerably in recent years. For example, newer community homes tend to be less restrictive and more normalized than homes that have been caring for people with mental retardation for longer periods of time (Baker, Seltzer, & Seltzer, 1977; Craig & McCarver, 1984), and a greater number of family care homes are located in urban and suburban neighborhoods than in past years (Kastner, Reppuci, & Pezzoli, 1979). The purpose of family care programs has shifted from being merely custodial to emphasizing habilitation with increased training activities (Craig & McCarver, 1984; Intagliata, Crosby, & Neider, 1981). Moreover, caregivers tend to be better educated and younger than in the past and claim to work with people with mental retardation for different reasons than those cited in earlier years (Gollay, Freedman, Wyngaarden, & Kurtz, 1978). The service systems in most states have also changed since the deinstitutionalization movement, and family care programs are usually not supervised by the large institutions. Perhaps the most dramatic differences related to change over time are found among the residents with mental retardation who have lived in the various settings. Evidence from demographic studies continue to restate the fact that people with more severe handicaps are being released from institutions to community placements and are remaining in the community (Eyman et al., 1984; Heal et al., 1978; Jacobson & Schwartz, 1983; Scheerenberger, 1980, 1982).

Philosophical differences have also emerged. As noted, in the earlier studies attributions for a placement "failure" emphasized a deficiency in the individual (who should be returned to the institution for additional training), whereas failures in more recent studies are often associated with the inability of the service delivery system to meet the individual's needs or determine the most appropriate placement (Craig & McCarver, 1984).

Placements in family care settings are currently made in the context of a comprehensive residential service system, as opposed to the early practice of simply releasing institutionalized individuals to foster care when it was the only community residential alternative. Hence today, individuals are placed in family care *in favor* of other options, e.g. group homes, health care facilities, semi-independent living. Moreover, people currently living in foster family care may have experienced a range of placement histories, that might have never included institutional living. Yet many published research studies on foster family care for people with mental retardation have focused on the follow-up of children and adults who have been deinstitutionalized. In the 1950s and 1960s the research question would have been, "Who are the individuals that can be moved from the institution to family care homes without being returned to the institution?" Instead, today the question asked is, "How can we determine the characteristics of people for whom foster family care placement is the best choice, given the range of available alternatives?"

Heterogeneity of Foster Family Care Homes

As noted in an earlier section, a large number of studies have attempted to compare and contrast the various placement alternatives using broad residence categories. These comparisons are often based on the assumption that characteristics of the environment and people who live in them are relatively homogeneous within broad classes of placement types. Research directed to this point has not found this to be so. For example, differences between the characteristics of institutions and of their effect on resident behavior have been documented in a number of studies (Butterfield & Zigler, 1965; Balla, Butterfield, & Zigler, 1974; Eyman et al., 1977; King, Raynes, & Tizard, 1971; McCormick, Balla, & Zigler, 1975). As previously noted, Bjaanes and Butler (1974) examined board and care homes and family care homes, and found as much variation within setting types as between them. Intagliata, Willer, and Wicks (1981) reviewed the literature in this area, and also concluded that there is great variation in the environments provided by any class of residences, and that the variation within broad classes of residential types may be as great or greater than between different types. Most studies focus on the varying characteristics of the homes without making judgments of home quality, although some investigators (e.g. Intagliata et al., 1981) have attempted to assign ranks of "quality" to family care environments. In either case, the importance of considering the interaction of features of the environment with characteristics of the individual has been emphasized.

Definitions of Success

In order to determine the characteristics of people for whom family care (or any alternative) is the most appropriate placement, there must be a general consensus with regard to the desired outcome, i.e., on what basis will a decision be made that a placement is best for an individual? The diversity of community adjustment criteria and outcome measures reported in the literature have been described as almost researcher specific (Craig & McCarver, 1984; Seltzer et al., 1981). Lakin et al. (1981) discussed the problems associated with the breadth of conceptualization of "adjustment" in research studies, and Crawford, Aiello, and Thompson (1979) noted similar difficulties with the many definitions of "success" in evaluations of community placement. The wide range of operational definitions may not lead to problems in interpreting the results of individual studies, but it does make it extremely difficult to compare research findings, and many reports appear to be contradictory and inconclusive (Lakin et al., 1981; McCarver & Craig, 1974).

While it might seem more straightforward to standardize the definition of adjustment (Eagle, 1967) this would oversimplify a complex issue. In fact, Lakin et al. (1981) suggest that adjustment is a matter of degree and personal preference, and is not easily quantified. They state:

> . . . the notion of adjustment as it has been operationalized in previous studies implies a standard or norm by which the adjustment of mentally retarded people can be determined—that is by which one can separate those who are "adjusted" from those who are not. Such a standard can be most easily criticized in that even among nonmentally retarded handicapped people adjustment is at best ill-defined and represents no particular pattern of behavior . . . . (p. 383).

Research conducted in the last decade has highlighted the importance of considering the many aspects of an individual's residential placement adjustment. Hence the question "who benefits from foster family care placement?" is a complex one, and demands an answer that takes the multidimensionality of adjustment into account.

FAMILY CARE VS. SMALL GROUP HOMES

In the field of mental retardation, family care homes have frequently been studied in relation to the characteristics of group homes, providing descriptive information in the context of the residential placement service system. These comparisons are common because group homes are often a reasonable alternative placement for people living in family care homes and because of the overlap in characteristics described above. In other words, of the different residential settings, people living in family care homes are most similar to those who have been placed in group homes and are less like those in institutions, health facilities, or parental homes (Borthwick et al., 1981; Borthwick-Duffy et al., 1987).

A great deal of variation *within* each of these two settings has been reported in the literature, however some studies have also drawn conclusions with regard to differences across the broad residential categories. The reviews are mixed. Whereas some investigators have found family care homes to be less normalized, more protective, and more custodial than group homes (Bjaanes & Butler, 1974; Baker, Seltzer, & Seltzer, 1974), others have concluded the opposite to be the case. Scheerenberger and Felsenthal (1977), for example, concluded that family care homes tended to be less structured, more flexible and individualized, and made better use of community services than group home programs.

Willer and Intagliata (1984) suggest these differences in findings may be due to factors that are unrelated to the actual characteristics of the setting type, e.g., variations in operational definitions of such terms as flexibility, normalization, autonomy, general satisfaction, etc. They cite examples of potential overlap and varying interpretation, e.g., overprotection vs. supervision, and autonomy vs. poor supervision.

Studies of this type also ignore the selection bias that is related to differences in characteristics of the people who do and do not live in them (Butterfield, 1985). Since group home residents are typically higher functioning, with fewer disabilities than individuals in family care (Borthwick et al., 1981), differences in levels of independence, protection, and autonomy found in the two types of homes are not surprising. Overall, people in family care tend to have fewer behavior problems than group home residents, and have been described as being more likely to be passive and unassertive (Willer & Intagliata, 1982).

Willer and Intagliata (1982) attributed differences in characteristics of people in family care and group homes to the impact of the different residential environments. However, their method of determining the "general initial comparability of the two groups" was not reported and adaptive behavior change was not examined at the individual level. By contrast, the majority of research findings support the position that differences in individual characteristics across residence types are related to placement selection criteria (Borthwick et al., 1981; Borthwick-Duffy et al., 1987). Finally, inconclusive results of comparisons between these two residence types might also be due to the possibility that family care homes with six residents are more similar to what are called group homes with seven residents than to family care with only one or two individuals who have mental retardation living in the home.

Landesman-Dwyer (1985) urged the research community to focus on characteristics of residential settings rather than on broad category labels that are frequently discussed in the literature. This seems to be the most effective way to interpret the findings of the longitudinal study reported in this monograph. The residences studied come closest to the broad category of foster family care, with one or two primary caregivers providing a home environment for a small number (one to six) of people with mental retardation. However, the relationships we found among characteristics of the homes and of the people who live in them might also be applicable to homes with similar characteristics that do not carry the foster family care label.

THE STUDY GOALS: CHARACTERIZING DEVELOPMENT AND QUALITY OF LIFE

Goal 1: Studying Changes in Adaptive and Maladaptive Behavior

For many years the authors have contended that the characterization of a person's behavior using assessments of adaptive behavior is more important and more useful than any other single global assessment of the retarded person and his or her behavior (Widaman, Borthwick-Duffy, & Little, 1991). Notwithstanding recent arguments regarding the supremacy of measures of intelligence for the classification of people as having mental retardation (e.g., Zigler, Balla, & Hodapp, 1984), measures of adaptive behavior reflect far more accurately than do intelligence test scores a person's everyday coping abilities, referring directly to self-help behaviors by people with mental retardation as well as behaviors they use to interact with or relate to others. Although assessments of intelligence and adaptive behavior may overlap statistically and conceptually to a certain degree, there is one difference between the two types of measures: whereas measures of intelligence provide an index of potential learning, measures of adaptive behavior provide indices of attained levels of behavior exhibited under the circumstances faced in the person's everyday life. Moreover, most inventories of adaptive behavior include indices of maladaptive behavior, a subdomain that provides critical information for educational placement and other programming decisions.

Measures of intelligence are deficient in this regard. The utility of adaptive behavior measures is well-supported by empirical studies, such as the study by Futterman and Arndt (1983), which found that adaptive behavior scores predicted program placement outcomes better than did IQ scores. These issues may be glossed over in discussions of the relative importance of measures of intelligence and adaptive behavior for classification, but researchers should not lose sight of the importance of measures of adaptive behavior. Assessments of adaptive behavior provide a more complete, accurate portrayal of the skills, behaviors, and competencies of people with mental retardation than do IQ scores. Thus, a theory of adaptive behaviors and their development is imperative for the field of mental retardation and developmental disabilities. It is the authors' hope that the findings of the Family Care Study will contribute to the development of such

a theory that will explain changes in adaptive and maladapti\
over the lifespan.

In a recent review, Clarke-Stewart (1988) summarized 10 years research
on parenting effects on five different domains of child behavior, including
socialization and cognitive development. Clarke-Stewart applauded the
wide-ranging work currently being done on a variety of fronts that is
relevant to the determination of parent effects on children's behavior,
however, she noted that many studies published during the past 10 years
allowed only ambiguous attribution of parent effects. To allow the disentan-
gling of effects, Clarke-Stewart concluded that studies of contextual effects
must utilize special designs. The chief distinguishing features of the required
designs are: 1) longitudinal form; and 2) use of multivariate data and
analyses. Longitudinal designs are needed to tease apart cause-and-effect
relations across time among contextual and child behaviors. Multivariate
designs and analyses are required to move beyond rather simplistic notions
that one single variable influences another single variable. Rather, research
must accommodate the relations among all of the variables, with structural
models formulated to account for the relations among behaviors, whether
direct effects, indirect effects, or simple correlations. These features—
longitudinal designs that are multivariate in nature—were characteristic of
the Family Care Study. Thus, this examination of contextual influences on
development (careprovider characteristics, residential environments, interpersonal relationships, and community involvement) should contribute
significantly to the research in this area.

The Family Care Study also utilized the process approach that Clarke-
Stewart stated was needed for studying contextual effects. That is, the study
was not one of "group differences," attempting to find differences between
groups (e.g., retarded versus non-retarded). Significant differences between
groups are frequently easy to find, are interpreted as consistent with one's
theory, and yet may be consistent with an almost infinite number of
alternative theories or explanations. Rather, the Family Care Study was
founded on process-oriented hypotheses that individuals influence one
another over time, assumes the presence of individual differences (here,
differences among people with mental retardation, environments,
careproviders) on variables of interest, and relies on analyses that represent
and test the causal influences across time among the variables. In the
authors' view, this is the state-of-the-art approach in research on contextual
effects that may serve as an extension of the work of Mink and Nihira (1986,
1987).

It has become popular in psychology to study the heritability, or genetic
determination, of psychological characteristics (Bouchard et al., 1990). But,
associated with the notion of genetic determination is the complementary
concept of *reaction range*, or the degree of malleability of behavior given the
genetic make-up of a person. The people with mental retardation in the

Family Care sample had genetic and other etiological characteristics that placed limits on their behaviors. Rather than studying the ways in which these factors limited development, the authors studied the reaction ranges of these individuals, i.e., the ways in which the proximal environment provided by caregivers and others contributed to change in adaptive and maladaptive behavior among the children and adolescents in the study. The findings of the Family Care Study that relate to behavior and development among people with mental retardation are presented in this monograph as an initial step in the development of an adequate theory of adaptive behavior. A direct outcome of such a theory will be to provide specific recommendations regarding environmental and other contextual variables that can maximize the development of people with mental retardation who live in family foster care settings. In Chapters 3 and 6 of this monograph the authors present findings related to changes in the behavior and development of the children and adolescents in the Family Care Study.

Goal 2: Studying Quality of Life

Although the behavior and development of people with mental retardation have been identified for many years as important criteria by which to measure the effectiveness of programs and the appropriateness of residential placements, a concomitant concern for the individual's quality of life has emerged in recent years. As discussed in Chapter 5, dimensions of quality of life (such as the residential environment, interpersonal relationships, community involvement, and stability) may be viewed as: 1) important outcomes; 2) impacting each other, and; 3) influencing or being influenced by changes in adaptive and maladaptive behavior. The longitudinal models described in Chapters 5 and 6 were proposed and tested in order to address these functions of quality of life dimensions.

Chapter 2

Design and Methods of the Family Care Study

The basic aim of the Family Care Study was to study the development of people with mental retardation within the family settings in which they were living. In doing so, the focus of measurement went beyond assessment of only the target individuals—the people with mental retardation. Rather, a more comprehensive approach to measurement was sought, which included assessment of the careproviders, the natural parents, and aspects of the home within which the target individuals were living. One outcome of this study was the determination of the merits and weaknesses of small family care settings as placements for people with mental retardation. A potentially more important outcome of the study was the investigation of factors that influence the development of adaptive and maladaptive behaviors in people with mental retardation and of the ways in which these individuals affect their careproviders and home environments. Thus, the Family Care Study involved a complex, multi-dimensional series of procedures related to the assessment of people with mental retardation and a large number of aspects of their environments in order to begin to tease apart the interplay of causes and effects in the lives of individuals with mental retardation. This chapter discusses the samples of individuals studied and how they were selected, the survey instruments employed, the data collection procedures, and the methodological and statistical procedures used.

DESIGN

The Family Care Study was funded by a grant from the National Institute of Child Health and Human Development, Grant NO1-HD-7-2847, with Richard K. Eyman as principal investigator. The basic design of the study was a three-year longitudinal study of people with mental retardation who were living in small family care settings with foster parents. Data were to be collected on a sample of people with mental retardation at yearly intervals for three consecutive years. Using such a design, it is possible to begin to untangle the influence of variables that affect the development of behaviors and skills of individuals with mental retardation, as well as initiating the study of the ways in which the behaviors and characteristics of people with mental retardation affect their surroundings over a period of time.

SAMPLES

The study sample was drawn from a four-county region of southern California. This region is served by one of the 21 regional centers in California providing services for people with developmental disabilities, including people with mental retardation. The regional center whose clients comprised the sample began serving the four-county region about five years before the study began. But, at the time the study started, small family care placements had been used for more than 20 years in this area of southern California. Moreover, the regional center from whose rolls the sample was selected had a long history of preference for community placements, small family care placements in particular, and considered institutionalization a reluctant choice. Thus, the data from the Family Care Study were collected in an area with a mature history of community placement and were not, therefore, derived as the result of a court order to deinstitutionalize clients en masse.

Persons with Mental Retardation

The total sample of persons with mental retardation in the Family Care Study consisted of 333 people who were 21 years old or younger at the time of initial data collection. Of these, 245 individuals comprised the First Year sample and were selected for inclusion in the study during the first year of measurement. The remaining 88 individuals were termed the Second Year sample, and these people were assessed for the first time during the second year of the study.

As shown in Table 2.1, 209 of the 245 individuals comprising the First Year sample were assessed again during the second year of measurement, and 196 of these people were assessed again during the third year. As a result, 80 percent of the people in the First Year sample were assessed during all three years of the study. Looking across the span of the study, the drop-out rate was somewhat larger between the first two times of measurement, as 14.7 percent of the First Year sample dropped out during this period. Between the second and third times of measurement, an additional 5.3 percent of the First Year sample dropped out, leaving an overall attrition, or drop-out, rate of 20 percent. The attrition rate of 20 percent suggests that some limitations on the ability to generalize the results of the study may be required. That is, the results may generalize only to somewhat selected portions of the population of individuals in small family care settings. However, the attrition rate for the First Year sample compares quite favorably with that from other short-term longitudinal studies. For example, Nesselroade and Baltes (1974) conducted a three-year study with yearly assessments, a study with the same general design as the current one, and had an attrition rate of approximately 40 percent over the span of their study.

TABLE 2.1

Samples of Persons with Mental Retardation
in the Family Care Study

| | | ASSESSED DURING | | | | | |
| | | YEAR 1 | | YEAR 2 | | YEAR 3 | |
SAMPLE	STATUS	N	PCT	N	PCT	N	PCT
First Year	Longitudinal	245	100.0	209	85.3	196	80.0
	Drop out	—	—	36	14.7	49	20.0
Second Year	Longitudinal	—	—	88	100.0	76	86.4
	Drop out	—	—	—	—	12	13.6

The 88 individuals in the Second Year sample were assessed for the first time during the second year of the study, and 76 of these people were assessed again during the third year. This left a one-year attrition rate of 13.6 percent, very similar to the one-year attrition rate of 14.7 percent shown by the First Year sample.

Across the 333 individuals with mental retardation in the First Year and Second Year samples, 285 individuals were assessed again one year after their first time of measurement, resulting in an overall one-year attrition rate of 14.4 percent. However, given the complexity of the analyses pursued in this monograph, the sample of 148 people with longitudinal data across the three times of measurement and with stable placement during the study period is the core sample on which most analyses will be based.

Careproviders and Their Homes

The sample of careproviders and facilities included in the study were those providing residential care to the clients in the sample during the three-year span of the project. The focus of the Family Care Study was on the development of the children and adolescents with mental retardation. As a result, the sample of facilities was limited to those licensed to care for people with mental retardation who were 21 years old or younger. The 151 homes in this study comprised virtually all of the homes in the catchment area that served children and adolescents, as well as some homes that also served adults. Further, the 151 homes comprised about 40 percent of all foster homes in the regional center's catchment area. When data were elicited from careproviders, the person who was the primary careprovider in a given small family care home was the one from whom responses were obtained.

Of the 151 facilities included in the study, 112 homes entered the study during the first year of data collection, 30 during the second year, and nine during the third year of the study. Of the 112 homes sampled during the first year of the study, 103 homes were included in the second year of the study, and 88 in the third year. Of the 30 homes entering the study during the second year, a one-year, follow-up survey was completed on 26 homes during the third year of the study.

Natural Parents

The natural parents of the people with mental retardation in the sample were contacted during the first year in which their child was involved in the study. More than 95 percent of the parents of the 333 persons with mental retardation in the sample were contacted. Of the 319 parents contacted, 315 agreed to be interviewed. The interviews of natural parents were conducted during the first year of study involvement by their child. The information was obtained from natural parents only during the first time of measurement, as most information obtained, such as basic demographic data and recollections of events surrounding the initial out-of-home placement of their child, would not be expected to change during the course of the study.

Case Managers

A case manager is routinely assigned to each person with mental retardation who receives services from the state of California through one of the 21 regional centers. Each person with mental retardation in the Family Care Study was assigned a case manager; for a total of 87 case managers in the study. Most of the sampled people with mental retardation in this study were served by different case managers across the three times of measurement, due to frequent changes in case assignments to case managers. Only a small portion of the clients, less than 10 percent, were served by the same case manager throughout the three-year span of the longitudinal study.

INSTRUMENTS

A set of nine instruments was used to collect the basic data for the Family Care Study. The first three instruments assessed primarily the target person with mental retardation, assessing both adaptive and maladaptive behavior, as well as qualities of the home environment in which the person was placed. The next two instruments assessed the careprovider, using a series of questions designed to obtain demographic information and the careprovider's preferences regarding characteristics and behaviors of the individuals with mental retardation living in their homes. Then, three questionnaires were used to measure aspects of the careproviders' homes, including the physical characteristics of the home, the degree to which the home was conducive to improving levels of adaptive and maladaptive behavior, and the quality of the relationship between the careprovider and the person with mental retardation. The final instrument consisted of a questionnaire obtaining information from the natural parent or legal guardian of the person with mental retardation. A summary of the instruments used in the Family Care Study is provided in Table 2.2, which lists the instrument, the persons responding to questions, the interviewer (if one was used), the person or situation that was the target of the assessment, and the domains assessed. Each of these nine instruments is discussed below.

TABLE 2.2

Instruments Used in the Family Care Study

INSTRUMENT	RESPONDENT	INTERVIEWER	TARGET OF RATINGS	DOMAINS ASSESSED
Behavior Development Survey	Careprovider	Case Manager	Person with MR	Three dimensions of adaptive and two of maladaptive behavior
Individual and Family Charac-teristics Form	Case Manager	None[a]	Person with MR	Demographic, back-ground items, place-ment information
Individual Client Assessment Form	Careprovider	Case Manager	Person with MR	Quality of personal relationships, com-munity involvement and health
Careprovider Questionnaire	Careprovider	Group testing by project staff	Care-provider	Demographic, back-ground items, experience and attitude items
Careprovider Preference Survey	Careprovider	Group testing by project staff	Care-provider	Seriousness, exper-ience with forms of problem behavior
Program Analysis of Service Systems	Project staff	None[a]	Facility	Normalization and other aspects of residential facility
Foster Home Observation for Measurement of the Environment	Careprovider	Project staff	Care-provider & Facility	Nine scales for aspects of the home environment
Home Quality Rating Scale	Project staff after home visit	None[a]	Care-provider & Facility	Five scales for intra-familial dynamics in the home
Responsible Parent Questionnaire, Parts I and II	Natural Parent or Guardian	I - Case Manager II - None[a]	Natural Parent or Guardian	Parental character-istics, attitudes about placement, interaction with child

[a]Instruments for which no interviewer is listed were completed individually by the Respondent with regard to characteristics of the Target of the ratings.

Measures of the Person with Mental Retardation

Behavioral Development Survey. The Behavioral Development Survey (BDS) is a behavioral assessment instrument designed to assist in the evaluation of the adaptive and maladaptive behaviors exhibited by people with developmental disabilities. The BDS was originally developed by the research group at Lanterman State Hospital (Neuropsychiatric Institute Research Group, 1979) as a shortened version of the AAMD Adaptive Behavior Scale (ABS) (Nihira, Foster, Shellhaas, & Leland, 1975), which is a well-standardized behavior rating instrument. When time and expense allow, the more comprehensive ABS may be preferred to the BDS, as the greater length of the ABS allows for greater variability on indices of behavior and potentially greater stability and reliability of the data. In addition, the descriptions and interpretations of behavior based on the ABS may be more precise and useful than those from the BDS. However, the BDS was carefully designed to yield scores on dimensions comparable to those from the ABS. Moreover, the BDS can prove valuable in the evaluation of client progress and development in research situations in which the longer ABS may prove unwieldy. This was the primary reason the BDS was used in the Family Care Study.

The 49 items on the BDS are grouped into five major scales, three indices of adaptive behavior and two of maladaptive behavior. The indices of adaptive behavior are derived from 34 items and parallel the dimensions found in factor analyses of the ABS by Nihira (1969a, 1969b, 1976)—Personal Self-Sufficiency, Community Self-Sufficiency, and Personal-Social Responsibility. On the BDS, the indices of adaptive behavior have the following characteristics: a) Personal Self-Sufficiency: 10 items, internal consistency reliability of .96, interrater reliability of .95, test-retest reliability of .84; b) Community Self-Sufficiency: 17 items, .92 internal consistency reliability, .94 interrater reliability, .80 test-retest reliability; c) Personal-Social Responsibility: seven items, .90 internal consistency reliability, .84 interrater reliability, .72 test-retest reliability.

The maladaptive behavior scales of the BDS consist of 15 items and assess Personal Maladaption and Social Maladaption, again paralleling the factor analytic findings by Nihira and others (e.g., Lambert & Nicholl, 1976). The psychometric properties of the maladaptive behavior scales are: a) Personal Maladaption: four items, .65 internal consistency reliability, .68 interrater reliability, .54 test-retest reliability; b) Social Maladaption: five items, .80 internal consistency reliability, .55 interrater reliability, .45 test-retest reliability. The remaining maladaptive behavior items on the BDS were not classified as representing either personal or social maladaption and were therefore analyzed separately.

The psychometric properties for the BDS scales listed in the preceding paragraphs were obtained from several sources. Internal consistency reliabilities for each scale were reported by Arndt (1981); interrater reliabilities were provided in the BDS manual (Neuropsychiatric Institute Research Group, 1979); and test-retest reliabilities were obtained over a one-year interval and were estimated on data from the current study. Although the

BDS is a shortened form of the ABS, the psychometric properties of BDS scales rival those of the longer ABS scales and provide impressive support for use of the BDS in research studies such as the Family Care Study.

As shown in Table 2.2, the BDS was completed by the case manager during annual interviews of the careprovider. This form of assessment is commonly termed the third-party informant method, as an interviewer makes ratings of the behavior exhibited by a target person after questioning someone who knows well the target person. The initial BDS assessment was made at the time the person with mental retardation was first placed into a family care home. Assessments on the BDS were then made at yearly intervals. The BDS data used in the Family Care Study were the annual assessments made during the three-year span of the study.

Individual and Family Characteristics Form. The Individual and Family Characteristics Form was an instrument with a variety of demographic and background items regarding the target person with mental retardation and his/her history of placement. In the first part of this form, a series of four items obtained demographic data, such as date of birth and ethnicity, for the person with mental retardation. Then, several questions inquired about the person's placement history, including the age at which the person was placed outside the home, whether the person had ever been placed back into his/her natural home after the initial out-of-home placement, and all residential settings in which the person with mental retardation had resided, including the current family care setting.

In the second section of the Individual and Family Characteristics Form, a set of questions regarding the person's parental figures at the time of initial placement were framed. These questions asked about both the mother and the father figures, gathering data on demographic items, such as ethnicity and marital status, as well as education and occupation. This form ended with inquiries about the number of people living in the home when the person was first placed and about reasons the parental figures gave for seeking an out-of-home placement for the person with mental retardation.

The Individual and Family Characteristics Form was completed on each person with mental retardation by the individual's case manager, as shown in Table 2.2. The case manager abstracted the information for this form from the client's personal file at the regional center. As the information for all items on this form remained unchanged throughout the study period, this form was completed only during the first year of the project.

Individual Client Assessment Form. The Individual Client Assessment Form contained a series of items assessing the person with mental retardation and his/her experiences that may be directly related to services obtained in the family care home and the success of the placement. One item inquired about the quality of the interpersonal relationships the target person had with a number of other people with whom he/she came into contact regularly, for example, careproviders, others living in the home, and school teachers. The degree of community involvement (e.g., attending church, joining clubs) and other social experiences (e.g., going to a shopping mall, to the movies) was indexed by other items, as was the careprovider's evaluation of the target person's potential for eventual self-sufficiency for independent living. A final set of items concerned the target person's general health and the degree to which the natural parents were involved in the person's life.

As shown in Table 2.2, the Individual Client Assessment Form was completed by the case manager during an interview of the careprovider at home. The information obtained using the Individual Client Assessment Form was expected to change across the span of the study, so this form was administered at each of the three times of measurement.

Measures of the Careprovider

Careprovider Questionnaire. The Careprovider Questionnaire was developed to compile information on careprovider characteristics and attributes that may be relevant to the adjustment and development of the people with mental retardation living in their homes. In addition to eliciting socio-demographic information (e.g., ethnicity, age), this questionnaire addressed, using both direct and indirect questions, issues such as the careprovider's motivation for becoming and remaining a provider of care for people with mental retardation and the careprovider's experience and knowledge in providing that care. Several items inquired about the careprovider's attitudes and practices related to child-rearing or parenting. The questionnaire ended with a set of items concerning a variety of procedural aspects of being a careprovider, such as dealing with staff from the regional center and with the natural parents of the person with mental retardation in their care.

The Careprovider Questionnaire was administered in group testing sessions during the first year a careprovider was in the study. Approximately 10 to 20 careproviders attended each of the group testing sessions. After staff of the Family Care Study read the instructions for the Careprovider Questionnaire, careproviders completed the questionnaire, taking as much time as needed. Careproviders who were unclear about particular questions were given additional help by the project staff person administering the instrument. The full Careprovider Questionnaire was administered only during the first year of participation, as information gathered on most items would not change across the three-year span of the study. Individual administration of this questionnaire to careproviders in their homes by project staff was necessary in a few cases in which the careprovider was unable to attend any of the scheduled group testing sessions.

Careprovider Preference Survey. The Careprovider Preference Survey (CPS) was designed for the study to examine the attitudes of careproviders toward a wide variety of physical and behavioral problems that may be displayed by clients in their care. The 50 items on the CPS were carefully written so that the behavior described corresponded to behavior delineated by the items on the BDS. A one-to-one match of CPS and BDS items, in terms of behavioral referents, was attempted, although this was not possible in a few isolated instances. All CPS items, however, were phrased in terms of problematic behaviors, such as maladaptive behaviors or the lack of adaptive behavioral skills. For example, one BDS item is titled DRINKING, and responses vary from "1 = Does not drink from cup or glass unassisted" to "4 = Drinks without spilling, holding glass in one hand." The corresponding CPS item stem is "When a client has trouble drinking from a glass or cup." Thus, BDS items tend to measure quality of specific performances or behaviors, whereas corresponding CPS item stems describe problems in executing well the specific performances or behaviors.

With regard to each CPS item, the careprovider made three ratings. First, the careprovider indicated whether the careprovider had experienced the presence of the particular problem behavior in his or her family care home. Then, the careprovider rated the behavioral problem for seriousness, on a scale ranging from "1 = not serious" to "3 = very serious." Finally, the careprovider indicated his/her willingness to deal with the behavioral problem on a dichotomous scale, "1 = would handle" or "2 = would rather not handle."

The CPS was administered in the same group testing session as was the Careprovider Questionnaire, during the first year a careprovider was in the study. As with the Careprovider Questionnaire, the staff of the Family Care Study read the instructions for the CPS; careproviders then completed the questionnaire, taking as much time as needed. In the few cases in which the careprovider was unable to attend any of the scheduled group testing sessions, the CPS was administered individually in the careprovider's home immediately after the Careprovider Questionnaire. The CPS was administered during each of the three years of the Family Care Study, in order to investigate the mutual influences between the behavioral capabilities of the persons with mental retardation from the BDS and the careproviders' perceptions of the behavioral problems assessed by the CPS.

Measures of the Home

Program Analysis of Service Systems. The Program Analysis of Service Systems (PASS) is a widely used instrument that provides a quantitative assessment of the quality of service systems, such as community residential programs for people with mental retardation. The PASS consists of 50 items that measure a wide array of aspects of residential programs. In the Family Care Study, the authors used the four factors derived from PASS items presented by Flynn (1980). These four factors are: a) Normalization of program, 19 items; b) Normalization of setting, 12 items; c) Administration, 8 items, and; d) Proximity and access, 4 items. Only seven of the PASS items are not included in the four factors; these items were not used further in the Family Care Study.

The PASS was completed on each home by Family Care Study project staff after a visit to the home, as shown in Table 2.2. The PASS was completed only during the first year a family home was part of the study, as it was unlikely that the characterization of a home using the PASS would change during the three-year span of the study.

Modified version of the Home Observation for Measurement of the Environment Scale. The Home Observation for the Measurement of the Environment (HOME) is an instrument designed by Caldwell (1968) and used in several studies by Caldwell and her associates (e.g., Bradley & Caldwell, 1979). The HOME assesses various aspects of the home environment and the daily care practices of the careprovider. The standard version of the HOME contains 100 items, which are grouped into nine scales. The scoring procedures for HOME scale items are quite explicit: each item is answered on a dichotomous, 0-1 scale, and there are clear and definite instructions regarding whether each item is to be answered on the basis of the observer's perceptions alone or whether the observer may query the careprovider to answer the item. All standard rules for scoring HOME items were followed in the Family Care Study.

For use in the Family Care Study, slight modifications of the HOME scale were necessary as several items were inappropriate for assessing the residential environments of people with mental retardation. As a result, the instrument used in the study was termed the Foster HOME, or FHOME. The FHOME had the same scales as the HOME; the scales were: a) Provision of stimulation through equipment, toys, and experiences, 17 items; b) Stimulation of mature behavior, 12 items; c) Provision of a stimulating physical and language environment, 12 items; d) Avoidance of restriction and punishment, seven items; e) Pride, affection, and thoughtfulness, 16 items; f) Provision of masculine role models, five items; g) Independence from parental control, seven items; h) Child-centered flexibility, 13 items, and; i) Family integration, seven items.

The FHOME was completed during the first year of the Family Care Study during a visit by a project staff member to the careprovider's home. Initially, the FHOME was to be administered during annual visits to the careprovider's home. However, because little variance across homes was shown on most items, the FHOME was administered only during the first year a home was included in the study.

Home Quality Rating Scale. The Home Quality Rating Scale (HQRS) was designed for use in the Family Care Study to complement the ratings obtained using the FHOME. The HQRS attempted to measure the sense of love and attachment of the careprovider to the person with mental retardation, the intrafamilial dynamics related to the target person, and family participation in providing care for the target person. The items on the HQRS are grouped into five factors, which are: a) Harmony of home and quality of parenting, seven items; b) Concordance in support of child care, four items; c) Openness and awareness of the careprovider, three items; d) Quality of the residential environment or dwelling, four items, and; e) Quality of the residential area or neighborhood, four items. Meyers, Mink, and Nihira (1981) reported satisfactory internal consistency reliabilities, between .70 and .86, for the first four factors, and somewhat lower reliabilities for the last factor.

As shown in Table 2.2, the HQRS was completed by the project staff member who visited the home during a given year of the project. The HQRS assesses domains that may change over time, so the HQRS ratings were completed during each of the three times of measurement.

Measures of Natural Parents

Responsible Parent Questionnaire. The Responsible Parent Question-naire was designed for the study to collect information from the natural parent of the child or adolescent with mental retardation. The respondent was the natural parent who had legal responsibility for the child or adolescent. The Responsible Parent Questionnaire assessed several do-mains, including basic demographic information on the natural parents, their reasons for placing the child outside the home, and their current attitudes toward and typical contact with their child. In addition, the Responsible Parent Questionnaire contained a series of items that inquired about the parents' developmental expectations for their children and their satisfaction with the child's current placement.

During the first year a person with mental retardation was involved in the Family Care Study, a project staff member contacted the natural parent who was to be interviewed. Then, each of these parents was interviewed individually by a project staff member in the parent's home. As mentioned above, the natural parent was interviewed only once, during the first year his/her child was in the Family Care Study, as the responses elicited from parents were not expected to change during the duration of the study.

PROCEDURES

Sample Selection

As noted previously, the people with mental retardation in the First Year sample consisted of individuals with mental retardation who met three criteria: a) they lived in a four-county area of southern California; b) they lived in a family care setting, and; c) they were 21 years old or younger at the start of the study. At initiation of the study, project personnel obtained lists of all people with mental retardation who met the preceding criteria. Case managers from the regional center helped project staff make contacts with the careproviders and natural families to enlist their participation in the study. Once their participation was ensured, the persons with mental retardation, their natural parents, their careproviders, and the careproviders' homes all became targets of assessment.

Data Collection

The data collected during the Family Care Study came from a variety of sources. As noted in Table 2.2, the three measures of the person with mental retardation—the BDS, the Individual and Family Characteristics Form, and the Individual Client Assessment Form—were completed by the person's case manager during the routine, state-mandated annual review of the person's case. In California, case managers typically monitor each of their assigned clients fairly closely, so a case manager's ratings on these forms constituted data from a person who knew each client well.

Two instruments were administered to careproviders, the Careprovider Questionnaire and the Careprovider Preference Survey. In most cases, these questionnaires were administered in group testing sessions at annual intervals. These group testing sessions had an average of 20-30 careproviders in attendance, and project staff provided detailed instructions for completing the forms and answered all questions careproviders had regarding any items on these forms.

Three forms were used to obtain information about the family care home in which the person with mental retardation was living; these forms were the PASS, the FHOME, and the HQRS. These three instruments were completed either during an interview in a careprovider's home by a project staff member (PASS and FHOME) or when the staff member had returned to the research office after completing the interview (HQRS). The careproviders' homes had high scores on most items on the PASS and the FHOME, as foster family care homes must meet many criteria to be licensed to care for people with mental retardation, and the licensing criteria are embodied in many of the PASS and FHOME items. As a result, many items on these inventories showed very little variability across homes, and the PASS and FHOME were completed on a home only during its first year in the study. The items comprising the HQRS revealed satisfactory levels of variability, so the HQRS was completed during each year a home was in the study.

The final instrument, the Responsible Parent Questionnaire, was administered only once, during the first year that a person with mental retardation participated in the study.

For instruments administered only once, data collection was completed during the first six months of the project. For instruments administered at each time of measurement, data were collected during a given month during a person's first year of participation in the study. Then, project staff ensured that, during the remaining times of measurement, data were collected from a subject at approximately 12-month intervals (± 1 month).

Monitoring Movement Between Placements

In order to obtain certain indices of successful placement, such as the stability of a person's placement in a given family care home, movements between placements were carefully monitored. Project staff received reports each month from case managers at the regional center regarding all changes in placement for subjects in the Family Care Study. These reports were then followed up through contact by project staff with careproviders in both the home from which the person with mental retardation was moved and the home to which the person was transferred. This close monitoring of movements between placements kept track of the home in which each person with mental retardation resided as well as providing a mechanism for recruiting into the Family Care Study the careprovider in the home to which person with mental retardation was transferred.

ANALYSES

The analyses for the Family Care Study were performed in a series of steps. The first task was to characterize people with mental retardation and their careproviders and home environments; these characterizations relied on descriptive statistics on a variety of scores obtained from the nine instruments used in the study. Next, control analyses were performed to determine whether differential drop-out of subjects would limit the generalizations that may be made based on the study. Finally, a series of structural equation models were fit to data from the study. These models represent the longitudinal relations among latent variables, or factors, representing characteristics of the persons with mental retardation, their careproviders, or their living conditions. These structural models, then, were the ultimate goal of the Family Care Study, providing models of important personal characteristics and how these characteristics change over time.

Basic Statistics

Certain basic forms of statistics were reported on people in the Family Care Study. Descriptive statistics reported on study variables consisted of the mean and standard deviation for quantitative, or continuous, variables or the percentage of individuals exhibiting some form of behavior for qualitative variables. These statistical indices can provide a useful description of the behavioral competencies and personal characteristics of various classes of subjects in the Family Care Study: the persons with mental retardation, their careproviders, and their parents.

To answer other questions, inferential statistics were also used. Here, correlations were computed among certain study variables to describe the linear associates among sets of variables. Also, analyses of variance were used to test the relationships of some outcome variables with qualitative variables, such as level of mental retardation.

Control Analyses

In longitudinal investigations, a major issue related to the ability to generalize results is the randomness of subject attrition. For more than 20 years, investigators (e.g., Riegel, Riegel, & Meyer, 1968) have found that attrition in longitudinal studies tends to be nonrandom—that is, subjects who drop out of a study tend to have less positive characteristics, e.g., lower intelligence, than do those remaining in the study. This pattern of nonrandom attrition has been reported across a variety of longitudinal investigations (e.g., Nesselroade & Baltes, 1974; Schaie, 1983), covering many domains of variables (e.g., ability, personality) and across the life span, from adolescence to old age. The purpose of the control analyses conducted was to investigate the limits to the ability to generalize results obtained on the core sample on which the most important statistical analyses were performed.

Drop-out control analyses. The drop-out control analyses used as dependent variables all of the important variables and scales from the Family Care Study that were assessed at the first time of measurement. The aim of the analysis was to determine whether the subjects who remained in the study for all times of measurement differed from those who dropped out at some point in the study. If differences between these groups arise, then the results from the Family Care Study should be generalized carefully only to populations of people who have the characteristics of the longitudinal subjects. Additional information on these analyses will be provided in Chapter 3.

Placement stability control analyses. A second type of control analysis contrasted longitudinal subjects who remained in the same family care home throughout the three-year span of the Family Care Study with longitudinal subjects who were shifted from one family care home to one or more homes during the span of the study. Certain of the most important forms of analysis to be pursued in this monograph could be performed only on subjects remaining in the same family care home throughout the study. If such subjects differ systematically from those who changed their residence during the study, then, once again, the results should be generalized carefully only to populations of people having characteristics similar to the people with stable placements. Further information on these analyses will also be presented in Chapter 3.

Structural Modeling of Longitudinal Relations

To investigate the longitudinal relations among constructs assessed during the Family Care Study, the authors employed structural equation modeling, using the LISREL 7 program (Jöreskog & Sörbom, 1988), to examine relations among latent variables across the three times of measurement. A latent variable is an unmeasured variable, a hypothetical construct that cannot be measured directly, but whose influence can be estimated on its indicators. For example, level of adaptive behavior is a latent variable that cannot be measured perfectly for any given person, but the effects of level of adaptive behavior can be estimated on indicators such as Personal Self-Sufficiency.

Using structural equation modeling with latent variables, it is possible to combine the latent variable representations of factor analysis with the linear relations between predictors and criteria of regression analysis to arrive at a useful representation of the patterns of causal relations among a set of latent variables or factors. In the Appendix, the authors discuss in more detail the way in which analyses were performed and then report more in-depth results from structural modeling of the data. Further detailed information on structural equation modeling is available in a number of standard sources, such as Jöreskog and Sörbom (1988), Hayduk (1987), and Bentler (1980; 1985), among others. The remaining parts of this chapter provide only an overview of the analyses, which should be sufficient to understand and interpret the results presented in later chapters.

Graphical conventions. The results of structural equation modeling are often presented in graphical form. For such a presentation to convey the outcomes of analyses well, certain graphical conventions are required. Two graphical conventions involve the figural symbols to represent types of variables; the authors have used conventions that are standard in literature using structural modeling. Specifically, the first convention is to use squares or rectangles to represent measured, or observed, variables. Measured variables correspond to scores on items or scales, the scores that can be observed on each individual. The second convention is to represent constructs, or latent variables, with circles or ellipses. As noted, latent variables correspond to hypothetical constructs that cannot be measured directly for each person; the most common form of latent variable encountered in research in the behavioral sciences is the factor underlying the representations of data achieved by factor analysis.

To illustrate the difference between measured and latent variables, consider the construct of adaptive behavior. Adaptive Behavior is a latent variable, which cannot be measured directly for any individual. In contrast, the three scales from the BDS—Personal Self-Sufficiency, Community Self-

Sufficiency, and Personal-Social Responsibility—are measured or observed variables in the current analyses. These measured variables consist of the sums of scores on specified sets of items and serve as indicators for the latent variable of adaptive behavior. In models pursued in this monograph, the three scales from the BDS (e.g., Personal Self-Sufficiency) would be placed inside squares or rectangles, whereas the latent variable of Adaptive Behavior would be placed within a circle or ellipse in figural presentations of models.

Two additional conventions were invoked to represent relations between variables. First, curved, double-headed arrows between variables represent symmetric relations, in which neither variable is presumed to have a causal influence on the other; essentially, such an arrow represents a correlation or covariance between the two variables. Second, a straight, single-headed arrow from one variable to another represents an asymmetric relation between the two variables, with the variable at the tail of the arrow exerting an influence on the variable toward which the arrow is pointed. Such a linear relation is frequently termed a direct effect or a direct causal relation. Using these conventions, it is possible to represent figurally all linear structural relations among variables in a structural model that may be specified identically using a series of linear equations.

Model specification. Model specification involves the selection of the set of linear relationships that are presumed to underlie the covariances among the observed variables in the model. In structural equation modeling, it is common to distinguish two aspects of a model that require specification, the measurement model and the structural model. The measurement model consists of the specified linear relations linking the unmeasured, latent variables (or constructs) to the measured variables that serve as their indicators. Each measured variable is presumed to be composed of two parts, one part linearly related to the latent variable(s) for which it is an indicator (i.e., the common part), and another part that is linearly unrelated to these latent variables. The latter part is termed the unique factor for the indicator, and reflects residual variance in the indicator after variance associated with the common latent variable(s) has been removed. For latent variable structural modeling, each construct must have two or more indicators; the resulting latent variables correspond to the factors derived in factor analyses. If a particular latent variable has only a single indicator, then the latent variable is essentially equated with its observed indicator, although it is possible to correct the latent variable for measurement error (see Jöreskog & Sörbom, 1988).

The second part of a structural equation model is often termed the structural model and consists of the relations among the latent variables in the model. These relations are of two types, correlations between latent variables or their residuals and directed (or causal) relations among latent variables. The directed relations correspond to partial regression coefficients in linear regression analysis. As with the observed variables, the variance of a latent variable may be decomposed logically and mathematically into two parts—one part linearly related to other latent variables that have causal impacts on the given latent variable, and a second part that is linearly unrelated to the predictor variables. The latter part of the variance of a latent variable is termed the residual variance of the variable and may be represented as the variance of a residual factor.

Parameter estimation. The parameters of a structural equation model are the path coefficients corresponding to: a) the regression coefficients associated with paths from latent variables to observed variables or from one latent variable to another; b) the linear covariances between variables, and; c) the variances of variables or their residuals. Once a structural model has been specified, each of the parameters of the model must be identified; this step is described in more detail in the Appendix. Then, each of the free parameters in the model must be estimated to maximize the fit of the model to the covariances among the observed variables.

For most structural modeling performed on data from the Family Care Study, maximum likelihood estimation of parameters was used. Maximum likelihood estimation is the most commonly used method of estimation. Moreover, use of maximum likelihood estimation is associated with a likelihood ratio chi-square measure of fit that allows one to test whether the given structural model is an adequate representation of the data. The one exception to this was the use of unweighted least squares in one analysis of quality of life dimensions in Chapter 5, in which the lack of multivariate normality in the data made use of maximum likelihood estimation injudicious.

Evaluation of the model. The evaluation of a structural equation model must be made on several levels. One way of doing so is to evaluate the fit of a given structural model to the data. Model fit was evaluated in two ways. The first method used the likelihood ratio test statistic that accompanies maximum likelihood estimation of parameters. The likelihood ratio statistic is distributed as a chi-squared variate, with degrees of freedom equal to the number of restrictions embodied in the model. According to this test, if the chi-square value is statistically significant, one may reject the current model in favor of an unstated, alternative model with at least one additional parameter estimate. Conversely, if the chi-square value is nonsignificant, then there is no statistical basis for rejecting the model, as its fit to the data resulted in nonsignificant deviations of predicted values from observed values.

The second way of evaluating the fit of a structural model is the use of a practical measure of fit. Here, the authors relied on the ρ coefficient, developed by Tucker and Lewis (1973), which was termed the "nonnormed fit index" by Bentler and Bonett (1980). Certain more technical points regarding the ρ coefficient are provided in the Appendix. In evaluating unrestricted factor analysis models, Tucker and Lewis advised that ρ values should be greater than or equal to .95 to conclude that a model adequately represents a set of data. However, Bentler and Bonett suggested that $\rho \geq .90$ was adequate for restricted structural equation models, such as those formulated in this monograph. Supporting the use of the ρ coefficient, Marsh, Balla, and McDonald (1988), on the basis of a large Monte Carlo study, concluded that the ρ coefficient was one of the best of the currently available indices of practical fit for covariance structure models.

Another level of evaluating the results of structural equation modeling is the evaluation of parameter estimates and their standard errors. The ratio of a parameter estimate over its standard error yields an asymptotic z-ratio to gauge the statistical significance of the parameter estimate. A common rule of thumb invoked in covariance structure modeling is that the z-value for a parameter estimate should be at least ± 2.0 to be considered statistically significant; that is, a parameter estimate should be at least twice as large as its standard error to be deemed statistically significant. A final check is on the relative levels of standard errors. Jöreskog and Sörbom (1988) stated that relatively large standard errors indicate that the corresponding parameter cannot be well estimated. As a result, standard errors should be approximately equal across different parts of a structural equation model for optimal estimation of all parameters.

Model respecification. If a structural equation model does not fit a set of data adequately, the model may be respecified, by adding one or more additional parameters to the model, to improve the fit of the model to the data. LISREL provides modification indices, which correspond to the estimated change in the chi-square statistic if a given fixed parameter were freely estimated. Using these modification indices, one may free parameters that will result in maximal improvement in the chi-square statistical index of fit. In the current study, the authors added parameters to inadequately fitting structural models based on modification indices and the theoretical meaning of the parameters. That is, in addition to modification indices, only additional parameters that made sense theoretically were estimated.

Confirmatory versus exploratory uses of structural equation modeling. Structural equation modeling was developed for use in confirmatory situations in which previous research and/or strong substantive theory supports the causal relations specified in the model. In this monograph, the authors pursued many analyses that were largely confirmatory, but were also partially exploratory. At present, there is considerable controversy regarding exploratory aspects of structural equation modeling, with some doubt regarding the replicability of models based on exploratory procedures (e.g., MacCallum, Roznowski, & Necowitz, in press).

The measurement models specified in the various chapters were primarily confirmatory in nature, with *a priori* specification of the indicators of each of the latent variables and with only a small number of additional measurement model parameters added to improve the fit of structural models to data.

The structural models in this monograph were more exploratory in nature than were the measurement models, yet even here there was a good deal of *a priori* specification of path coefficients. That is, the three times of measurement in the Family Care Study enabled considerable *a priori* specification, and therefore confirmatory analysis, of each structural model. For each construct measured at each of the three times of measurement in the study, the latent variable at Time 1 was presumed to affect the same latent variable at Time 2, which in turn was presumed to affect the like-named latent variable at Time 3. Such a specification, in which status at Time t on a given latent variable is represented as a function of status on the same variable at Time t-1 and an unrelated residual, conforms to a first-order autoregressive pattern of relationships, a common model for repeated measures data. Under such a specification, the effect of the latent variable at Time t-2 on the same variable at Time t is mediated fully by the variable at Time t-1. Of course, sometimes patterns of data require deviation from the first-order autoregressive pattern. In the context of this study, deviation from the first-order autoregressive pattern would take the form of a direct effect of the latent variable at Time 1 on the like-named latent variable at Time 3, a parameter that was readily entertained, if this proved to be a statistically significant parameter estimate.

More exploratory was the specification of cross-lagged paths between different constructs across time. But, because of the time-ordered nature of data collection, only certain paths were theoretically meaningful ones to estimate, so that model modifications were not fully exploratory. Given the somewhat exploratory nature of some of the model specifications, the models presented in this monograph should be considered preliminary statements of the causal influences among the constructs in the models. The ultimate utility of these models will only be determined by future research that attempts to replicate and extend these findings.

Chapter 3

Individuals With Mental Retardation in The Family Care Study

This chapter aims to describe the sample of persons with mental retardation, attempting to characterize them and their behavioral characteristics. In the first part of the chapter, data on personal characteristics are presented to provide a useful summary of the sample of the people in our study. These personal characteristics include basic demographic information, general level of health and ability, problem behaviors, placement history, reasons for initial out-of home placement, and reasons for current family care placement. This is an important task, as the results of this study should be generalized only to the population of which the sample is representative. That is, the patterns of results in the Family Care Study should not be generalized to populations of people with mental retardation with rather different personal characteristics. In the first part of this chapter, the authors attempt to characterize the subjects in terms of many different personal and behavioral characteristics, to more carefully delineate the sample of subjects and thereby prescribe the limits of the generalizations.

In the second part of the chapter, two control analyses are presented. The first analysis examines whether the Longitudinal subjects, who remained in the study for its three-year duration, differed from the Drop-out subjects, who dropped-out at some point during the study. The second analysis examines whether any differences exist among people with stable placements during the term of the study and those who remained in the study but moved to a new home during the study period (i.e., had unstable placements). These analyses have a most important function; the analyses will determine whether the results for the Longitudinal subjects can be generalized to the entire sample that entered the study or only to those subjects who remained in the study or in the same residence throughout the span of the project.

In the last part of the chapter, the authors present an initial structural model of the longitudinal relations among important personal characteristics, including the person's age, level of mental retardation, general health, level of adaptive behavior, level of social maladaptive behavior, and level of personal maladaptive behavior. This model forms the core of models that will be presented in Chapter 6, which focus on various contextual features, such as careprovider characteristics and quality of life dimensions, that influence or are influenced by these core personal characteristics of the persons with mental retardation in the Family Care Study.

CHARACTERIZING THE PERSONS WITH MENTAL RETARDATION IN THE FAMILY CARE STUDY

Personal Characteristics

Chronological age. Among the 333 people with mental retardation comprising the sample, nearly 65 percent were children or adolescents under 18 years of age at the first time of measurement in the Family Care Study; the remaining 35 percent were between the ages of 18 and 21 when entering the study. These proportions are not representative of all people with mental retardation in family care placements in the catchment area sampled or in California in general. For example, throughout California, about 50 percent of the persons with mental retardation who are placed in family foster care homes are older than 21. However, the principal aim of the Family Care Study was to focus on the impact of family care settings and their characteristics on the development of children and adolescents living in these settings. Thus, an age restriction for inclusion in the study was employed to define the sample. By restricting the sample to persons who were 21 or younger when the study was initiated, the developmental impact of an array of contextual variables, such as characteristics of the careprovider and the family setting, could be investigated during a time when development of the person is most malleable.

Other demographic variables. With regard to gender, the sample of 333 persons with mental retardation in the study was 56 percent male and 44 percent female. The majority of people were functioning in the mild (17 percent) or moderate ranges (45 percent) of mental retardation, using the standard AAMR classification (Grossman, 1983). The remaining individuals were identified as severely (31 percent) or profoundly (seven percent) mentally retarded. With regard to ethnicity, most of the people with mental retardation in the sample were White (84 percent). Hispanic persons comprised nine percent of the sample, Blacks three percent, and other ethnic origins four percent.

Comparison of the Family Care Study Sample to other people in family care settings. In this section, the demographic distributions of people in the sample are compared with three comparison groups. As discussed in Chapter 2, the people with mental retardation in the sample came from a four-county region of southern California that was served by a single regional center (Inland Counties Regional Center). These individuals comprised all people who were 21 years old or younger at the start of the study, lived in the four-county region, and lived in a family care setting. One comparison group comprised people who were 22 or older and who were living in family care settings in the same catchment area. The remaining two comparison groups consisted of all people with mental retardation throughout the state of California who were living in family care settings at the time of the study, again dividing this sample into people who were 21 or younger and those 22 or older. The use of these comparison groups enabled: a) comparisons of the sample from the Family Care Study with a state-wide sample of individuals within the same age range, and; b) comparisons of the sample with samples of older individuals living in similar settings.

As noted above, the age restriction for inclusion in the Family Care Study led to a sample of people with mental retardation with an age distribution that was nonrepresentative of all persons with mental retardation living in family care settings. On the other hand, the age distribution of the individuals in the sample is rather representative of the age distribution for individuals throughout the state of California who are 21 or younger and who are living in family care settings. The mean age of individuals in the Family Care Study sample was 14.1 years (SD = 3.8), and the mean age of people 21 or younger in the state-wide sample was 13.8 (SD = 3.7). For comparison, the mean age of people from the four-county catchment area 22 or older and living in family care settings was 39.3 (SD = 12.3), and the mean age of persons from the same age range in the state-wide sample was 39.1 (SD = 13.1). Thus, it appears that people with mental retardation from the four-county catchment area from which the sample was drawn are representative of persons with mental retardation throughout the state of California with regard to chronological age distribution. Thus, the results from this study with regard to the effects of chronological age require no major qualification when generalizing to the population of people with mental retardation who are 21 or younger throughout the state who live in family care settings.

Table 3.1 displays data on the three demographic variables of gender, ethnicity, and level of mental retardation for the Family Care Study sample as well as for the three comparison samples. The gender breakdown was very similar across all four samples. The state-wide sample of people 21 or younger had a somewhat higher percentage of males (60.8 percent) than did the Family Care Study sample (55.9 percent), but this difference is neither large nor especially noteworthy.

The breakdown by ethnicity revealed some differences in ethnic composition when comparing the Family Care Study sample with the state-wide sample of people in the same age range. Specifically, the Family Care Study sample had more White (83.5 percent versus 54.2 percent), fewer Black (3.3 percent versus 14.9 percent), and fewer Hispanic (9.3 percent versus 18.3 percent) people than did the state-wide sample. In general, the catchment area we sampled contained fewer persons of Asian origin when compared to the two age groupings of the state data. Interestingly, the ethnic distribution of subjects in the Family Care Study was very similar to the samples of people who were 22 or older in both the same catchment area as well as in the state-wide sample. Regardless of this similarity, some qualification may be necessary when generalizing the results from this study to the population

TABLE 3.1

Comparison of Demographic Characteristics of the
Family Care Study Sample with Three Comparison Samples

PERSON CHARACTERISTIC	STUDY SAMPLE AGE ≤ 21 (N = 333)		SAME STUDY SITE AGE ≥ 22 (N = 896)		STATE DATA AGE ≤ 21 (N = 3623)		STATE DATA AGE ≥ 22 (N = 9142)	
	N	%	N	%	N	%	N	%
Gender								
Female	147	44.1	407	45.4	1420	39.2	4167	45.6
Male	186	55.9	489	54.6	2203	60.8	4975	54.4
Ethnicity								
Asian	3	0.9	3	0.3	114	3.1	171	1.9
White	278	83.5	715	79.8	1965	54.2	7042	77.0
Black	11	3.3	65	7.3	539	14.9	716	7.8
Hispanic	31	9.3	98	10.9	662	18.3	914	10.0
Other	10	3.0	15	1.7	343	9.5	299	3.3
Level of Mental Retardation								
Unclassified	0	0.0	18	2.1	247	8.3	300	3.3
Mild/Moderate	209	62.8	600	66.9	1854	56.5	5754	63.4
Severe/Profound	124	37.2	278	31.0	1159	35.3	3028	33.4

of people who are 21 or younger throughout the state, as the population has a larger minority and smaller White representation than held for the sample in the Family Care Study.

The last characteristic evaluated was level of mental retardation. As shown in Table 3.1, the breakdown for people in the sample was quite similar to those in the same age range who were living in family care homes throughout the state of California, as well as for the two older groupings. For all four categories, the mild/moderate levels of mental retardation ranged from 56.5 to 66.9 percent and the severe/profound levels of mental retardation ranged from 31.0 to 37.2 percent. In summary, the demographic characteristics of the sample appear to be representative of people in family care facilities, except with regard to ethnicity, where the Family Care Study sample had a somewhat lower representation of persons from minority groups relative to the population.

General Levels of Physical Impairments and Health

Previous research has indicated that small family care settings are usually provided for people with mental retardation who do not have serious functional impairments or health problems (e.g., Borthwick, Meyers, & Eyman, 1981; Eyman & Borthwick, 1980; Eyman & Call, 1977; Lei & Eyman, 1979). More recently, however, deinstitutionalization and a corresponding reluctance to place people with mental retardation in institutions have resulted in increasing rates of family care placement of people who are lower functioning and have additional handicapping conditions than was the case in past years. The characteristics of the persons in the Family Care Study reflect each of these trends. The sample comprises a rather heterogeneous group that is less handicapped than most institutionalized groups, yet is far from being self-sufficient. More specifically, the people in the sample present a variety of special needs that must be met by caregivers and community resources.

Vision and hearing. The majority of persons in the study sample were free from sensory deficits, although some individuals were living in family care in spite of severe hearing (5.2 percent) or vision (4.8 percent) difficulties.

Seizures. Only four percent of the individuals in the sample of persons with mental retardation had problems with epileptic seizures that were rated as severe enough to impede developmental progress. However, an additional 16 percent were receiving medication to control seizure activity. The impact of the medication on behavior and development could not be determined in the context of the study.

Health. For the most part, the general health of persons in the sample was reported as good or excellent. For a substantial number (18 percent), however, their health was described as only fair or poor. Visits to the doctor for illness or injury averaged at least once a month for 27 people (9.1 percent) in the sample. Illnesses reported for persons in the study ranged from asthma (4.5 percent), chronic colds (16.8 percent), chronic skin problems (18.0 percent), enlarged colon or chronic constipation (7.8 percent), history of tuberculosis (0.6 percent), diabetes (0.6 percent), and heart conditions (11.7 percent)

Levels of Behavioral Skills and Abilities

Ambulation. The majority of the people studied were fully ambulatory (80.2 percent), whereas some walked with difficulty (11.3 percent), and a smaller proportion (8.4 percent) could not move about without assistance from others. With regard to basic body coordination, three percent of the people studied could not stand unassisted, 4.8 percent could not sit unassisted, and approximately five percent were unable to sit or stand, even with assistance. Approximately 36 percent of the people comprising the sample were in need of crutches, and six percent needed a walker, however, only one percent were restricted to a wheelchair. Comparative data published by Borthwick, Meyers, and Eyman (1981) are quite similar to this sample, even though the age range studied by Borthwick et al. was unrestricted.

Self-help skills. Basic self-help skills frequently have been named as selection criteria for community placement and as important predictors of successful adjustment to a community placement. Of the persons in the sample, the majority (56.5 percent) were considered fully toilet trained, and only 12 percent were not trained at all, with about 32 percent being partially toilet trained. In addition, about 22 percent were unable to bathe or wash their hands and faces by themselves, and approximately 35 percent required assistance when dressing.

Regarding the performance of purposeful activities around the home, 62 percent of the persons in the sample were able to clean and maintain their own rooms, and about 69 percent were able to perform simple chores around the home, such as gardening, emptying trash, and mopping floors. On the other hand, only 45 percent of the persons studied could focus attention on purposeful activities for at least 15 minutes, and 23 percent could not focus attention on activities at all.

With regard to food-related activities such as cooking, eating, and drinking, most of the persons comprising the sample were reasonably self-sufficient, with only about 12 percent unable to feed themselves, and about eight percent unable to drink from a glass or use table utensils without help from others. However, approximately 60 percent of the people in the sample did not prepare any foods or meals for themselves. Borthwick et al. (1981) reported that 51 percent of the people in their sample did not prepare meals for themselves. The higher percentage reported for the current sample may be due to the restricted age range that was sampled. However, it is unclear whether the high percentage in this study is due to the careproviders assuming responsibility for the task or an inability on the part of the persons studied to perform the food preparation tasks, as the BDS does not allow this type of distinction to be made.

Another facet of self-help skills involves interacting with the community environment through such activities as shopping, exchanging money, ordering food, and navigating the neighborhood around one's home. Approximately 23 percent of the people in the sample were reported to get lost whenever he/she left his/her own living area, and very few (3.3 percent) of the people studied could tell time. More than 60 percent never handled money; moreover, although 33 percent handled money, few could make change correctly. Only about 14 percent were able to make simple purchases without help, and less than eight percent of the sample had the skills requisite for ordering meals in restaurants.

Communication skills. The number of persons in the family care sample who were nonverbal was striking. More than one-third (40.4 percent) were unable to express themselves with words. Twelve percent of the individuals could not express anger or pleasure by vocal noises, and six percent did not even laugh or chuckle when happy. Only 30 percent of the sample could speak in simple sentences. This inability to communicate has serious implications for careproviders, in terms of additional workload and, in some cases, lack of positive feedback and affective reinforcement for caregiving efforts. With regard to reading and writing, 74 percent of the persons were unable to read, and 81 percent could not write or print any words, although 26 percent could print his/her own name. The dangers associated with an inability to read simple warning signs, for example, extends additional responsibility to the careprovider.

Maladaptive Behaviors

The Behavior Development Survey contains numerous items that identify the frequency of maladaptive behaviors exhibited by persons in the sample. In general, the sample of subjects in the Family Care Study showed moderate levels of maladaptive behaviors, either in the form of socially maladaptive behaviors or personally maladaptive behaviors. Certain forms of problem behavior were exhibited fairly frequently by the persons in the sample. Specifically, persons frequently (20.5 percent) or occasionally (16.3 percent) displayed stereotypical behaviors, frequently (15.4 percent) or occasionally (11.1 percent) exhibited forms of hyperactive behavior, frequently (12.5 percent) or occasionally (41.0 percent) showed forms of rebelliousness (such as ignoring restrictions and instructions), frequently (10.3 percent) or occasionally (33.4 percent) damaged his/her own or other's property, and frequently (9.9 percent) or occasionally (35.2 percent) were disruptive of others' activities.

On the other hand, several other, more serious types of maladaptive behavior were shown fairly infrequently by the people in the sample. These more serious problem behaviors included physical violence, hostile or profane language, running away, stealing or cheating, tearing off one's own clothing, self-inflicting physical violence, performing socially unacceptable sexual behaviors, or requiring seclusion and/or restraint. These behaviors were rated as frequent occurrences for less than five percent of the people with mental retardation in the sample.

The persons in the sample displayed many behaviors that can be considered maladaptive. Although these problem behaviors often require additional care and monitoring on the part of the careprovider, the frequency of the maladaptive behaviors exhibited was not notably high. The more serious forms of maladaptive behavior were shown rather infrequently by the people in the Family Care Study. Comparative data from Borthwick et al. (1981) for the same forms of maladaptive behavior revealed lower frequencies for almost all categories of behavior than held for the persons in this sample. However, the differences in frequency rates are not large for any particular form of maladaptive behavior. Also, it is likely that the differences in results reported by Borthwick et al. and in the current study are due to differences in the age ranges covered. That is, as mentioned above, Borthwick et al. studied persons in family care settings regardless of their chronological age, whereas this sample was restricted to people who were 21 or younger. There is some evidence that levels of maladaptive behavior show systematic age-related changes (e.g., Eyman & Widaman, 1987), so the inclusion of older subjects in the Borthwick et al. study may account for the lower frequency rates for maladaptive behaviors reported in that study.

PATTERNS OF RESIDENTIAL PLACEMENT

Placement History

The importance of considering an individual's background with regard to residential living experiences cannot be overstated. Variables such as the length of time a person spends with his/her natural family before being placed outside the home, the types of out-of-home placement a person has experienced, the number of times a person has been moved from one setting to another, and the number of times a person has been returned to his/her own family can affect significantly the quality of life for the individual as well as his/her currently attained levels of adaptive and maladaptive behavior. A wide range of residential placement histories were evidenced in the Family Care Study sample.

Time with natural families. A small group (N = 52, or 16 percent) of the persons with mental retardation were placed immediately after birth and had never lived with their natural families. By contrast, 27 of the people (or seven percent) had lived at home during two or more time periods in their lives. The remaining 254 people in the sample (comprising 76 percent of the total sample of 333 persons) had lived with their parents for some time, but only until the initial out-of-the home placement, and had never returned home for more than a brief visit.

Age at first placement. Most (78 percent) of the individuals with mental retardation had been placed outside the natural home before their tenth birthday, and 47 percent of these were placed within four years of birth. As expected, children with more severe handicaps were placed at somewhat younger ages than were those functioning at higher levels. Representing this trend, the mean age for initial out-of-home placement was 6.21 years (SD = 4.83) for persons with mild or moderate mental retardation, and 5.02 years (SD = 4.17) for persons with severe or profound retardation.

Family care placements. For slightly more than half (54 percent) of the sample, the family care home in which they lived at the time of the study was the only family care setting in which they had been placed. In contrast, 33 percent of the sample had lived in two or three family care homes, and the remaining 13 percent had lived in from four to twelve different family care homes since leaving their natural homes.

Institutional history. Whereas the majority (53 percent) of persons with mental retardation had never been placed in an institution, 40 percent had had at least one residential stay in a state institution. Moreover, the remaining seven percent had been returned to an institution after having been moved from an institutional placement into a community setting for the initial time. Of the 155 persons who had at one time lived in a state hospital, 68 people, or about 44 percent, had spent more than two years in state hospital placements.

Prior placements. Among the 333 people with mental retardation, 31 percent (N = 103) were in their initial out-of-home placement. On the other hand, 29 percent of the sample were people who had been deinstitutionalized, and the remaining 40 percent were transferred from other community residential facilities, the majority of which were other small community care homes. Generally, the people who were in their first out-of-home placement were considerably younger (mean age 12.50 years, SD = 5.68) than were the persons who either were previously institutionalized or had other experiences in out-of-home placement (mean age 15.83 years, SD = 5.00). A surprisingly high number of people in the study had experienced rather unstable placement histories, with nearly 43 percent of the Family Care Study sample having resided in four or more placements prior to the time of the study.

Reasons for Initial Out-Of-Home Placement

The reasons for initial out-of-home placement that were reported by parents whose children were initially placed during the duration of the study were examined, as well as reasons given in retrospect by parents who were interviewed at the time of the study regarding the prior placement of their children. Parents were also questioned regarding the source of greatest influence in the decision to place their children outside their natural home and regarding some of their feelings about the decision they had made.

The reasons natural parents gave for initial out-of-home placement fell into three major categories: Family problems at home, including marital difficulties, psychological problems such as inability to cope, and financial difficulties; the need for professional supervision and training, due to such issues as a physical inability to handle the child's self-care and/or medical needs, the need for professional supervision of problem behavior, or a desire for appropriate environmental advantages for the child, including education and training, living with peers of similar IQ, and having a life as normal as possible for the child; and other less common reasons, such as abandonment by parents or unavailability of services in the community for parents who had originally placed their children in institutions. Parents were also allowed to respond to this question by noting that they decided upon out-of-home placement for the child immediately after birth. Unfortunately, no specific reason for this decision was available on the questionnaire, so that parents choosing this answer may have based their decision on any of the three types of reasons outlined above.

Overall, the most commonly stated reason for the initial out-of-home placement was to alleviate family problems of one sort or another, a reason selected by 171, or more than 54 percent, of the 313 natural parents interviewed. The next most frequent reason, selected by 83 parents, more than 26 percent of the sample, was to obtain professional supervision, training, or appropriate living experiences for the child. The remaining 60 parents stated that they placed their children either immediately after birth (34, or 11 percent) or for some other reason not subsumed within the previous categories (26, or 8 percent).

Personal and Family Characteristics Related to Reasons for Placement

Table 3.2 shows the breakdown of reasons for initial out-of-home placement by relevant personal and family characteristics. In addition to placement immediately after birth, Table 3.2 provides the tabulation of responses in the three categories of reasons: a) family problems; b) supervision and training, and; c) other reasons, as a function of other variables of interest.

Person's level of mental retardation. One initial hypothesis was that the person's level of mental retardation would be related to reasons for placement. The more profound the person's level of mental retardation, the more obvious the physical and behavioral pathology at birth. As a result, placement immediately after birth was expected to be more common for persons at the severe/profound level of mental retardation relative to those at the mild/moderate level. Interestingly, reasons for the initial out-of-home placement were unrelated to the person's level of mental retardation ($p > .50$). As shown in Table 3.2, the distribution of reasons for placement of persons in the mild and moderate ranges of mental retardation was very similar to that for persons in the severe and profound ranges.

Person's chronological age at placement. In contrast to level of mental retardation, the chronological age of the person with mental retardation at the time of placement appeared to be strongly related to parental reasons for the placement of their child, χ^2 (9, N=310) = 171.88, $p < .0001$, as shown in Table 3.2. This test of significance was affected, however, by the fact that the 34 natural parents who placed their children immediately after birth were required to provide no other reason for placement. Discarding these parents from the analysis, there was a nonsignificant overall relationship between the child's age at placement and the reasons stated for placement, χ^2(6, N=296) = 7.60, ns.

Despite the nonsignificant overall chi-square, there were meaningful trends exhibited in the reasons for placement as a function of the child's age at placement. Specifically, parents citing the alleviation of family problems as the reason for placement decreased systematically from about 71 percent for children placed before their second birthday to approximately 58 percent for children placed after the age of 5 years. A similar trend held for parents citing "other" reasons for placement, which fell from approximately 17 percent for children placed before their second birthday to around 7 percent

TABLE 3.2

Type of Initial Out-of-Home Placement for Persons with Mental Retardation as a Function of Personal and Family Characteristics

CHARACTERISTICS	REASONS FOR OUT-OF-HOME PLACEMENT				
	IMMEDIATELY AFTER BIRTH[1]	FAMILY PROBLEMS	SUPERVISION AND TRAINING	OTHER	TOTAL
Person's MR level[a]					
Mild/Moderate	18	107	51	17	193
	(9.3)	(55.4)	(26.4)	(8.8)	(100.0)
Severe/Profound	16	57	30	9	112
	(14.3)	(50.9)	(26.8)	(8.0)	(100.0)
Person's age at placement[b]					
0–1 year	34	17	3	4	58
	(58.6)	(29.3)	(5.2)	(6.9)	(100.0)
		(70.8)[c]	(12.5)[c]	(16.7)[c]	(100.0)
2–5 years	0	71	28	12	111
	(0.0)	(64.0)	(25.2)	(10.8)	(100.0)
6–10 years	0	52	32	6	90
	(0.0)	(57.7)	(35.6)	(6.7)	(100.0)
11+ years	0	30	17	4	51
	(0.0)	(58.8)	(33.3)	(7.9)	(100.0)
Mother's age[d]					
Under 30	17	57	16	13	103
	(16.5)	(55.3)	(15.5)	(12.6)	(100.0)
30 and over	13	104	63	8	188
	(6.9)	(55.3)	(33.5)	(4.3)	(100.0)
Family Composition[e]					
Both biological parents	7	102	44	10	163
	(4.3)	(62.6)	(27.0)	(6.1)	(100.0)
One biological parent	1	52	35	11	99
	(1.0)	(52.5)	(35.4	(11.1)	(100.0)
Other	25	17	4	5	51
	(49.0)	(33.3)	(7.8)	(9.8)	(100.0)
Number of Siblings[f]					
None	10	26	9	2	47
	(21.3)	(55.3)	(19.1)	(4.3)	(100.0)
1 or 2	14	85	42	10	151
	(9.3)	(56.3)	(27.8)	(6.6)	(100.0)
3 or more	3	54	30	7	94
	(3.2)	(57.4)	(31.9)	(7.4)	(100.0)

Note. [1]No specified reason for placement. Tabled values are frequencies, with row percentages in parentheses.

[a]χ^2 (3, $N = 305$) = 1.89, *ns*

[b]χ^2 (9, $N = 310$) = 171.88, $p < .0001$, and χ^2 (6, $N = 276$) = 7.60, *ns*. Parents selecting "immediately after birth" were excluded from computation of the latter chi-square value, because they were constrained, by definition, to have children falling at only one of the four levels of "age at placement."

[c]Row percentages based only on the 24 parents giving a specific reason for placement (i.e., excluding the 34 parents selecting "immediately after birth" as reason for placement).

[d]χ^2 (3, $N = 291$) = 20.31, $p < .001$

[e]χ^2 (6, $N = 313$) = 104.02, $p < .0001$

[f]χ^2 (6, $N = 292$) = 13.5, $p < .05$

for children placed at the age of 6 or later. The similarity of this trend was supported by analyses, $\chi^2(3, N=196) = 1.21, p > .70$.

In contrast, the percentage of parents stating that the need for professional supervision or appropriate training and life experiences led to their decision for out-of-home placement increased steadily as a function of child's age at placement, with 12.5 percent, 25 percent, and about 35 percent of parents placing their child at 0-1 year, 2-5 years, or 6+ years of age, respectively, providing such a reason. The difference between the systematic decreases in citing family problems or other reasons for placement and the corresponding systematic increases in citing supervision and training as the reason for placement was statistically significant, $\chi^2(1, N=296) = 4.59, p < .05$.

Maternal age at placement. The natural mother's age at the time of placement was also related significantly to reasons given for placement, as shown in Table 3.2. For this analysis, mothers were divided into two categories: a) younger, or under 30 years of age when the child was initially placed outside the home, and; b) older, or 30 years or older when the child was placed. Regardless of maternal age, the majority of natural mothers (55 percent) reported placing their child outside the home to ease family problems. However, younger mothers tended to cite professional supervision or training/life experiences less often as a reason for placement of their children relative to older mothers (15.5 percent and 33.5 percent for the younger and older mothers, respectively). On the other hand, younger mothers had a greater tendency either to place their children immediately after birth (16 percent) or to cite other reasons (13 percent) than did older mothers, of whom only seven percent placed their children immediately after birth and four percent cited other reasons.

Family composition. The reasons provided for initial out-of-home placement were significantly related to family composition at the time of placement. As shown in Table 3.2, almost two-thirds (63 percent) of families with both biological parents present stated that family problems were the primary reason that motivated the initial out-of-home placement. Slightly more than one-quarter (27 percent) of the families with both biological parents cited the need for professional supervision or training as the reason for the initial placement, and relatively few of these families provided other reasons for placement (6 percent) or placed their children immediately after birth (4 percent).

A similar pattern of reasons for initial out-of-home placement was provided by families in which only one of the child's biological parents was present. In these families, about half (53 percent) mentioned the alleviation of family problems as the reason for initial out-of-home placement, more than one-third (35 percent) noted the need for professional supervision or training, one-ninth (11 percent) gave other reasons, and only one family (1 percent) placed their child immediately after birth.

In contrast, a rather different pattern of reasons for placement was given by parent figures for families for which neither biological parent was present. Of these families, almost half (49 percent) placed their children immediately after birth, one-third (33 percent) cited the easing of family problems at home as a motivating factor, and smaller percentages of families cited either the need for professional supervision or training (8 percent) or gave other reasons for the initial placement (10 percent).

Number of siblings. Finally, families with different numbers of children showed some differences in reasons given for the initial out-of-home placement for the child with mental retardation, as shown in Table 3.2. Regardless of the number of siblings of the child with mental retardation, the majority of families (approximately 56 percent) stated that the primary reason for the initial placement was to alleviate family problems in the home that surrounded caring for a child with mental retardation. But, placement immediately after birth was inversely related to the number of children in the family, with such placements being much more common in families in which the child with mental retardation was the only child (21 percent) than if the child with mental retardation had one or two siblings (nine percent) or three or more siblings (three percent). On the other hand, citing the need for professional supervision or training was positively related to the number of siblings, increasing from 19 to 28 percent to 32 percent for families in which the child with mental retardation had no siblings, one or two siblings, or three or more siblings, respectively. The percentages of families mentioning other reasons for placement were fairly constant across number of siblings in the family.

Other Placement-Related Variables

Primary source of advice regarding initial placement. Natural parents were asked to recall the person who had the greatest impact on their decision to place their retarded child in his/her initial out-of-home placement. Family physicians, ministers, social workers and psychologists, spouses, and other family members were among the sources named by the majority of parents. Some differences in the source of placement influence were observed in relation to the child's level of mental retardation. Whereas parents whose children had severe or profound retardation were more likely to have been influenced by a physician, parents of children with less retardation were more often influenced by a spouse or other family member. The impact of professional counselors or psychologists on out-of-home placement was important regardless of level of retardation.

A moderate relationship existed between the reason given (in retrospect) for initial placement and the source of primary influence. As expected, parents who cited "physically unable to handle the child" were most often influenced by physicians, "psychological pressures/problems in the home" by counselors and psychologists, and "environmental advantages to the child" (special education/training, normalization) by spouses or other family members.

Parental reflection on decision to place child. Parents who had placed their children for physical or environmental reasons tended to be the least sure that they would make the same placement decision again. These parents decided to place their children in order to secure better supervision or training opportunities for their children. In essence, these parents made their decision with the child's best interest as the primary basis for the decision. These placements were seen as a way to improve the child's life situation, with less weight given to the parents' own wishes to keep their child living at home.

Conversely, those parents who had placed their children for psychological reasons, such as to alleviate problems in the family, seemed most certain that their original decision had been correct. For these parents, the primary reason for placement was the fact that the retarded child was a disruption to family functioning. As a result, their placement decisions were based less on concern for improvement in the child's life situation than on improving the living situation for the family. Because placement outside the home for the "disruptive" child with mental retardation led to improved family functioning, these parents looked back on their placement decisions and tended to be quite confident that they had made the correct decision.

Parental visits and reason for out-of-home placement. Nearly all (95 percent) of the parents visited their children at least once or twice a year, and only a small group (five percent) never saw their children. Parents who visited their children most often (at least once a month) were those who had placed them for physical or reasons of environmental advantage. In contrast, parents whose children were placed for psychological reasons or had been placed immediately at birth were most likely to be those who never visited their retarded children in the current family care home.

Possibility of child's return to natural home. The majority (55 percent) of parents felt that they might one day take their children back into their homes on a permanent basis. Of these, 23 percent felt certain that this would occur. Parents who had placed their children to ensure a normalized environment with education and training were most likely to consider taking their children back home. Parents of younger children (one to five years) were also more optimistic about this possibility. Conversely, the parents whose children who had been placed for reasons of psychological pressure at home or who were 18 years or older were least likely to take their children back. Parents of school-age children tended to be most uncertain about the prospect of the child's return.

Few parents (three percent) cited financial problems as the primary reason for the out-of-home placement decision, but 21 percent of parents indicated they would be more willing to take their children home if the state would agree to pay them what the careprovider was currently receiving.

Whereas parents who had placed their children because they could not physically handle the child were more likely to consider reimbursement, parents who had placed for reasons of environmental advantage to the child were less inclined to consider this possibility.

Reasons Given for Current Family Care Placement

Table 3.3 shows the relationship between the individuals' prior living arrangements (excluding first placements) and reasons for placement in their current family care home, a relationship that was statistically significant ($p < .0001$). The results clearly indicate that a majority of the persons previously residing in non-institutional settings were relocated due to problems associated with the service system or with the child and his/her relations with others. That is, few of these people were relocated to achieve a normalized environment. More specifically, transfer from another community care facility was most likely due to "other" reasons for placement (74 percent), of which the majority were due to conflict in previous placement (37 percent) or to closure of the prior facility (23 percent). Placement from the home of parents, relatives, or friends was primarily the result of the inability of the caregivers to cope with the child or with caregiving demands.

In contrast, the clear majority (more than 75 percent) of people whose prior living arrangement was a state institution or convalescent hospital were placed in their current family care home in order to achieve a more normalized environment. Rather small numbers of these people had been placed because their parents could not cope or for other reasons.

TABLE 3.3

Reasons for Current Placement for Persons with Mental Retardation As a Function of Previous Living Arrangement

	REASONS FOR CURRENT PLACEMENT			
PRIOR LIVING ARRANGEMENT	PARENTAL INABILITY TO COPE	TO ACHIEVE NORMALIZED ENVIRONMENT	OTHER (E.G., CLOSURE OF FACILITY)	TOTAL
Other community facility	17	15	91	123
	(13.8)	(12.2)	(74.0)	(100.0)
Home of parents, relatives, or friends	87	5	11	103
	(84.5)	(4.9)	(10.7)	(100.0)
Institution or convalescent hospital	16	74	8	98
	(16.3)	(75.5)	(8.2)	(100.0)

Note. Tabled values are frequencies, with row percentages in parentheses. Association between prior placement and reason for current placement was significant, χ^2 (4, $N = 324$) = 291.24, $p < .0001$.

CONTROL ANALYSES: DETERMINING THE REPRESENTATIVENESS
OF SUBJECTS IN THE FAMILY CARE STUDY

When presenting results from any research investigation, it is important to delineate the population to which results may be generalized. To do so, one must consider the method by which subjects were selected, the "population" from which they were selected, and the relevant characteristics of the subjects who comprised the sample. These issues were dealt with in the preceding section of this chapter. As discussed in the preceding section, the sample consisted of all persons in the requisite age range who lived in a four-county area of southern California and resided in family care settings. This procedure—taking all individuals with given characteristics—guarantees that the group studied is representative of the population. In one sense, the authors obtained virtually the entire population in the area studied. Moreover, the study sample seemed fairly representative of other people living in family care settings throughout the state of California with regard to several basic personal characteristics. These findings suggest that there is considerable justification for generalizing the results to all people in the state of California living in family care settings, at least those under the age of 22.

However, additional issues surrounding the generalization of results arise in the context of longitudinal investigations. In such investigations, the final sample of people observed across all times of measurement may become systematically less and less representative of those who constituted the initial sample if subject attrition is related to important variables in the study. In many previous longitudinal studies, whether long-term (e.g., Damon, 1965) or short-term (e.g., Nesselroade & Baltes, 1974), analyses suggested that results could not be generalized to the population at large. Rather, generalization of results was justified only to rather positively selected portions of the population. In this section, two forms of control analyses are reported. Both analyses bear on the issue of the ability to generalize the results of the longitudinal relations obtained in the Family Care Study.

Although hundreds of pieces of information on the individuals, careproviders, and care facilities were collected, most of these pieces of information were used to create scales or composite indices of more general characteristics. For example, a Health index for each person in the sample was created by averaging across seven pieces of information: frequency of doctor visits, asthma attacks, colds, seizures, skin ailments, colon problems, and heart problems. Table 3.4 contains a list of the 25 variables, scales, and indices that were examined in order to characterize better the individuals in the sample. These 25 variables associated with people with mental retardation were then used to compare the individuals who remained in the study for the duration of the study (the Longitudinal group) with those who withdrew from the study at any point during data collection (the Drop-out

TABLE 3.4

Description of the Variables Used in the Drop-out Control Analyses

VARIABLE	DESCRIPTION
Person Age	Chronological age of person at the first time of measurement
Level of Mental Retardation	Standard AAMR four category classification: mild, moderate, severe, and profound, coded numerically such that higher numbers mean higher level of dysfunction.
Careprovider Age	Chronological age of primary careprovider at the first time of measurement.
Careprovider Education	Highest grade completed by primary careprovider (e.g., college graduate = 16).
Careprovider Experience (Yrs)	Number of years careprovider has participated in family care.
Careprovider Involvement	Amount of time careprovider spends in care for person.
Health Index of Person with MR	Average of seven items: frequency of doctor visits, asthma attacks, colds, seizures, skin ailments, colon problems, and heart problems.
Health Rating of Person with MR	Overall rating of person's health as judged by the primary careprovider.
Careprovider Preference Survey	The CPS contains items to which the careprovider gave two responses: 1) How serious is a behavior (not serious, somewhat serious, very serious) and 2) Is the behavior something the careprovider is willing to handle (yes or no). An item score was the seriousness rating but was scored as 0 if the careprovider was unwilling to handle the behavior.
Personal Self-Sufficiency	The average of 8 items about the person in the family home: spilling while eating, unsteadiness on feet, trouble drinking from glass, toileting accidents, help toileting, bed wetting, help bathing, help dressing.
Community Self-Sufficiency	The average of 4 items about the person in the family home: help using money, unable to clean room properly, unable to fix simple foods, unable to do simple chores.
Personal-Social Responsibility	The average of 4 items about the person in the family home: unable to pay attention to activities, unable to take care of own things, does not play or talk with others at home, nonparticipation in group activities.
Social Maladaption	The average of 16 items about the person in the family home: wandering off, threatens with words/gestures, physically slaps or punches others, purposefully breaks things, disrupts activities, swears, refuses to follow instructions, takes others' things, runs away, inappropriate sexual behavior, homosexual behavior, masturbatory behavior, too friendly, too bossy, unable to get along with others, and continually hangs onto careprovider.

(continued on next page)

TABLE 3.4 *(continued)*

VARIABLE	DESCRIPTION
Personal Maladaption	The average of 9 items about the person in the family home: constant drooling, stereotypical behavior (e.g., head banging, rocking), makes strange noises (e.g., groaning, teeth grinding), tears off clothing, deliberately hurts self, hyperactivity, uninterested in anything, extreme emotionality, and peculiar habits (e.g., eating dirt).
Behavior Development Survey Personal Self-Sufficiency	10 items from the BDS measuring personal self-sufficiency attributes were summed: toilet training, self-care at toilet, bathing, washing hands and face, donning clothes, donning shoes, walking and running, body coordination, drinking with a glass, and using table utensils.
Community Self-Sufficiency	15 items from the BDS measuring community self-sufficiency attributes were summed: understanding complex instructions, handling money, job complexity, preparing food, sense of direction, maintaining own room, clearing table, eating in public, making purchases, telling time, number skills, reading, writing, sentence complexity, and vocabulary.
Personal-Social Responsibility	7 items from the BDS measuring personal and social responsibility attributes were summed: care of clothing, care of personal belongings, paying attention, activity initiation, awareness of others, interactions with others, and participation in group activities.
Social Maladaption	8 items from the BDS measuring attributes of social maladaption were summed: threatens or does physical violence, damages property, disrupts activities, uses profane/hostile language, rebelliousness, attempting to run away, and untrustworthiness.
Personal Maladaption	4 items from the BDS measuring attributes of personal maladaption were summed: displaying stereotypical behavior, removing/tearing off own clothing, self-inflicting physical violence, and hyperactivity.
Activities in Public Places	Average number of public activities in which the person participated during the preceding 4 months. The places were: going to a 1) mall, 2) store, 3) restaurant, 4) park, picnic area, and 5) library, museum, zoo.
Participation in Clubs, etc.	Average number of club affiliations from eight items: 1) church, 2) scouts, 4H, etc., 3) YMCA or YWCA, 4) parks recreation programs for nondisabled, 5) athletic team (e.g., soccer), 6) athletics for developmentally disabled, 7) music, band, choir, etc., and 8) other specified clubs.
Participation in Events	Average number of events in which the person participated during the preceding 4 months. The events were: 1) movies, 2) amusement parks, 3) day trips (e.g., beach), 4) overnight trips (e.g., camping), 5) single activity (e.g., dancing, bowling), and 6) spectator sporting events.

(continued on next page)

TABLE 3.4 *(continued)*

VARIABLE	DESCRIPTION
Stability of Placement	Total number of different living arrangements that a person has been in (e.g., institution, group home, foster care, parents, relatives, etc.).
Normalization of Placement	Average of 28 items from the PASS. The instrument measures the degree to which the family home facility approximates a normal home environment (higher scores) or an institutional setting (lower scores).
Quality of Environment	Average of 44 MHOME and 12 HQRS items assessing the quality of the home environment (e.g., affective, physical, cognitive). Higher scores indicate higher quality.
Relationships	Average of 5 point ratings of the harmoniousness of a person's relationships with: 1) Foster mother, 2) foster father, 3) other disabled children in home, 4) other non-disabled children in home, 5) natural mother, 6) natural father, 7) school teacher, 8) friends or school-mates, 9) neighbors, 10) pets, and 11) other specified relationships. Higher scores indicate higher quality.

group) as well as to compare persons with and without stable placements during the study period.

Drop-Out Comparisons

The first type of control analysis performed on data from the Family Care Study investigated whether subjects remaining in the study during all possible times of measurement differed from subjects who dropped out at some point during their participation in the study. All of these analyses were performed using data from the first occasion of measurement, as the Drop-out group had missing data for later occasions of measurement.

As shown in Table 3.5, of the 25 variables presented, only four variables revealed significant differences between the Longitudinal group and the Drop-out group. Two of these four variables involved placement-related characteristics: a) stability, indexed by the number of placement changes prior to initiation of the study, and; b) normalization of placement, measuring the degree to which the care facility approximates a normal home environment. As shown in Table 3.5, the Drop-out group showed fewer placement changes and greater normalization of placement relative to the Longitudinal group.

The third variable on which the Longitudinal and Drop-out groups differed was careprovider involvement, the only one of the nine careprovider variables to differ across groups. The careproviders for the Drop-out group showed less involvement in caregiving than did those for the Longitudinal group. This may explain why the people in the Drop-out sample became

TABLE 3.5

Drop-out Control Analyses: Testing Differences between Longitudinal
And Drop-out Samples on Variables Collected at the
First Time of Measurement

VARIABLE	LONGITUDINAL		DROP-OUT		
	M	SD	M	SD	F RATIO
Person Age	15.45	5.30	14.72	5.70	1.50
Level of Mental Retardation	3.28	0.82	3.13	0.87	1.35
Careprovider Age	52.00	9.77	51.46	10.53	0.52
Careprovider Education	11.34	2.92	11.80	2.60	1.89
Careprovider Experience (Yrs)	8.42	5.05	8.62	6.70	0.04
Careprovider Involvement	2.17	2.03	1.47	1.65	5.68*
Health Index of Person with MR	0.72	0.27	0.68	0.27	1.15
Health Rating of Person with MR	1.89	0.75	1.85	0.95	0.07
Careprovider Preference Survey					
Personal Self-Sufficiency	4.16	4.16	4.39	3.93	0.03
Community Self-Sufficiency	1.07	1.65	1.25	1.66	0.42
Personal-Social Responsibility	2.53	2.35	2.49	2.22	0.06
Social Maladaption	12.89	8.83	13.29	7.62	0.07
Personal Maladaption	6.78	5.95	6.10	4.78	1.29
Behavioral Development Schedule					
Personal Self-Sufficiency	31.39	13.32	32.44	14.74	0.08
Community Self-Sufficiency	17.13	10.76	20.02	13.62	3.07+
Personal-Social Responsibility	11.92	6.32	12.70	6.73	0.49
Social Maladaption	2.57	2.65	3.05	3.01	1.47
Personal Maladaption	1.40	1.81	1.39	1.94	0.00
Activities in Public Places	0.81	0.22	0.80	0.25	0.31
Participation in Clubs, etc.	0.24	0.17	0.24	0.17	0.03
Participation in Events	0.58	0.29	0.58	0.29	0.01
Stability of Placement	2.38	0.58	1.85	0.57	6.07*
Normalization of Placement	3.00	1.85	3.13	1.47	5.03*
Quality of Environment	3.24	0.50	3.21	0.47	0.52
Relationships	2.86	0.35	2.78	0.34	1.18

Note. Sample sizes for all variables except Relationships were: Longitudinal $N = 272$, Drop-out $N = 61$. For Relationships, Longitudinal $N = 270$, Drop-out $N = 60$. F ratios had 1 and 329 degrees of freedom; F ratio for Relationships had 1 and 326 degrees of freedom.
$^+p < .10$
$^*p < .05$

drop-outs during the course of the study: their careproviders were less involved in providing care and were therefore likely to be less interested in ensuring continued presence in a study of child and adolescent development in family care settings.

The fourth and final variable noted as revealing differences across the two groups was Community Self-Sufficiency as measured by the BDS. This difference between the groups was of marginal significance ($p < .10$), but the magnitude of the difference was not large, less than a quarter of one SD unit for the Drop-out sample.

On the remaining 21 person and careprovider characteristics, nonsignificant differences between the Longitudinal and Drop-out groups were found. Moreover, the between-group differences in means and SDs for most variables were quite small in magnitude. Thus, across all variables listed in Table 3.5, the Longitudinal and Drop-out groups appear to be more similar than different. This is a welcome outcome, as it means that subject attrition during the study was a fairly random occurrence, not strongly related to any important variables in the study. Indeed, the only nonrandomness to subject attrition may have occurred through the lower levels of involvement exhibited by careproviders in the Drop-out group, as noted above. The lack of large between-group differences means that the results presented in later chapters on the longitudinal relations among personal, careprovider, and residential characteristics can be generalized to the population represented by those people initially selected for the study, as the Longitudinal sample was quite representative of this initial sample.

Comparisons of Subjects with Stable and Unstable Placements

The second set of control analyses involved the comparison of two subgroups of longitudinal subjects—those who remained in the same home during the three times of measurement of the study (Stable group) and those who changed homes at some time during the span of the study (Unstable group). This is an important control analysis for this reason: In the modeling of longitudinal relations among personal, caregiver, and residential characteristics, only people with stable placements can be included in the primary analyses. It would make no sense to ask whether persons with mental retardation influenced their careproviders across time if the careproviders constituted different individuals at the multiple times of measurement. Given this constraint, any large differences between people with stable placements and those with unstable placements would require some restriction in the generalizations made, hence the importance of the current set of comparisons.

The results of the tests of differences between individuals with stable placements and those with unstable placements are presented in Table 3.6. As with the Drop-out control analyses, very few of the variables analyzed showed significant differences between the Stable group and the Unstable group. The three variables showing a difference between the two groups were: a) careprovider involvement, with the Stable group experiencing greater careprovider involvement than the Unstable group; b) Social Maladaption, with the Stable group evincing lower levels of social maladaptive behaviors than the Unstable group, and; c) Relationships, with the Stable group enjoying a higher quality of relationships than the Unstable group. This set of findings may explain why people in the Unstable group did not stay in the same family care setting during the span of our project. The people in the Unstable group had careproviders who were less involved and with whom they had poorer quality relationships. Coupling these differences with the higher levels of social maladaptive behavior shown by the Unstable group, these individuals appear to be at greater risk for unstable placement.

On the other hand, the results of this set of analyses revealed that the Stable group appears to be quite similar in behavioral and other characteristics to the Unstable group on the clear majority of variables. As shown in Table 3.6, nonsignificant differences were found on 22 of the 25 variables, and on most variables the between-group differences in means and *SD*s were fairly small. Thus, stability of placement is not strongly related to any of the important personal or careprovider variables in the study. Therefore, the Stable group, on which most of the core analyses will be based, are fairly representative of all people in the Family Care Study. As a result, no obvious restrictions on the generalization of the results to the population of persons with mental retardation living in family care settings must be made.

LONGITUDINAL CHANGES IN PERSONAL CHARACTERISTICS DURING THE THREE-YEAR SPAN OF THE FAMILY CARE STUDY

Mean Change Across Times of Measurement

One form of change that may take place across time is change in the mean level of a behavior or personal characteristic. The covariance structural modeling to be presented in the next section of this chapter disregards changes in mean level, concentrating instead on the structural relations across time among constructs. As a prelude to these analyses, the authors performed analyses of variance on core aspects of the behavior of persons with mental retardation in the Family Care Study, to determine whether these behaviors or attributes exhibited significant change across time.

The analyses of variance were performed on four behaviors or attributes—adaptive behavior, socially maladaptive behavior, personally maladaptive behavior, and health problems of the persons with mental retardation. Each analysis of variance had the same form, a 4 (Level of Retardation) X 3 (Time of Measurement) analysis of variance, with Level of Retardation a between-subjects factor and Time of Measurement a within-subjects factor. The multivariate approach to repeated measures analyses (McCall & Appelbaum, 1973) was taken in testing all within-subjects effects.

The main effect of Level of Retardation reflects whether, averaging across times of measurement, individuals at different levels of mental retardation show significantly different mean levels of the given behavior; the main effect of Time of Measurement on any dependent variable represents a test of overall mean change across time. Finally, the Time of Measurement by Level of Retardation interaction tests whether persons at different levels of mental retardation exhibit different forms of mean change across time. This interaction effect has important implications for the covariance structure models to be pursued later. If people at different levels

TABLE 3.6

**Stability Control Analyses: Testing Differences on Variables
Collected at the First Time of Measurement Between
Longitudinal Sample Subjects with Stable and Unstable
Placements During the Family Care Study**

VARIABLE	STABLE		UNSTABLE		
	M	SD	M	SD	t RATIO
Person's Age	16.21	4.72	16.02	5.22	.23
Level of Mental Retardation	3.28	.80	3.13	.76	1.21
Careprovider Age	53.45	9.26	53.77	10.93[a]	−.19
Careprovider Education	10.99	2.92	11.23	3.33	−.47
Careprovider Experience (Yrs)	8.28	4.71	9.29	6.12[a]	−1.04
Careprovider Involvement	2.25	1.93	1.45	1.29[a]	3.29**
Health Index of Person with MR	0.72	.27	.75	.27	−.60
Health Rating of Person with MR	1.89	.78	1.88	.84	.08
Careprovider Preference Survey					
Personal Self-Sufficiency	4.29	4.08	5.60	5.01[a]	−1.65
Community Self-Sufficiency	1.18	1.64	1.29	1.86	−.41
Personal-Social Responsibility	2.66	2.30	2.81	2.57	−.38
Social Maladaption	12.90	8.91	14.28	9.48	−.92
Personal Maladaption	6.99	5.20	7.58	5.04	−.69
Behavioral Development Schedule					
Personal Self-Sufficiency	33.01	12.18	33.50	11.75	−.24
Community Self-Sufficiency	17.39	10.28	17.27	9.26	.07
Personal-Social Responsibility	12.57	6.35	12.04	6.07	.51
Social Maladaption	2.24	2.16	3.56	3.53[a]	−2.46*
Personal Maladaption	1.26	1.57	1.75	2.11[a]	−1.47
Activities in Public Places	.81	.22	.82	.21	−.17
Participation in Clubs, etc.	.26	.16	.27	.17	−.30
Participation in Events	.58	.29	.63	.26	−1.16
Stability of Placement	2.72	1.73	2.46	1.78	.88
Normalization of Placement	2.94	.47	2.88	.57[a]	.73
Quality of Environment	3.24	.32	3.14	.43[a]	1.51
Relationships	2.94	.59	2.71	.58	2.39*

Note. Sample sizes for the two groups were: Stable $N = 148$, Unstable $N = 48$. All t-ratios had 194 degrees of freedom, unless otherwise noted.

[a]Within-group variances differed significantly ($p < .20$) between the Stable and Unstable groups. As a result, degrees of freedom were adjusted according to the inequality of variances; degrees of freedom for these t-ratios varied between 59 and 121.

*$p < .05$

**$p < .01$

of mental retardation exhibited significantly different change across time, then this might cast some doubt on the feasibility of specifying and testing structural equation models across all levels of mental retardation, implying that separate structural models must be developed for each level of retardation.

Adaptive behavior. The analysis of variance on adaptive behavior revealed a significant effect of Level of Retardation, $F(3,144) = 9.59, p < .0001$. Not surprisingly, the mean level of adaptive behavior was approximately linearly related to level of mental retardation. That is, persons with mild mental retardation had the highest mean levels of adaptive behavior, and mean level of adaptive behavior declined as level of mental retardation became more profound. The means for people at the mild, moderate, severe, and profound levels of retardation were $M = 79.1$, $M = 69.3$, $M = 63.3$, and $M = 40.3$, respectively. The major deviation from linearity of these means occurred for individuals at the profound level of retardation, but the small number of people at this level ($N = 9$) resulted in this mean being less stable than for the other levels of retardation.

The main effect of Time of Measurement was also significant, $F(2,143) = 15.77$, $p < .0001$. Means increased approximately linearly, with $M = 63.0$, $M = 65.8$, and $M = 70.8$, at the three times of measurement, respectively, replicating previous research by Eyman and Widaman (1987) on development during the years of childhood and adolescence.

The interaction of Time of Measurement and Level of Retardation was nonsignificant, $F(6,286) < 1.0$, ns, suggesting that people at the different levels of mental retardation exhibited approximately equal forms of mean change across the three times of measurement.

Social maladaption. None of the main or interaction effects for social maladaption reached statistical significance. The main effect of Level of Retardation was marginally significant, $F(3,144) = 2.16$, $p > .09$, the main effect of Time of Measurement was nonsignificant, $F(2,143) < 1.0$, ns, and the Time of Measurement by Level of Retardation interaction was also nonsignificant, $F(6,286) = 1.66$, $p > .10$. The basic upshot of this analysis was a verification that levels of social maladaption were unrelated to level of mental retardation and showed little change across the three times of measurement.

Personal maladaption. The main effect of Level of Retardation was statistically significant, $F(3,144) = 6.87$, $p < .0005$. Inspection of the means revealed that there was an approximately linear relationship between level of retardation and level of personal maladaption, with persons at the mild level showing the lowest levels of personal maladaption and those at the profound level the highest levels of personal maladaption. The means were $M = 1.1$, $M = 1.2$, $M = 1.5$, and $M = 2.5$ for the mild, moderate, severe, and profound levels of retardation, respectively.

Neither of the remaining two effects—the main effect of Time of Measurement and the Time of Measurement by Level of Retardation interaction—were statistically significant (both $Fs < 1.0$). Thus, although levels of personal maladaption were related to level of retardation, little mean change across the three times of measurement was evident, whether across the sample as a whole or within levels of retardation.

Health problems. With regard to health problems, neither of the two main effects attained statistical significance, and the interaction of Time of Measurement and Level of Retardation was also nonsignificant (all $ps > .30$). As a result, the mean level of health problems in the Family Care Study was essentially unaffected by level of retardation and did not change across the three years of the study.

Modeling Structural Relations Among Latent Variables Across the Three Times of Measurement

As discussed in Chapter 2, structural equation modeling was used to represent the important dimensions of behavior for the 148 persons with stable placements for whom there was complete data across all three times of measurement. In order to model longitudinal relations across time, it is necessary to specify indicators, or observed measures, of each construct. In the structural model, a total of 14 constructs related to personal and behavioral characteristics of persons with mental retardation were identified; these constructs are shown in Figure 3.1. The first two constructs were the person's chronological age and his/her level of mental retardation. Both Client Age and Level of Retardation were single-indicator latent variables, as the measured variables of age and level of mental retardation define directly the two constructs, respectively. Each of these two constructs was perfectly stable across time (e.g., age at Time 1 correlated perfectly with age at Times 2 and 3), so both of these constructs are represented in the model at only the first time of measurement.

The third through fifth dimensions or latent factors corresponded to the construct of Health Problems at the first through third times of measurement, respectively. At each time of measurement, Health Problems had two indicators of the person's health, a Health Index and a Health Rating. As noted in Table 3.4, the Health Index was the average of seven items that reflected the frequency of health-related symptoms or behaviors, such as frequency of doctor visits, and the Health Rating was an overall rating of the person's health made by the primary careprovider. The basic health of a person was included in the model for at least two reasons. First, health is an important variable in its own right; if certain variables were found to influence health across time, this would be an important outcome for both theoretical and practical reasons. Second, health was included because the authors assumed that health might influence the person's level of behavior, whether reducing adaptive behavior or increasing maladaptive behavior. Especially interesting in this regard are questions of cross-lagged influences. That is, the authors attempted to determine whether Health Problems influenced a persons' level of adaptive or maladaptive behavior, whether adaptive or maladaptive behaviors influenced the person's health, or whether Health Problems and forms of adaptive and maladaptive behaviors followed essentially unrelated paths of development.

The sixth, seventh, and eighth latent variables included in the model were Adaptive Behavior at the first, second, and third times of measurement, respectively. The scores on the indicators of the Adaptive Behavior

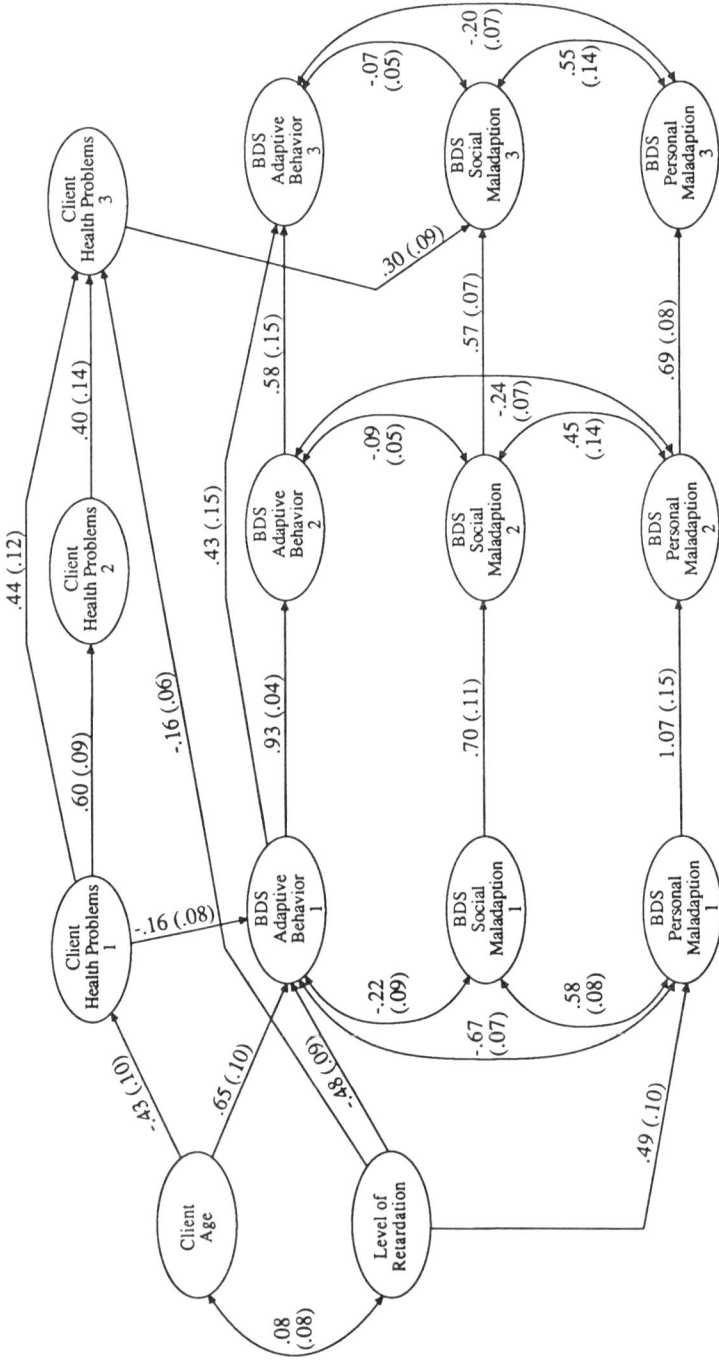

FIGURE 3.1. Structural model representing relations among personal and behavioral characteristics of the persons with mental retardation across the three times of measurement (maximum likelihood parameter estimates are listed, with associated standard errors in parentheses).

constructs were obtained from the BDS, so these latent variables are labeled BDS Adaptive Behavior at each of the three time points. Based on the structure of the BDS, three indicators of a general Adaptive Behavior, or Adaptive Competence, construct were obtainable. These three indicators correspond to the three factors described by Nihira (1976), termed Personal Self-Sufficiency (PSS), Community Self-Sufficiency (CSS), and Personal/ Social Responsibility (PSR). The items from the BDS that were used to create these scales are described in Table 3.4. Currently, a range of opinions have been offered on the structure of the adaptive behavior domain. These range from single-factor views (e.g., McGrew & Bruininks, 1989) to multiple-factor conceptions (e.g., Widaman, Borthwick-Duffy, & Little, 1991). As Widaman et al. argued, the optimal model for the adaptive behavior domain is likely a hierarchical one, with a single, general factor at the apex, but with at least four factors at the next lower level. For many purposes, the multiple factors of the adaptive behavior domain should be considered in order to represent the domain adequately. However, given the fairly short duration of this study, the age restriction of the sample, and the structure of the BDS, the authors focused only on the single, general Adaptive Behavior construct in the current analyses.

Two different forms of maladaptive behavior appear in the current models, Social Maladaption and Personal Maladaption. These maladaptive behavior dimensions, although highly correlated, have been shown to be rather distinct types of maladaptive behavior (e.g., Nihira, 1969a, 1969b; Widaman, Gibbs, & Geary 1987). The ninth through eleventh constructs in the model represented the Social Maladaption factor at the first through third times of measurement, respectively. At each time of measurement, the Social Maladaption factor had two indicators. These indicators were formed in the following way: the first five items listed in Table 3.4 were averaged and comprised one indicator of social maladaption (SMAL A), and the last four items were averaged to comprise the second indicator (SMAL B).

The final three constructs—the 12th through 14th—reflected Personal Maladaption at the three times of measurement, respectively. Paralleling the specification of Social Maladaption, two indicators of Personal Maladaption were formulated for each time of measurement. These two indicators were formed as follows: the first two items listed in Table 3.4 were averaged and comprised the first indicator (PMAL A), and the remaining two items were averaged and comprised the second indicator (PMAL B).

The 14 constructs described above are shown as circles in Figure 3.1, arrayed from left to right along the dimension of time. Given the specification of indicators for each construct, or latent variable, at each point in time, the authors initiated the fitting of a model of the longitudinal relations among the 14 constructs. The first step in the model building process was to specify an initial model on an *a priori* basis, using theory and the structure of the data collection sequence to guide the specification. After this, additional parameters (e.g., directed paths or covariances) that were interpretable theoretically and that were necessary to obtain adequate fit of the model to the data were estimated. In this section, only a basic introduction to the model fitting is provided, so that emphasis can be placed on the interpretation of the final model estimates provided in Figure 3.1. However, interested readers will find the details regarding the steps in model fitting described in the Appendix. There the fixing of the scale for each latent variable, constraints on the measurement model parameters, and the steps taken to build the final model that is presented below are explained.

The initial *a priori* model contained three sets of estimates. First, for each construct that was measured at each time of measurement, only first-order autoregressive paths were estimated. Such autoregressive paths presume that status on a given variable at one point in time can be represented as a function of two components: a) status on the same variable at the immediately preceding time of measurement, and; b) an independent residual component. For example, Adaptive Behavior at Time 2 was presumed to be influenced by Adaptive Behavior at Time 1, and Adaptive Behavior at Time 3 was influenced by Adaptive Behavior at Time 2, but Adaptive Behavior at Time 3 was assumed to be uninfluenced directly by Adaptive Behavior at Time 1, although there would be an indirect influence of Adaptive Behavior at Time 1 through its influence on Adaptive Behavior at Time 2.

Second, the three BDS factors—Adaptive Behavior, Social Maladaption, and Personal Maladaption—were allowed to intercorrelate freely at each time of measurement. Third, the latent variables for the two personal characteristics of Client Age and Level of Retardation were allowed to correlate and to influence directly all four of the remaining latent variables at Time 1.

The initial, *a priori* measurement model had a reasonable level of practical fit, $\rho = .91$. However, there were indications that model respecifications would significantly improve the fit of the model to the data. Making these modifications, which involved the deletion of a total of 63 parameter estimates, resulted in the estimated relations among constructs shown in Figure 3.1. The final model exhibited adequate levels of fit, with $\chi^2(340) = 530.04$, and an ρ value of .93.

The authors consider first the relations of the two personal characteristics to the remaining constructs in the model. The first characteristic, Client Age, had two sizable path coefficients, one on Health Problems ($\beta = -.43$, *se* $= .10$) and the second on Adaptive Behavior ($\beta = .65$, *se* $= .10$). The first of these paths, which explained about 20 percent of the variance in Health Problems at the first time of measurement, indicated that older subjects in the sample tended to be healthier, with health improving as a function of age. The second path, relating Age and Adaptive Behavior, explained approximately 40 percent of the variance in Adaptive Behavior at Time 1. This path represents the well-documented rise in forms of adaptive behavior during childhood and adolescence (e.g., Eyman & Widaman, 1987). Of importance for theory regarding these behaviors, the failure to find significant relations between Client Age and forms of maladaptive behavior is also consistent with previous findings. Eyman and Widaman (1987) reported that social and personal maladaption were not highly related to age in their state-wide sample of persons with mental retardation.

The second personal characteristic, Level of Mental Retardation, also had two significant effects on Time 1 latent variables, Adaptive Behavior and Personal Maladaption. The former effect (β = -.48, se = .09) explained about 24 percent of the variance in Adaptive Behavior at Time 1, whereas the latter effect (β = .49, se = .10) explained about 24 percent of the variance in Personal Maladaption at Time 1. The negative sign of the path coefficient to Adaptive Behavior at Time 1 reflects the inverse relation between these two constructs, but is consistent with the way in which Level of Mental Retardation was scored (i.e., scores going from 1 = mild to 4 = profound). Thus, the more profound the level of mental retardation (i.e., the higher the score on Level of Retardation), the *lower* the level of adaptive behavior. The positive sign of the path coefficient to Personal Maladaption at Time 1 also has a ready interpretation: the more profound the level of mental retardation, the *higher* the level of personally maladaptive behavior exhibited by the person with mental retardation, with persons with mild retardation having the lowest level of personal maladaption. Level of Mental Retardation did not have significant direct effects on the remaining two constructs—Client Health Problems and Social Maladaption—at Time 1. The findings that level of mental retardation had a nonsignificant relationship with social maladaption, but a significant relation with personal maladaption also replicates findings by Eyman and Widaman (1987), who found that level of mental retardation was much less highly related to levels of socially maladaptive behaviors during childhood and adolescence than to levels of personally maladaptive behaviors.

The autoregressive relations across times of measurement for the remaining four constructs—Client Health Problems, Adaptive Behavior, Social Maladaption, and Personal Maladaption—are shown in Figure 3.1. As hypothesized, the first-order autoregressive paths were strong and significant for each of these constructs. Moreover, the simple, first-order autoregressive model was quite sufficient for both Social Maladaption and Personal Maladaption, as the influence of Time 1 level of each of these two constructs on Time 3 level of behavior was mediated by Time 2 measurements. However, two deviations from the initial hypotheses must be noted: a) Health Problems at Time 3 was directly influenced by Health Problems at Time 1, and; b) a similar pattern of influence was noted for Adaptive Behavior at Time 3. These two path coefficients were estimated in order for the model to fit the data. Whether these departures from a strict first-order autoregressive represent substantive phenomena for which the authors must account or reflect model misspecification (i.e., failure to include other relevant characteristics, such as careprovider and residential setting measures, in the model) will only be determined in later chapters, when other domains of variables are added to the basic model in Figure 3.1.

The final set of direct relations that must be discussed are three paths that were not hypothesized on an *a priori* basis. The first path was from Health Problems at Time 1 to Adaptive Behavior at Time 1, $\beta = -.16$ ($se = .05$), which represents an inverse relationship between health and adaptive behavior: the higher (i.e., poorer) the level of health problems, the lower the level of adaptive behavior. The second path was a direct path from Level of Mental Retardation to Health Problems at Time 3. This path ($\beta = -.16$, $se = .05$) suggests that people at the less profound levels of mental retardation (i.e., mild and moderate) had somewhat worse levels of health than did those at the more profound levels of retardation. The third path was from Health Problems at Time 3 to Social Maladaption at Time 3, a path coefficient of $\beta = .30$ ($se = .08$). This path suggests that the poorer one's level of health, the higher the level of social maladaption. Because each of these path coefficients was rather small and the effects were rather evanescent (i.e., they occurred only at a single point in time), little interpretive stress should be given to these paths. As other domains of variables are added to the model in later chapters, these path coefficients may become nonsignificant, due to model respecification.

The patterns of explained variance for the variables shown in Figure 3.1 are fairly consistent across times of measurement. That is, at each time of measurement, predictor variables explained more variance in Adaptive Behavior than in the remaining three constructs of Social Maladaption, Personal Maladaption, and Health Problems ($R^2 = .42, .90$, and $.87$, at the three times of measurement, respectively). Health Problems and Personal Maladaption displayed somewhat lower, but approximately equal levels of explained variance, with R^2 values of $.16, .47$, and $.66$, respectively, for Health Problems, and R^2 values of $.20, .72$, and $.46$, respectively, for Personal Maladaption, across the three times of measurement. Social Maladaption consistently had the lowest levels of explained variance, with $R^2 = .00, .34$, and $.41$, at the three times of measurement, respectively. However, these figures demonstrate that even the construct with the lowest levels of explained variance, Social Maladaption, was a moderately stable construct. Also, there was a consistent pattern across constructs in the levels of explained variance as a function of times of measurement. Explained variance figures are relatively low for all constructs at Time 1, as only age and level of mental retardation were considered as primary predictors. At Times 2 and 3, when autoregressive paths were added, levels of explained variance climbed rapidly, as hypothesized.

As a final note about the relations shown in Figure 3.1, the correlations among the three BDS factors were quite consistent at each of the three times of measurement. Specifically, Social and Personal Maladaption were rather strongly and positively correlated. In contrast, Adaptive Behavior was correlated negatively and much less strongly with the two maladaption factors, but consistently exhibited a stronger inverse correlation with Personal Maladaption than with Social Maladaption. The similarity of these patterns of correlation provides evidence of the consistency with which these three dimensions of behavior derived from the BDS were assessed.

Summary

The structural relations among constructs displayed in Figure 3.1 are largely consistent with the *a priori* hypotheses about the structure among these characteristics and behavioral tendencies. That is: a) age was related to health and adaptive behavior and was not related to levels of maladaptive behavior; b) level of mental retardation was related primarily only to adaptive behavior and personally maladaptive behavior and was unrelated to levels of socially maladaptive behavior, and; c) there were moderate to high levels of stability, or large autoregressive paths, for the four constructs of Health Problems, Adaptive Behavior, Social Maladaption, and Personal Maladaption. The deviations from these *a priori* patterns tended to be fairly small. Determining whether the deviations must be explained or resulted from inadequate model specification will await the results of later chapters. But, most importantly, constructs depicted and the relations among these constructs shown in Figure 3.1 provide a baseline model of personal characteristics for the people in this study, against which the impact of other contextual influences, such as careprovider characteristics and perceptions as well as environmental and quality of life variables, can be evaluated as these are added in later chapters.

Chapter 4　Careproviders of Small Family Homes

BECOMING A CAREPROVIDER

A person who wishes to become a careprovider in California for individuals with mental retardation must apply for licensure as a residential service provider. If the careprovider intends to care for children (under 18 years of age), a Small Family Home license must be obtained. A Small Family Home means "any residential facility in the licensee's family residence providing 24-hour a day care for six or fewer children who are mentally disordered, developmentally disabled or physically handicapped and who require special care and supervision as a result of such disabilities" (Title 22, *California Code of Regulations,* sec. 80001). Careproviders who wish to provide residential care in their homes for persons with mental retardation who are age 18 and above must obtain a license for an Adult Residential Facility. The Adult Residential Facility license is much broader than the Small Family Home license; for example, it enables the careprovider to care for larger groups of people. However, all persons in the Family Care Study who were between the ages of 18 and 21 lived in small homes with fewer than six persons with mental retardation that closely resembled the Small Family Homes in which the younger persons resided.

The Title 22 regulations provide minimal standards that are to be met by both the careprovider and the physical setting. Prospective careproviders must show evidence of training or experience in providing family home care to the type of children being served. As careproviders, they must provide a safe physical environment in which there are planned leisure activities as well as training related to the development of individual goals (Cal. Code Regs., tit. 22, sec. 83064).

CHARACTERISTICS OF CAREPROVIDERS

Previous work has suggested that the careprovider's age, education, and experience may each influence the quality of care provided in community settings (Boyle & Comer, 1990). Careprovider characteristics may also affect the lives of clients outside the home, including levels of community involvement and the development of friendships with both handicapped and non-handicapped people (Crapps & Stoneman, 1989). For example,

Coates and Vietze (1987) hypothesized that very young and very old careproviders may provide less adequate care than those in the middle age group, though for different reasons. That is, less adequate care may be due to inexperience and concern for self-fulfillment for young careproviders, but due to lack of stamina or physical strength for older providers.

It has been consistently reported in the mental retardation literature that, on average, family care parents tend to be older women who have a high school education and are married (Crapps & Stoneman, 1989; Intagliata, Crosby, & Neider, 1981; Sanderson & Crawley, 1982; Willer & Intagliata, 1984). The majority of studies report that careproviders are about 50 or more years old, which is somewhat older than has been reported for those who care for nonretarded children. Providers who are unmarried tend to be widows, and most careproviders have had children of their own.

The above characteristics of family home providers are somewhat different than those that have been reported for group home employees. Janicki, Jacobson, Zigman, and Gordon (1984) reported that most group home employees in New York were well-educated and had a fair amount of experience. The majority were young (mean age = 31 years) and fairly well educated (more than 60 percent had two or more years of college and 38 percent were college graduates). In addition, most of the group home staff in New York had had specialized training related to their jobs and had been employed in human service jobs for about four years. Variability in these characteristics was associated with different levels of responsibility in the group homes, with more qualified individuals holding positions carrying more responsibility.

Janicki et al. suggested that although the quality of care might be enhanced by the rather impressive qualifications of group home staff, these characteristics in combination with relatively low pay for the level of education might also contribute to high turnover rates and thus reduce the overall effectiveness of the group home environment. Sanderson and Crawley (1982) reached a similar conclusion after studying 55 family caregivers, by comparing those who continued to provide care with those who had closed their homes. Those who persisted were older and less educated than those who left. The results of that study supported earlier findings that stable staff tended to be older and less educated, were hired at older ages, and were motivated by other than career interests (Burchard & Thousand, 1988). Because it is generally believed that clients benefit from stable associations with caregivers by promoting long-term relationships and providing consistent caregiving practices, the trade-off between stability and education may be an important factor to consider when evaluating caregiver qualifications.

Careproviders in the Family Care Study

Overall, the careproviders of the children and adolescents who were studied fit the descriptions of family care home providers that have been reported previously in the literature. Distributions of gender, age, ethnicity, marital status, education, and other family and social characteristics were examined among the primary careproviders of the 151 small family homes in the study sample (See Table 4.1). The average age of careproviders was 52.8 years, with a range from 24 to 75 years. Ninety-six percent of the primary caregivers were female, and 45 percent were White. Among the non-white careproviders, the majority were Black. Other non-white careproviders (15.9 percent) included persons of Hispanic, Asian, and other ethnic backgrounds. The distribution of providers by marital status showed that approximately 78 percent of the homes were two-parent families which is consistent with other reports (e.g. Intagliata, Willer, & Wicks, 1981; Justice, Bradley, & O'Connor, 1971). Thus, most of the foster homes had a male figure as a secondary careprovider and appeared to function as a traditional family with both paternal and maternal figures. Approximately 44 percent of the careproviders also had children of their own living at home. The foster family care homes provided care for one to six people with mental retardation, with an average of 3.7 clients in each home. Sixty-six percent of the careproviders had more than five years of experience in serving people with developmental disabilities, with 35 percent also having been careproviders of people who did not have developmental disabilities. Approximately 64 percent of the providers had at least a high school education, and 70 percent had also taken at least one special training class designed to assist them in caring for people with mental retardation.

The characteristics of the careproviders in the study were similar to the figures reported recently by Stoneman and Crapps (1988), whose sample of 104 careproviders averaged 51 years of age and 51 months tenure in careprovision. On average, the Stoneman and Crapps sample had a high school education and were married (64 percent). One difference between the small family homes in the two samples is that the average number of clients per home was slightly larger in the Family Care Study (three to four people per home) than in the Stoneman and Crapps study (one to two people per home).

Careprovider and Client Characteristics

Lei, Nihira, Sheehy, and Meyers (1981) previously reported on the relationship between careprovider characteristics and the types of clients served in the sample. Since the current data set was used in that report, the findings are summarized below.

The majority of clients studied lived in family care homes for children. However, clients in the sample who were ages 18 to 21 were living in homes that were licensed to care for adults. Some associations were found between careprovider characteristics and the age and gender of the people cared for

TABLE 4.1

Characteristics of Careproviders
In the Family Care Study

CHARACTERISTICS	FREQUENCY (N=151)	PERCENT
Gender		
Male	6	4.0
Female	145	96.0
Age		
Under 50 years	61	40.4
51 years or older	90	59.6
Ethnicity		
White	69	45.7
Black	58	38.4
Hispanic	14	9.3
Other	10	6.6
Marital status		
Married/marriage-like	118	72.2
Widowed	14	9.3
Separated/Divorced	18	12.0
Never married	1	.7
Education		
Less than high school	55	36.4
High school	49	32.5
Some college	47	31.1
Experience		
5 years or less	52	34.4
More than 5 years	99	65.6
Number of clients		
One	15	9.9
Two	24	15.9
Three	30	19.9
Four	33	21.9
Five	18	11.9
Six	31	20.5
Number of own children at home		
No children	85	56.3
One	23	21.9
Two	22	14.6
Three	7	4.6
Four	4	2.6

in the homes. As shown in Table 4.2, a significantly higher proportion of the careproviders who served only older people were non-White, without any of their own children living at home, and caring for four or more residents. On the other hand, the careproviders of homes providing care for children and young adults were more likely to be White, better educated (at least completion of high school), have their own children living in the same residence, and provide home care for fewer than four people.

Whether the homes provided cared for only males or females was not

TABLE 4.2

Careprovider and Home Characteristics —
Classified by Age of Residents

| | RESIDENTS SERVED (%) | | |
CHARACTERISTICS	ADULTS ONLY (N=59)	CHILDREN UNDER 18[a] (N=92)	χ^2
Age			
Under 50	30.5	44.6	2.98
50 or over	69.5	55.4	
Ethnicity			
White	25.4	58.7	16.04**
Non-White	74.6	41.3	
Education			
Less than 12 years	44.1	31.5	2.44
12 years or more	55.9	68.5	
Own children at home			
No	71.2	46.7	8.73*
Yes	28.8	53.3	
Number of clients			
1 to 3	32.2	54.3	7.10*
4 to 6	67.8	45.7	
Years of experience			
5 years or less	37.3	31.5	.53
More than 5 years	62.7	68.5	

[a]Including 15 homes in the transitional period of license change for providing services to young adult clients
*$p < .01$
**$p < .001$

associated with any careprovider characteristics. However, as shown in Table 4.3, significant differences were found between the homes providing services to people of the same gender (either male or female) and those homes having residents of both genders. It appeared that careproviders of the homes caring for people of the same gender were older, non-White, with more than five years of experience in foster care, and without any of their own children living at home. In contrast, careproviders of the homes serving both males and females were more likely to be under 50 years of age, White, less experienced, and with their own children living at home. Neither educational levels of careproviders nor the number of residents in the home were related to whether the provider cared for clients of the same gender or both males and females.

REASONS FOR PROVIDING FOSTER CARE

Intagliata, Crosby, & Neider (1981) noted in their review of the literature on foster family care that most careproviders give altruistic reasons for taking clients into their homes. For example, providers cite reasons such as

TABLE 4.3

Careprovider and Home Characteristics — Classified by Gender of Residents

| | RESIDENTS SERVED (%) | | |
CHARACTERISTICS	SINGLE GENDER (N=92)	BOTH GENDERS (N=57)	χ^2
Age			
Under 50	32.6	50.9	4.91*
50 or over	67.4	49.1	
Ethnicity			
White	40.2	56.1	3.95*
Non-White	59.8	43.9	
Education			
Less than 12 years	37.0	36.8	.00
12 years or more	63.0	63.2	
Own children at home			
No	64.1	43.9	5.88*
Yes	35.9	56.1	
Number of clients			
1 to 3	42.4	52.6	1.48
4 to 6	57.6	47.4	
Years of experience			
5 years or less	28.3	43.9	3.85*
More than 5 years	71.7	56.1	

*$p < .05$

wanting the personal satisfaction that comes from caring for someone or from knowing that they are doing something useful for the community. Interviews of careproviders in the sample revealed similar results. They were asked to describe their initial reasons for taking individuals with mental retardation into their homes, as well as reasons why they continued to do so. In the majority of responses they stressed the desire to help others develop their own competencies, as shown in the following examples of comments from the caregivers in the study:

"I'm doing something that's helping someone else—it gives me self-worth."

"I want to see them be able to learn and do for themselves, to learn independence."

"It gives me great pleasure to see the clients advance and become more socially acceptable."

"Yes, I enjoy helping people to care for and help themselves."

"Something in me needs to help."

"I had needs, they had needs, together we could meet them."

"It's hard to express the feeling of helping someone to be independent."

Other caregivers mentioned reasons related to the benefits of having other people present in their homes:

"It gives me a family and someone to talk to and things to do."

"All my kids were gone, I wanted to be a grandmother."

"It's like a new family with my children gone."

"I can be at home with my own children and I enjoy the clients that are now with me."

"It's fulfilling. Having children in our home is a pleasure and a very rewarding experience."

"It provides companionship for my daughter and provides a home for Rick."

"I wanted to share my home."

It seemed that in spite of the very real fact the caregivers benefit financially from caring for individuals with mental retardation, the individuals interviewed were also sincere in their desire to help others and were honest about some of their own emotional needs being fulfilled by their roles as careproviders. In short, even in homes with as many as six residents, care provision is viewed as much more than a business endeavor.

CAREPROVIDER ATTITUDES ABOUT CLIENT NEEDS AND BEHAVIOR PROBLEMS

In the Family Care Study, four objectives were associated with the examination of caregiver attitudes. First, the authors wanted to know the extent to which personal characteristics of the caregivers affected their levels of tolerance of client dependencies and behavior problems. Second, the relative "match" of caregiver attitudes and the reported abilities and behaviors of the people in the sample was explored. Third, it was of interest to know whether a careprovider's willingness to handle different problems was based on actual experience or on speculation of how they might react to certain problems. Finally, the impact of caregiver attitudes on changes in levels of maladaptive behavior over a two-year period was examined.

Careprovider Characteristics and Attitudes About Behavior

In geographic areas where small family care homes are in demand, careproviders may be in a position to select clients according to the characteristics they are most willing to handle. Thus, it was of interest to identify the dependencies and problem behaviors that careproviders were least willing to handle in their homes. In the Family Care Study the

Careprovider Preference Survey (CPS) listed 50 dependent or problem behaviors that might be characteristic of people living in family foster care homes. These behaviors or dependencies require physical assistance from the caregiver (such as dressing, toileting, or feeding clients) and can drain the caregiver's emotional energy (such as temper tantrums, disruption of others' activities, or inappropriate public behavior). Caregivers were asked in the survey to indicate whether each behavior was something they would a) be willing to handle, or b) rather not handle in their homes.

Attitudes and Experience: Item Analyses

As Table 4.4 indicates, the behaviors that careproviders were least willing to handle were when clients tended to run or wander away. In addition, sexually-related behavior (masturbation, homosexual behavior, inappropriate behavior with the opposite sex), self-injurious and stereotyped behavior, aggression and inability to get along with others in the home, bed wetting and toileting accidents, seizures, inability to understand instructions, and not doing for oneself were the behaviors most frequently cited by careproviders as preferring not to handle.

TABLE 4.4

Careprovider Experience and Willingness to Handle Client Needs

QUESTION	% WITH EXPERIENCE	% PREFER NOT TO HANDLE
1. When a client is unsteady on his/her feet	65.6	19.2
2. When a client eats with lots of spilling	76.2	5.3
3. When a client has trouble drinking from a glass or cup	58.9	6.6
4. When a client is not toilet trained or has many accidents during the day	71.5	28.5
5. When a client wets the bed frequently	68.2	23.8
6. When a client needs help going to the toilet	74.8	9.9
7. When a client needs help bathing	95.4	1.3
8. When a client needs help getting dressed	92.7	.7
9. When a female client has difficulty caring for herself during her menstrual period	47.7	14.6
10. When a client wanders off	44.4	31.1
11. When a client does not know how to use money	86.8	2.0
12. When you cannot understand a client's speech	86.8	5.3
13. When a client cannot understand instructions of any kind	60.9	25.2
14. When a client cannot clean a room properly	88.1	1.3
15. When a client cannot fix simple foods to eat	84.1	2.0
16. When a client cannot do simple work like emptying trash, pulling weeds, mopping floors	77.5	3.3
17. When a client will not do anything him/herself	62.3	24.5
18. When a client does not pay attention to an activity for even five minutes	75.5	11.3
19. When a client does not take care of his/her own things	80.1	4.0
20. When a client does not play or talk with others at home	63.6	7.9

continued on next page

TABLE 4.4 *(continued)*

Careprovider Experience and Willingness to Handle Client Needs

QUESTION	% WITH EXPERIENCE	% PREFER NOT TO HANDLE
21. When a client does not take part in group activities	73.5	5.3
22. When a client threatens others with words or gestures	70.9	15.2
23. When a client slaps, pinches or punches another resident	78.8	20.5
24. When a client breaks his/her things or another client's things on purpose	78.1	10.6
25. When a client disrupts other's activities	77.5	5.3
26. When a client swears or says mean things to others	62.3	6.6
27. When a client refuses to follow an instruction	74.2	11.3
28. When a client takes another's things	76.2	6.0
29. When a client runs away	39.1	47.0
30. When a client acts inappropriately toward member of the opposite sex	35.8	25.8
31. When a client shows homosexual behavior	26.5	45.7
32. When a client masturbates in public	30.5	41.7
33. When a client is too friendly in a local store by talking to or touching others too much	61.6	5.3
34. When a client is too bossy	70.2	2.0
35. When a client just cannot seem to get along with others in your home	44.4	39.1
36. When a client bangs head, rocks back and forth, or flaps his/her hands or a piece of paper for a long period of time	70.2	25.8
37. When a client makes strange noises such as groaning, grunting, snorting, teeth grinding	77.5	16.6
38. When a client continually hangs on to you	52.3	3.3
39. When a client removes or tears off his/her clothing at the wrong time	45.0	25.2
40. When a client deliberately burns him/herself	59.6	33.8
41. When a client is hyperactive and just cannot sit still	74.2	13.9
42. When a client shows no interest in anything at all	56.3	21.9
43. When a client is extremely emotional and cries easily	49.7	18.5
44. When a client has a peculiar habit such as eating dirt	41.7	20.5
45. When a client has trouble seeing	54.3	17.9
46. When a client has trouble hearing	52.3	12.6
47. When a client has seizures	64.2	27.2
48. When a client drools	57.6	17.2
49. When a client has difficulty using his/her hands	56.3	7.3
50. When a client requires several medications at different times during the day	72.8	9.9

With regard to attitudes and experience, it appears that most opinions were based on actual experience. Self-injury and stereotyped behavior, aggressive behavior, toileting needs, and seizures had been experienced by at least half of the respondents. By contrast, sex-related behaviors had been experienced by fewer than 40 percent of providers in the study. Those behaviors that were not named as being problematic were also of interest. For example, careproviders were not concerned about problems with eating, dressing, toileting assistance, expressive language, lack of household skills, non-participation, or being overly friendly with strangers, even though these appeared to be common among the people in their homes. In summary, careproviders seem willing to assist clients with their needs if they are indeed true dependencies. Certain behaviors that cause fear among careproviders (seizures, running away, self-injury, physical aggression) or may create additional work for careproviders (changing sheets, doing tasks for clients when they have the ability, inability to communicate) are those they are least willing to handle. However, careprovider willingness to deal with most of the dependent behaviors suggests these people realize these problems and needs will be characteristic of children and adolescents with mental retardation who are placed outside their natural homes.

Careprovider-Client Match

The notion of a careprovider-client match emerged in the literature in conjunction with the belief that community placement "failures" might not all be due to characteristics of clients that predisposed them to an inability to remain in a particular setting. Whereas the early studies of community adjustment focused on characteristics of people with mental retardation that were associated with successful community adjustment, in the Family Care Study the authors were interested in the match between careproviders' feelings about client dependencies and problem behaviors and the characteristics of the clients they served. The importance of matching the feelings and preferences of caregivers with characteristics of people who might live in their homes was initiated by Fanschel (1965) and emphasized later by Adams (1975). Fanschel found that some foster parents actually preferred to care for highly dependent children with long-term care requirements while others showed an interest in working with children who had problems with aggressive or acting-out behavior. Landesman (1987) suggested that residential environments should probably not be evaluated in terms of being "better or worse" by any absolute criteria. Instead, we should be most concerned with the optimal match between available resources, environmental demands, and characteristics of the individual with mental retardation.

A pilot study of careprovider attitudes conducted by the study's research group confirmed that there were widely divergent feelings about the seriousness of different behavior problems and the careprovider's willingness to handle them (Nihira, 1977). This area of study was pursued with the hypothesis that caregiver preferences and client-caregiver matches would impact the quality of life for people in small family homes.

In addition to the personal attitudes of foster parents, Adams (1969) also discussed the importance of the professional aspect (management of medical, behavioral, and developmental deficits) of caregiving that is unique to children with mental retardation, as opposed to the more common need for surrogate parenting. The professional image and monetary rewards might also provide compensation for the lack of intellectual and social achievements which frequently reinforce foster parents of non-retarded children.

Although it is possible that these benefits might influence the careprovider's willingness to handle additional behaviors and dependencies, the fact remains that in many cases it is a "seller's market," in which caregivers can reject or accept clients on the basis of their own preferences. Depending on the policies of the service system, the rejection can be outright, by refusing to take clients with certain problems into their homes, or it can be more subtle and affect caregiver relationships with clients who are overly dependent or display troublesome behaviors.

Careprovider-client match in the Family Care Study. The *Careprovider Preference Survey* (CPS), and the *Behavior Development Survey* (BDS) had corresponding items. For example, the CPS item "When a client needs help bathing . . ." corresponds to the BDS bathing item which describes the client's level of independence related to bathing. This correspondence provided the opportunity to observe both the caregiver's willingness to handle different behaviors and the actual dependencies and behavior problems of people who lived in their homes.

If a caregiver indicated that he or she would prefer not to handle a particular behavior or problem, and a client in the home evinced that behavior, a score of "0" was assigned, indicating a mismatch of caregiver and client. If a caregiver was not willing to handle the problem and his or her clients did not have that problem, a score of "1" was assigned for each client, indicating a match. Finally, if a caregiver was willing to handle a problem, a score of "1" (indicating a match) was also assigned, regardless of whether or not the client displayed the problem behavior.

The 37 match and mismatch scores were summed within the appropriate domains of the *Behavior Development Survey*, i.e., Personal Self Sufficiency, Community Self-Sufficiency, Personal-Social Responsibility, Personal Maladaption, and Social Maladaption. The higher the score, the better the match between caregiver and client. Then, domain scores by client age groups (0-10 years, 11-15 years, 16-18 years, and 19-21 years), gender, and mental retardation levels (mild, moderate, severe-profound), were examined to see whether the level of client-caregiver matches were related to characteristics of the persons with mental retardation.

Overall, the people in the sample were well matched with their caregivers in terms of their willingness to handle behaviors and the actual abilities and behaviors displayed by the people in their homes. For 32 of the 37 behaviors examined, five or fewer people were mismatched with their caregivers. With regard to the remaining five behaviors, a person's inability to understand instructions was a dependency that 52 (15.6 percent) people displayed whose caregivers preferred not to deal with in their homes. This item was the source of the greatest mismatch. Other behaviors that were mismatched with their careproviders were: people who did not take part in group activities (6 pairs mismatched), head banging or stereotypic behavior (12 pairs), hyperactivity (6 pairs), and requiring several medications at different times of the day (12 pairs).

Given the fact that overall, clients were well-matched with caregivers according to the study's criteria (hence there was a lack of variability among domain matching scores), it was not surprising that most characteristics of the person with mental retardation were not associated with differences in mean domain scores of matches across subgroups of people. The only significant relationship revealed in the analysis of variance procedures was that the oldest group of people in the sample (19-21 years) was less well matched in the Community Self-Sufficiency domain than people in younger age groups (F=3.13, p<.05). However, since so few behaviors in this domain were mismatched, even for the oldest age group, the difference between age groups may not be practically meaningful.

LONGITUDINAL EXAMINATION OF CAREPROVIDER CHARACTERISTICS

As described in Chapters 2 and 3, our longitudinal sample consisted of 148 clients and their careproviders who participated in the Family Care Study for three times of measurement. The variables considered in the analysis were: 1) careprovider age; 2) careprovider education; 3) careprovider experience working with people with mental retardation; 4) careprovider involvement in ongoing training opportunities; 5) careprovider feelings about the seriousness of the client's lack of adaptive behavior skills, and; 6) careprovider feelings about the seriousness of maladaptive behaviors. Careprovider views on seriousness of behaviors (the last two variables) were measured once a year for three years in order to determine the stability of these attitudes over time and to identify possible cross-lagged causal paths.

The initial model had inadequate levels of statistical and practical fit, rho=.84. Adding a total of nine estimates to the initial model led to the final model, which had an adequate level of practical fit, rho=.94, although this model was still rejectable statistically, p <.001.

The relationships among careprovider characteristics from the final model are shown in Figure 4.1. The significant autoregressive paths between Careprovider Seriousness of Adaptive Behavior Problems across the three years reflect the stability of this construct from Year 1 to Year 2 and Year 2 to Year 3. Similar stability estimates were present for Careprovider Seriousness of Maladaptive Behavior. In other words, Careprovider views on seriousness can be viewed as stable from year to year for both adaptive and maladaptive domains. The longitudinal relations for Careprovider Seriousness of Adaptive Problems deviated from a first-order autoregression

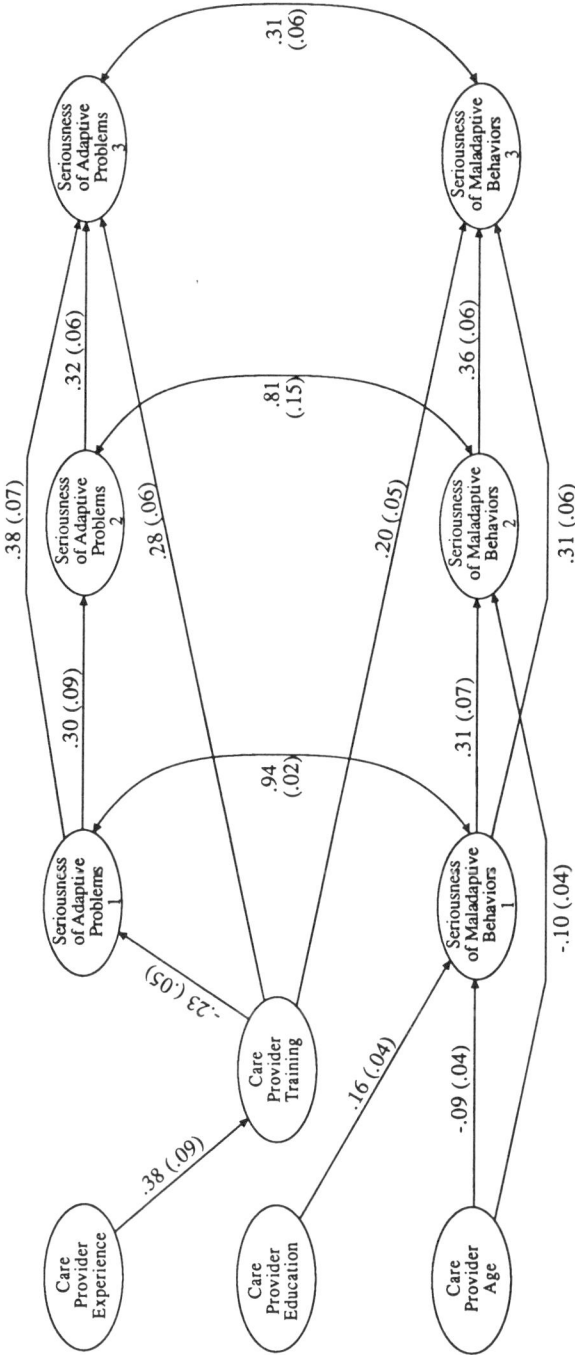

FIGURE 4.1. Structural model representing relations among personal and behavioral characteristics of the careproviders across the three times of measurement (maximum likelihood parameter estimates are listed, with associated standard errors in parentheses).

pattern, as the latent variable at Time 3 was influenced by the latent variables at both Times 1 and 2. A similar pattern of relations was shown for Careprovider Seriousness of Maladaptive Behavior.

It was also important to note that careprovider views on the seriousness of problems in adaptive and maladaptive behavior were correlated rather strongly in each of the three years, although the strength of the association decreased at the third time of measurement. These correlations suggest that careproviders who view client needs for adaptive assistance as less serious are also those who consider maladaptive behavior to be a less serious problem.

This is especially interesting given the negative correlation between Client Adaptive Behavior and Personal Maladaption reported in Chapter 3. This finding suggests that the lower a client's level of adaptive behavior, the higher his or her level of personal maladaption is likely to be. Thus, the fairly high concordance between client adaptive and personally maladaptive behaviors is paralleled by the high concordance between careprovider's perceptions of the seriousness of client problem behaviors in the adaptive and maladaptive domains.

The direct path from Careprovider Experience to Careprovider Training, $\beta=.38$ ($se=.09$), suggests that careproviders with more experience are more likely to be involved in additional training programs. Moreover, it suggests that additional training might eliminate fears and increase competencies, since careproviders who had been more involved in training programs in the first year were also more likely to view client dependencies as less serious than those with less training, $\beta=-23$ ($se=.05$).

Given the preceding finding, the positive path from Careprovider Training to Seriousness of adaptive problems in Year 3, $\beta=.28$($se=.06$) was somewhat puzzling, however, a positive path was also present from Careprovider Training to Seriousness of Maladaptive Behavior in Year 3, $\beta=.20$ ($se=.05$). Thus, careproviders with more training in the first year viewed both adaptive behavior needs and maladaptive behavior as *more* serious in Year 3.

A possible explanation of this reversal in signs for adaptive behavior problems is that careproviders come to view the problem behaviors as more serious as the effects of their training "sink in" over time. An alternate hypothesis is that initially careproviders may have felt they had been provided with the knowledge and ability to handle adaptive behavior problems, but that hope was later diminished by the realities of challenging client care.

Neither Careprovider Education nor Careprovider Age was related to careprovider attitudes about client dependencies (Seriousness of adaptive problems). However, younger and better educated careproviders considered behavior problems to be more serious than older providers or those with less education, $\beta=.09$($se=.04$) although these relationships were rather weak.

SUMMARY

In this chapter the authors focused primarily on the characteristics of people who provide family care services to individuals with mental retardation. Overall, careproviders had altruistic reasons for their involvement in foster family care. Their demographic characteristics were similar to those of family careproviders reported in other studies.

Caregivers in the Family Care Study reported their willingness to handle different client dependencies and behavior problems. In general, the careproviders were willing to handle most client needs that stemmed from the physical or cognitive limitations of the clients in their care.

Behaviors identified as particularly problematic by careproviders tended to be those that may have caused unnecessary work (e.g. clients not doing what they were able, toileting accidents) or made careproviders fearful of some outcome (e.g. seizures or running away). For the most part careproviders' opinions were based on their experience with the different behaviors and they seemed to accept that clients with mental retardation were likely to display dependencies and problem behaviors.

When examining careprovider willingness to handle behaviors in connection with the actual needs and behavior problems of the clients they cared for, the clients were generally well-matched with their providers. In only a few instances did a client display a behavior or need that the careprovider preferred not to handle.

The structural model describing relationships among careprovider characteristics, including attitudes about the seriousness of adaptive and maladaptive behavior problems of their clients, suggested that careprovider attitudes are relatively stable from year to year. Younger and better educated providers were less tolerant of maladaptive behavior, while careprovider age and education were unrelated to views on adaptive behavior needs.

It was of primary interest in the Family Care Study to move beyond the examination of careprovider characteristics alone to a study of their impact on client quality of life measures and on the behavioral development of the client over time. Relationships between careprovider characteristics and client quality of life factors will be discussed in Chapter 5, and the cross-lagged causal relationships between careprovider attitudes and changes in levels of client adaptive and maladaptive behavior will be described in Chapter 6.

Chapter 5

Quality of Life For Persons With Mental Retardation

Rather than simply monitoring an individual's ability to remain in a community placement, mental retardation professionals have shifted their concern in recent years to an emphasis on the *quality* of the individual's life in a given residential setting. Putting into operation this abstract construct of quality of life, however, is much more difficult than recognizing its importance.

Concerns about quality of life have been identified as the major impetus for improved mental retardation services and outcomes in the 1990s, just as deinstitutionalization, normalization, and community adjustment served this function in the past two decades (Schalock, 1986). Beyond the need to evaluate programs, Schalock cited "America's current concern for the general welfare and well-being of its citizenry" as a justification for evaluating a person's quality of life.

Landesman (1986) referred to quality of life as a new "buzz word" in mental retardation and as an outcome that was badly in need of a formal, measurable definition. In her proposal that the American Association on Mental Retardation develop guidelines to help measure this concept, Landesman identified some of the problems associated with utilizing and summarizing the existing literature. For instance, it seems that public policy decisions that affect people with mental retardation (e.g., mainstreaming, deinstitutionalization) are often made either in the absence of or without regard to theoretical and empirical advances in the study of adaptation to different environments (Emerson, 1985; Landesman, 1986). Furthermore, lacking a definitional structure of desired outcomes and estimated relationships of those outcomes to one another, the overall evaluation of the effects of these policies has been less than systematic and has occurred outside a conceptual framework.

What exist in the literature are reports of many well-executed studies that have examined numerous outcome variables, each important to an individual's quality of life, yet bearing ambiguous relationships with other studies that focused on related but different objectives. Research that specifically addresses the construct of quality of life, by contrast, is still in its infancy (Schalock, Keith, & Hoffman, 1990).

The explanation for the wide range of outcomes that have been studied and for the lack of definitional uniformity lies both in the evolution of the residential care systems for people with mental retardation and in changing perspectives regarding the important factors to consider when evaluating residential placement decisions. The administrative control and delivery of services to people with mental retardation has shifted during the past 25 years from institutions to community settings (Best-Sigford, Bruininks, Lakin, Hill, & Heal, 1982; Eyman, Borthwick, & Tarjan, 1984; Intagliata, Crosby, & Neider, 1981; Lakin, Hill, & Bruininks, 1988). In the 1970s and 1980s, emphasis on deinstitutionalization and the community placement of people with mental retardation led to the rapid development of a wide range of community residential placement alternatives (Baker, Seltzer, & Seltzer, 1974; Best-Sigford et al., 1982; Bruininks, Hauber, & Kudla, 1980; Emerson, 1985; Lakin et al., 1988; Switzky & Haywood, 1985). As a result, placement decisions became increasingly more complex and difficult to evaluate.

Parents and professionals who have responsibility for residential placement decisions are faced with an important question: How can one determine whether an individual with mental retardation is living in a home situation that affords him or her the greatest opportunity to reach his or her cognitive potential, to live with maximum dignity and respect, and to enjoy the pleasures and comforts of associations with other people?

In short, what factors determine residential placement outcomes (Bell, Schoenrock, & Bensberg, 1981), and how can we know what type of person belongs in which kind of setting (Landesman, 1988; Seltzer, 1981)? Serious attention has been given to these questions for more than 20 years, as research studies have addressed a multiplicity of issues related to the out-of-home placement of individuals with mental retardation. What seem to be relatively straightforward questions, however, have been examined from so many different perspectives that the results are difficult to interpret.

GENERAL ISSUES IN RESEARCH ON QUALITY OF LIFE

Difficulties Associated with Summarizing Placement Literature

Without exception, reviews of the literature on the adjustment of people with mental retardation who have been placed in community residential facilities have included discussions of the wide range of criteria used to define operationally "adjustment" or "quality of life" and of the concomitant problems associated with summarizing this literature (e.g., Bell et al., 1981; Craig & McCarver, 1984; Eagle, 1967; Heal, Sigelman, & Switzky, 1978; McCarver & Craig, 1974; Seltzer, 1981; Windle, 1962). At first glance, much of the literature appears to be contradictory and inconclusive (Craig & McCarver, 1984).

Eagle (1967), for example, found that published data on more than 40 characteristics of people with mental retardation at the of time of their release from institutional placements showed wide disagreement regarding relationships between these client characteristics and successful placement outcomes. In response, Eagle stressed the need for standardized outcome measures. McCarver and Craig (1974) later reviewed 75 published studies and were also unwilling to conclude that any characteristics of the individual were unambiguous predictors of the "success" of community placement.

McCarver and Craig suggested that a reason for the apparently inconsistent results may have reflected the lack of a standard outcome measure. Heal et al. (1978) concluded from their review that "given the state of the literature at present, it is impossible to test whether certain correlates of adjustment are more powerful predictors at one state of placement than another." In later reviews, Jacobson and Schwartz (1983), Craig and McCarver (1984), and Heal and Fujiura (1984) also discussed the problems associated with summarizing the results of studies that have examined different aspects of the many dimensions of placement outcomes.

Overlapping terminology. A number of concepts have been used to describe the positive outcomes that are related to residential placement, including "adjustment," "adaptation," "success," and "quality of life." Yet, regardless of the concept label used, the specific operational criteria employed in research studies have been used interchangeably, suggesting that these concepts may not be distinguishable in the literature. For example, friendships (operationally defined) have been said to reflect an individual's *adjustment* (Seltzer, 1981), his *adaptation* (Bell et al., 1981), and *quality of life* (Schalock, 1986). Hence, it is likely that these differing labels represent the same underlying concept when evaluating residential placements.

The terms *adjustment, adaptation,* and *success* reflect the evaluation of a person's lifestyle after movement to a new placement from another residential setting, very often the institution. The frequent usage of these terms reflects the fact that a large percentage of research studies have evaluated the impact of deinstitutionalization on individuals with mental retardation, comparing life in the institution to life in the community. Craig and McCarver (1984) noted, however, that the number of residents in community-based facilities who come directly from their natural homes is nearly as large as those who have been released from institutions.

Although the goal of most studies has been to identify the factors that are predictive of successful placements (in whichever way success is defined), the ultimate objective is to determine the optimal environments for individuals with different needs, abilities, and personalities (Switzky & Haywood, 1985) and to assess the quality of their lives, regardless of placement histories or current living arrangements.

"Eye of the beholder". A second general problem is the subjective nature of the concept of quality of life, the definition of which has been dependent on the perspectives and biases of the people doing the evaluation. An illustration of this point emerged from a study conducted by Intagliata, Willer, and Wicks (1981), who found that social workers and nurses assigned very different ranks of importance to various aspects of the lives of individuals in their care. For example, social workers ranked "encouraging independence" last, while nurses ranked it as most important in client care.

In contrast, social workers placed a higher value on stability and organization of the home and knowledge of individual needs. Similarly, Bartnik and Winkler (1981) found that employers, training staff, and parents had discrepant opinions regarding the importance of various criteria for evaluating the community adjustment of adults with mental retardation. These results clearly point out that criterion measures likely reflect the investigator's view of residential care and the purpose it should serve, whether it be custodial, habilitative, or otherwise (Butterfield, 1985; Intagliata, Willer, & Wicks, 1981), rather than representing criteria with a more objective status. Even though quality is often precisely defined in individual research studies, these studies suggest that quality of life is a subjective concept and its interpretation may be "in the eye of the beholder."

The diversity of quality of life criteria has been described as almost researcher specific, with no outcomes that are universally accepted as being most important (Craig & McCarver, 1984; Landesman, 1988; Seltzer, Sherwood, Seltzer, & Sherwood, 1981). In a discussion of community adjustment, Lakin, Bruininks, and Sigford (1981) stated that the wide range of operational definitions may not lead to problems in interpreting results of single studies, but it does make comparing and summarizing research findings more difficult.

In some ways, this relatively undeveloped research field is faced with a dilemma. While it would be more straightforward to standardize measures of life quality (Craig & McCarver, 1984; Eagle, 1967; McCarver & Craig, 1974), this would oversimplify an extremely complex phenomena. In fact, Lakin et al. (1981) suggested that adjustment is a matter of degree and of personal preference and is not easily quantified. They stated:

> . . . the notion of adjustment as it has been operationalized in previous studies implies a standard or norm by which the adjustment of mentally retarded persons can be determined—that is by which one can separate those who are "adjusted" from those who are not. Such a standard can be most easily criticized in that even among nonmentally handicapped persons adjustment is at best ill-defined and represents no particular pattern of behavior (p. 383).

The problem seems to lie in the task of summarizing the literature, rather than in the research process itself. Without a conceptual model of residential placement outcomes, reviewers who would prefer to take into account varying perspectives and operational definitions resort instead to using one or another "admittedly imperfect criterion—such as remaining in the community versus returning to the institution—as a baseline or standardized criterion" (Craig & McCarver, 1984, p. 114).

Breadth of criteria used in quality of life studies. Operational definitions of an individual's quality of life based on a single variable or set of dependent variables have been criticized because they reduce "a complex process into a one-sided variable" (Heal & Fujiura, 1984; Taylor & Bogdan, 1981). Heal and Fujiura, for example, discussed the "sampling of referent generalities" (i.e., dependent measures) and the importance of selecting a referent that adequately represents the effects of residential placement. They concluded that most studies fall far short of sampling the range of outcomes that can be expected from community placements.

The research questions associated with community adjustment are multivariate in nature, and studies that examine causal relationships of predictors with single outcomes may be guilty of oversimplification (Heal, 1985). The range of outcomes that are selected depends upon the research question of interest, and it may be justifiable to take an in-depth look at a single outcome.

Research conducted by Intagliata, Willer, and Wicks (1981) clearly demonstrated the importance of taking criterion measures into account when summarizing the literature. They cited results of earlier studies that had utilized community tenure as the central criterion variable, which suggested that older people were more likely to "succeed" in the community (Sternlicht, 1978; Windle, 1962).

However, quite different results were found when successful placement was defined in terms of normalization and the promotion of client development rather than just community tenure. In contrast to the earlier findings, Intagliata et al., 1981 found that *younger* people seemed to be living more active and satisfying lives than older people in family foster care settings. However, the younger children presented more management problems to their caregivers in this study, thus being in jeopardy of movement out of the family care homes. If tenure had been the criterion for "success," then the earlier findings that older people were more likely to succeed might have been substantiated, rather than contradicted. Hence, the factors identified as predictors of life quality or of successful placement depend on the way the criterion of success is defined.

Toward a Quality of Life Model

Quality of Life dimensions. One objective of the Family Care Study was to develop and to empirically evaluate a "Quality of Life Model" that would assist in the evaluation of the small family homes that were studied. Ultimately, a model such as the one described will contribute to a theory of quality of life and will facilitate the interpretation and summarization of the research related to the life experiences of people with mental retardation. The model will also contribute to the establishment of criteria for assessing outcomes of treatments and experiences, responding to Landesman's (1986) challenge to define and operationalize quality of life.

Most importantly, the Quality of Life Model should not require a consensus of opinion on the relative *importance* of the various dimensions of this complex concept. It is believed that the priorities assigned to quality of life dimensions will vary according to the perceived needs and characteristics of the individual.

Relationships among quality of life dimensions. Quality of life measures have been used interchangeably as predictor or criterion variables, depending on the perspectives and purposes of the investigators. For example, a number of studies have regarded environmental normalization as an important criterion variable, describing a person's quality of life (e.g. Blunden, 1988; Intagliata et al., 1981; McCord, 1982; Wolfensberger, 1980a, 1980b), while others focused on the potential impact of normalized environments on other aspects of life quality, such as community involvement (Butler & Bjaanes, 1978) or placement stability (Nihira & Nihira, 1975).

Likewise, community integration has been considered a quality of life measure (Schalock & Harper, 1978), as well as a process by which other goals are achieved (Blunden, 1988; Emerson, 1985; Schalock & Keith, 1984). The implication of this is that although the relative *importance* of quality of life dimensions might reflect personal needs or perspectives and may not be testable, the causal impact of one dimension upon another can, and should, be evaluated empirically. As Blunden (1988) noted, the dimensions of quality of life are not mutually exclusive, and aspects of one dimension often influence the other. Thus, another objective of this study was to examine the relationships among the dimensions described in the Quality of Life Model.

Origins of Quality of Life Models

Although quality of life issues per se are relatively new to the field of mental retardation, quality of life models are common in community psychology and have been studied for several decades. The first of such models focused on characteristics of the community (*Quality of Life Index,* Thorndike, 1939) and was based on the assumption that the characteristics of a city were indicative of the quality of life of the people who lived in that city. These models were later expanded to include assessments of life quality experienced by *individuals* who live in the communities being studied (Zautra, 1983).

With the exception of studies that have assigned an overall goodness score to cities, the concern of most model-builders has been to select clusters of dimensions that are useful for understanding and evaluating community life, rather than to identify a single underlying dimension of quality of life (Zautra, 1983). A review and summary of the community psychology literature (Borthwick-Duffy, 1992) suggested that there are four salient dimensions of quality of life, including: 1) Residential Environment; 2) Interpersonal Relationships; 3) Community Involvement, and; 4) Stability.

Need for an Empirically Tested Quality of Life Model

In spite of repeated discussions about the confusing state of the litera-ture and the many different ways in which the lives of people with mental retardation are being examined, there have been few attempts to provide testable models for understanding the quality of life domain. Heal et al. (1978) and Emerson (1985) emphasized the need for this research to be guided by theoretical models, that, until recently, have been virtually nonexistent.

One could argue that a number of theories are represented in the research literature, unstated, but still implicit in the emphases given to different criterion measures examined in research studies. But, these implicit theories are not necessarily competing theories. Investigators who study community involvement and interpersonal relationships of individuals with mental retardation probably believe these criteria are important aspects of an individual's quality of life, yet most would acknowledge that quality is not restricted to these dimensions alone. Hence, quality of life appears to be a multidimensional construct, based on research efforts that attempt to explain the life circumstances of people with mental retardation.

Two testable quality of life (or community adjustment) models (Halpern, Nave, Close, & Nelson, 1986; Schalock, Keith, & Hoffman, 1990) have been proposed in mental retardation literature, both evolving from efforts to evaluate the rehabilitation and community adjustment of adults with mental retardation who live in semi-independent and independent residential settings. Not surprisingly, the elements of the Halpern et al. and Schalock and Keith models are similar in content to the community psychology models and can be explained in terms of similar dimensions.

For relatively high functioning people with mental retardation, the desired goal of residential placements is that the residents conduct normal life activity to the greatest extent possible. Although certain achievements and activities may occur less frequently among people with mental retarda-tion, quality of life for those with mild disabilities is likely to be explained with rather straightforward generalizations from normal community psy-chology, i.e., employment, income, residential environment, leisure activi-ties, education, civic activities and citizenship, marriage, etc.

Schalock (1986) summarized different approaches to operationalizing a person's quality of life by integrating models from both the community psychology and mental retardation literature. The Schalock review revealed considerable overlap among the elements of the various approaches and subdomains of life quality, again suggesting that the important indicators of quality of life are similar for non-retarded and relatively high functioning people with mental retardation. More recently, Schalock et al. (1990) and Goode (1990) also concluded that quality of life for people with disabilities is comprised of the same factors and relationships as has been found for people without disabilities.

The work of Schalock and his associates (Schalock, 1986; Schalock & Harper, 1978; Schalock, Harper, & Carver, 1981; Schalock & Keith, 1984) has been primarily at the level of the conceptual model and has proven extremely useful in the evaluation of programs and of individual outcomes. Halpern et al. (1986) proceeded one step further and empirically tested the relationships among the hypothesized components of the four dimensions in their Community Adjustment Model.

A confirmatory factor analysis, using structural equation modeling techniques, supported the hypothesis by Halpern et al. that the 12 measured variables in the analysis would provide an interpretable four-factor definition of community adjustment for the population studied. Halpern et al. (1986) distinguished between external dimensions (Occupation, Social Support, and Residential Environment) and an internal dimension (Satisfaction).

This distinction is similar to that made by Schalock (1990) between social indicators (external) and psychological (internal) indicators that focus on a person's subjective reactions to life experiences. An examination of the Halpern et al. data showed that scores on the external dimensions were uncorrelated; the internal dimension, Satisfaction, was strongly correlated with Social Support and moderately correlated with Residential Environment. An implication of the lack of correlation among external dimensions is that program interventions must aim specifically at the dimension of interest, without assuming that adjustment or life quality in one area will necessarily affect quality of life in another (Halpern et al., 1986).

Quality of Life for all levels of retardation and for all ages. The community psychology field has contributed considerably to the development of quality of life models that are appropriate for non-retarded individuals. Although the operational definitions differ somewhat across models, the same four dimensions (residential environment, interpersonal relationships, activities/involvement, and stability) seem adequate to describe the major aspects of a quality of life model. In general, conceptual and measurement models for high functioning adults with mental retardation closely resemble community psychology models, although increased emphasis is given to utilization of community resources and leisure activities in mental retardation studies. Operational definitions of measured variables in studies of people with mild mental retardation can also be explained in terms of the above mentioned four dimensions.

The application of quality of life models to groups of people with more severe degrees of retardation has not yet been tested, although the need for such a study has been acknowledged (Halpern et al., 1986). Whereas some researchers believe that quality of life is comprised of the same dimensions for handicapped and non-handicapped people (Goode, 1990; Schalock et al., 1990), Flanagan (1982) asserted that the dimensional structure itself might require modification for people with various disabilities.

In either case, the relevance of the specific questions asked about quality of life is likely to differ according to an individual's skills and ability level (Flanagan, 1982). For example, a community involvement dimension may be judged by "civic activities or service projects" for a non-retarded person or a person with mild retardation, whereas the same dimension might be measured by "visits to the library, shopping mall, or grocery store" for a person with severe retardation who lacks the basic skills to function independently in these settings.

Moreover, stability can be interpreted as length of time in a job, marriage, or educational program for a person with mild retardation or a non-retarded person. By contrast, among persons with severe retardation, stability might be viewed as certainty in living arrangements, such as the lack of frequent movement from placement to placement (Willer & Intagliata, 1984). Many of the same arguments apply to the consideration of children and adolescents with mental retardation whose quality of life should not be judged on the basis of occupation, income, civic involvement, and other outcomes that are indicators of adult adjustment. The same broad categories of life quality might be appropriate for all people, regardless of age or disability, however, the specific criteria for evaluating these dimensions is likely to be different for children and adults.

DEVELOPING A COMPREHENSIVE QUALITY OF LIFE MODEL

After examining existing models in the mental retardation and community psychology literature, the logical place to begin model development was with outcomes that had been examined in previous deinstitutionalization and community adjustment studies. As noted, a number of investigators have conducted studies on groups of people with varying levels of retardation and have examined rather wide ranges of outcome variables.

Although the measured outcomes have seldom been identified as quality of life variables per se, or as components of a conceptual model, the stated purposes of many of the studies run parallel to quality of life evaluations. Hence, an examination of outcome variables that have been associated with adaptation, success, or appropriateness of community placement for people with mental retardation provided a basis for the development of the model.

Satisfaction Measures

The consideration of the preferences and perceptions of the person whose quality of life is being evaluated is a recurring theme in recent studies of community adjustment (Blunden, 1988; Emerson, 1985; Landesman-Dwyer, 1985; Sigelman et al., 1981; Wyngaarden, 1981). Satisfaction with a current lifestyle is frequently examined in relation to a previous experience in a different placement and is often discussed in the context of quality of life (i.e., people are asked whether they would rather live in the current setting or a different one). As such, personal satisfaction seemed a potential candidate for a fifth dimension in the Quality of Life Model. There were several reasons, described below, that the satisfaction dimension was *not* included in the model.

Client satisfaction has been identified as: 1) synonomous with quality of life (Stark & Goldsbury, 1990; Taylor & Bogdan, 1990); 2) a dimension of quality of life (Blunden, 1988; Bruininks, 1986; Halpern et al., 1986); 3) a concept distinguishable from quality of life (Edgerton, 1990; Landesman, 1986), and; 4) an approach to assessing quality of life (Schalock, 1986).

Satisfaction, like quality of life, is multidimensional. People can be satisfied with their homes, *or* with their social activities, *or* their interpersonal relationships, but may not feel similarly satisfied in each area. Thus, indicators of personal satisfaction may provide an additional perspective or impression of each of the four aspects of life quality already discussed, rather than representing a separate dimension. This may explain the significant correlations of the Halpern et al. (1986) Satisfaction dimension with the "external factors," as well as the lack of correlation among the external factors. Halpern et al. found that the measured satisfaction variables were sufficiently intercorrelated to support the existence of a separate satisfaction factor. However, it is still possible that personal satisfaction may have been correlated with the external dimensions because it represented another method of evaluating those dimensions (i.e., common trait variance).

A practical concern regarding personal satisfaction information is that the reliability and validity of interview data have not been established for populations of people with mental retardation. Sigelman et al. (1981), for example, found that more than 40 percent of the subjects in each of three samples responded "yes" to both questions "Are you usually happy?" and "Are you usually sad?"

Sigelman et al. found this problem to be highly related to IQ. Moreover, 13 of the 16 profoundly retarded subjects in that study failed the initial screening for the interview process. After a series of studies, Sigelman and her colleagues (e.g., Sigelman et al., 1981; Heal & Sigelman, 1990) concluded that the ability to respond to quality of life questions increased with IQ and that many individuals with severe and profound retardation were unable to provide meaningful responses to verbal questions about their lives.

Nevertheless, measurement issues do not pose limitations to a conceptual model, and there is still a strong commitment on the part of some researchers (e.g. Blunden, 1988; Emerson, 1985; Sigelman et al., 1981) to continue to develop creative techniques for soliciting information from the individual.

The Quality of Life Model developed during the Family Care Study, integrates aspects of personal satisfaction into what Halpern et al. (1986)

referred to as external dimensions of adjustment (e.g., environment, activities), so that personal satisfaction does not constitute a meaningful dimension in and of itself. Thus, if measures of personal satisfaction were obtained, they would be embedded within corresponding quality of life dimensions, rather than being combined and treated as a separate factor.

Unfortunately, this aspect of our Quality of Life Model can only be discussed conceptually and was not tested empirically in the Quality of Life Model. Existing methods of measuring personal satisfaction were clearly inadequate for many of the family care subjects studied, as they lacked the communication skills required to provide meaningful responses to questions about their quality of life (Heal & Sigelman, 1990).

The Quality of Life Model proposed in the Family Care Study consists of the four dimensions previously suggested: Residential Environment, Interpersonal Relationships, Community Involvement, and Stability. The following sections review the mental retardation literature in these areas and provide a rationale for the sub-structures of each of the four dimensions. The specific operational criteria introduced are those expected to provide meaningful descriptors of the life quality of people with mental retardation, regardless of their ages or levels of functioning.

DIMENSION 1: RESIDENTIAL ENVIRONMENT

Prior Research and Theory

Studies of special living arrangements for people with mental retardation typically seek to learn how the environment influences behavior (Butterfield, 1985). However, even though a major focus of research efforts has been on the role of the environment as a "means to an end", (i.e., development, community involvement, stability), it is generally agreed that, at any point in time, an individual's quality of life is at least partly defined by the characteristics of his residential environment (Balla, 1976; Emerson, 1985; Landesman-Dwyer, 1985; Willer & Intagliata, 1984).

It has been argued that placement in the least restrictive environment is justifiable on humanitarian grounds, regardless of its effect on behavior or development of the individual. According to Seltzer et al. (1981), an individual may not adapt to his environment in terms of behavioral change, yet "the quality of that person's life may still be improved, given the improved qualities of the environment, such as increased cleanliness and personalization and stimulation" (p. 85).

In recent decades, official policies and legislation have committed service systems to the concept of placement in the least restrictive environment (Bachrach, 1985; Flynn, 1980; Maloney & Ward, 1979). Moreover, perceptions of environmental quality are now judged on the basis of adherence to the principle of normalization. Although empirical studies have not overwhelmingly concluded that "smaller is better" or that "normalized environments promote greater development" (Landesman, 1987,1988; Landesman-Dwyer, 1983; Landesman-Dwyer & Sackett, 1978), the commitment to these values does not appear to be in jeopardy. To the extent that normalization, or other sociophysical aspects of the home enhance an individual's quality of life, regardless of their effect on other outcomes, environmental quality can be considered a quality of life goal in itself (Aanes & Haagenson, 1978; McCord, 1982; Seltzer et al., 1981).

Dimensions of the Residential Environment

Volumes have been written about the issues and research related to the residential living environments of people with mental retardation and were reviewed elsewhere (e.g. Bruininks & Lakin, 1985; Haywood & Newbrough, 1981; Janicki, Krauss, & Seltzer, 1988; Kernan, Begab, & Edgerton, 1983; Landesman & Vietze, 1987). Rather than providing a general review, the purpose of this section is to discuss the rationale for defining the structure of the Residential Environment dimension as it appears in the Quality of Life Model.

It seems obvious that residential environments must be viewed as complex and multidimensional. Novak and Berkeley (1984) discussed the "innumerable, and potentially infinite components" that have emerged from attempts to describe and evaluate residential living environments. Yet, environments have also been perceived of as a whole, rather than as a collection of separate attributes that affect those who are exposed to them (Ittleson, 1978; Landesman-Dwyer, 1985).

Landesman (1988) discussed the challenge that the description and evaluation of environments presents to the scientific community, since there are no clear-cut guidelines for doing this. Hence, the assessment of residential environments is rather undeveloped relative to the measurement of the characteristics of the individuals who live in them (Elardo & Bradley, 1981; Landesman-Dwyer, 1985).

For many years, category labels of facility types were frequently used as crude environmental distinctions in the majority of studies, even though the heterogeneity within these broad classifications had been well documented (Bjaanes & Butler, 1974; Landesman-Dwyer, 1985; Rotegard, Bruininks, Holman, & Lakin, 1985). The rationale for doing this is based on the notion of a continuum of residential alternatives, from most restrictive (or institutional) to least restrictive (or homelike). However, as Landesman (1988) pointed out, community residences are also vulnerable to providing care that can be characterized as institutional (i.e., suboptimal, routinized, and depersonalized) and substantial variance among residences in the community can be found that is unrelated to residence type.

In the evaluation of the Quality of Life Model, the multidimensionality of residential environments as well as the interrelationships among environmental dimensions were empirically tested. The possibility that the environment could be conceptualized at different levels was also examined. Previous studies found dimensions of environmental care were uncorrelated in large institutions (Raynes, Pratt, & Roses, 1979) and in smaller community residences (Pratt, Luszcz, & Brown, 1980). Conversely, Ittleson's (1978) theory of a single higher-order factor reflects the perception of the environment as a whole. One of the authors' objectives was to examine these competing hypotheses for the sample of homes.

The proposed structure for the Residential Environment dimension of the Quality of Life Model was drawn primarily from Bradley (1986), Jacobson and Schwartz (1983), and Crawford, Aiello, and Thompson (1979). Three comparable dimensions have been described by these researchers. Bradley (1986) described three salient attributes of the environment, including Socioemotional/Affective, Cognitive, and Physical factors, that contribute to an individual's quality of life. Crawford et al. summarized three similar domains, including the social environmental climate, treatment programs and skill training, and the physical environment.

Nihira, Mink, and Meyers (1984) studied the child-rearing attitudes and adjustment of families with children with mental retardation and identified similar dimensions of the environment. Finally, Jacobson and Schwartz (1983) cited the social environment (client-caregiver interactions and attitudes toward the individual), habilitation and structured activities, and physical setting components as important dimensions. In addition, Jacobson and Schwartz discussed the importance of a fourth area, called "homelikeness," which is an application of the normalization principle to residential environments.

Integrating the frameworks just described, four dimensions of the environment were identified and proposed for the Residential Environment aspect of the Quality of Life Model: 1) Affective Environment; 2) Cognitive Environment; 3) Physical Environment, and; 4) Environmental Normalization. Figure 5.1 displays the conceptual factor structure of the Residential Environment dimension.

Affective component. The affective qualities of a home environment are important to the quality of life of any human being, but particularly to those individuals whose early attachments may have been less than ideal or even cut off within the first years of their lives by out-of-home placement. Moreover, for individuals with mental retardation who have been placed outside their natural homes, there is an instability built into the placement, referred to by Evans (1983) as a "conditional belongingness."

Foster care homes can offer a family-oriented environment, with opportunities for interaction with other foster children who also have mental retardation, non-retarded children of the foster parents, and close relation-

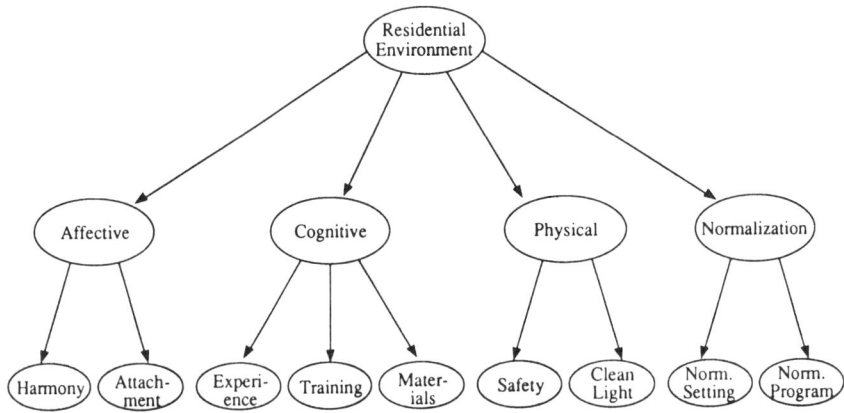

FIGURE 5.1. Proposed hierarchical structure for the Residential Environment dimension, relating levels of latent variables represented from measures obtained in the Family Care Study.

ships with foster parents. These qualities, however, are not always present (Evans, 1983).

A home that reflects positive and accepting attitudes toward its residents, and toward people with mental retardation in general, enhances the quality of life experienced by all who live in the home (Bjaanes & Butler, 1974; Jacobson & Schwartz 1983).

Characteristics of the affective home environment have been described as responsiveness, warmth, nurturance, encouragement of independence, discipline styles, and the overall positiveness of the socioemotional climate (Bradley, 1986). These qualities were summarized in the Quality of Life Model in the subcategories of 1) *harmony* in the home, and 2) *emotional attachment* to the individual with mental retardation.

Cognitive component. The importance placed on the cognitive or training aspects of the home environment in the proposed model represents a departure from the quality of life models that have been developed for people with mental retardation who are high functioning or are non-retarded groups of people. Whereas employment, occupation, schooling, or workshop behavior and attendance are all training-*related*, they actually reflect a degree of independence and stability; an entirely separate issue is the degree and quality of *cognitive stimulation* that occurs within the home.

Landesman (1988) and Berkson and Landesman-Dwyer (1977) discussed the role of the caregiver as a natural teacher, as well as the fact that some characteristics of resident behavior appear to be related to the environments in which individuals spend most of their time, such as the home. Cognitive aspects of the home environment involve such characteristics as the cognitive/affective investment of caregivers, variety of stimulation, intellectuality in the home, encouragement of achievement, etc. (Bradley, 1986). The sub-components of the Cognitive Environment were conceptualized as including: 1) cognitively stimulating *materials*; 2) *skill training*, and; 3) cognitively stimulating *experiences*.

Physical component. Physical aspects of the residential setting have been shown to be related to quality of life by influencing motivation, activity levels, affective behavior, and stress (Rotegard et al., 1985). The physical qualities of a home environment have also been found to reflect a resident's well-being and general lifestyle (Willer & Intagliata, 1984). Robinson (1988), for example, asserted that dignity is promoted when an individual lives in a home that looks and functions like those of other nonhandicapped citizens, by "incorporating beauty, convenience, and comfort . . ." (p. 328).

Frequently cited concerns regarding physical features include cleanliness, attractiveness, noise level, lighting of the home (Bradley, 1986; Willer & Intagliata 1984), and safety aspects of the house and outdoor yard area (Groner, 1988; Halpern et al., 1986; Robinson, 1988). Most other physical attributes mentioned in the literature reflect the environment's adherence to the principle of normalization (see Robinson, 1988). Thus, in the Quality of Life Model, these elements were incorporated into the Normalization component, rather than the Physical component. The sub-elements of the Physical Environment were proposed to be *cleanliness and lighting* of the home as well as concern for individual *safety*.

Normalization component. The philosophy of normalization has been identified as the main catalyst for restructuring several aspects of the service delivery system in mental retardation (Landesman, 1987; O'Connor, 1976; Zigler & Balla, 1976). The Scandinavian principle of normalization was first articulated in Denmark by Bank-Mikkelson (1980) and written into the Danish Mental Retardation Act of 1959. Quite simply, the act stated that people with mental retardation should be given the opportunity to obtain an existence as close to normal as possible.

In the 1970s the normalization principle was introduced with what might be considered an evangelistic fervor in the United States by Wolfensberger (1972, 1980a, 1980b). He defined normalization as: 1) the use of culturally valued means in order to enable people to live culturally valued lives; 2) the use of culturally normative means to offer people life conditions at least as good as that of average citizens, and as much as possible, enhance or support their behavior, appearances, experiences, status, and reputation, and; 3) utilization of means which are as culturally normative as possible.

According to Wolfensberger (1980b), normalization does not necessarily mean doing what everyone else does, and the application of the principle is not intended to make people with mental retardation normal. Rather, normalization should make their life conditions as close to normal as possible, by "realistically assessing and respecting the degrees and complications of their handicaps" (Nirje, 1980).

Butler and Bjaanes (1980) distinguished between environmental normalization and client normalization and suggested that both types are equally important. Whereas *environmental normalization* is the process of developing culturally normative and appropriate residences and services, client normalization is the acquisition of necessary skills for assuming culturally normative social roles and responsibilities.

In summary, the principle of normalization affirms that treatment of people with mental retardation should be guided by the realization that they are first and foremost human beings who are to be afforded dignity. The goal of any residential program should be to provide experiences and living conditions that are as normal as possible. Normalization has been referred to as the spirit behind the letter of the law.

Given the relatively abstract definition and the consciousness-raising goals of normalization, the concept would seem especially difficult to evaluate or quantify. Responding to this challenge, Wolfensberger and Glenn (1975) developed the Program Analysis of Service Systems (PASS), which breaks normalization into hierarchically arranged ratings, grouped according to integration, age and culture-appropriate interpretations and structures, developmental growth orientation, quality of setting, and model coherency. According to Wolfensberger (1980a), the principle of normalization is embodied in the PASS and allows one to quantify objectively the implementation of the principle in a particular service setting. Two of the four PASS factors, Normalization of Setting and Normalization of Program, provide quantitative measurements of environmental normalization, as defined by Butler and Bjaanes (1980), and these were used to evaluate the normalization component of the Residential Environment dimension in the Quality of Life study.

DIMENSION 2: QUALITY OF INTERPERSONAL RELATIONSHIPS

Prior Research and Theory

The importance of interpersonal relationships to the quality of life of people with mental retardation has been well documented in the literature on community adjustment (Gollay, Freedman, Wyngaarden, & Kurtz, 1978; Heal et al., 1978; Intagliata, Crosby, & Neider, 1981). Approaches to studying the quality of life and appropriateness of residential placements also include social ecology, in which the individuals studied are seen as "embedded in sets of interpersonal relationships" (Romer & Heller, 1983).

Willer and Intagliata (1984) concluded that residents of family care homes actively participate in the daily activities of family care homes and are provided social support through relationships with their caregivers and peers in the home. Another important relationship that can contribute to the quality of life of people with mental retardation is involvement with their natural families.

These three types of relationships, including the "family" in the residential environment, the natural family, and non-family members, comprise the dimensions of interpersonal relationships that were proposed in the Quality of Life Model shown in Figure 5.2. These three categories represent the components of the social networks of people living in foster family care settings, and, as pointed out by Lewis, Feiring, and Brooks-Gunn (1987), individuals in these categories may have different social and practical functions.

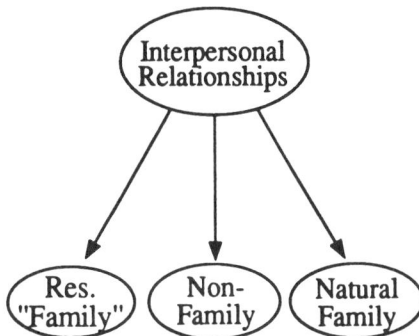

FIGURE 5.2. Proposed hierarchical structure for the Quality of Interpersonal Relations dimension, relating latent variables represented from measures obtained in the Family Care Study.

Dimensions of Interpersonal Relations

Relationships with residential family. A number of authors have reported that the presence of helpers or benefactors is crucial to the adjustment of adults with mental retardation who are attempting to live "independently" in the community (Bell et al., 1981; Edgerton, 1967; McDevitt, Smith, Schmidt, & Rosen, 1978). Likewise, based on a review of previous studies, Intagliata, Crosby, and Neider (1981) concluded that residents of family care homes were well integrated into the family unit (Baker et al., 1974; Scheerenberger & Felsenthal, 1977), and that the most positive social support reported for residents of family care homes was offered by careproviders who actively attempted to help and to establish reciprocal relationships with those in their care (Willer & Intagliata, 1980). Conversely, conflicts with caregivers have been cited as a primary reason for movement out of homes located in the community, often to more restrictive settings (Pagel & Whitling, 1978; Eyman, 1981), hence the term "conditional belongingness" (Evans, 1983).

Relationships with natural family. One of the stated advantages of family foster care placement is that it provides opportunities for residents to maintain close contacts with their natural families (Intagliata, Crosby, & Neider, 1981), with the hope that some individuals might eventually return to their natural homes (Adams, 1970). Unlike the family care programs within the Child Welfare system, there is usually no distinction between temporary and permanent family care placements for people with mental retardation. Hence, in a family foster care home for people with mental retardation, there may be residents whose long-term involvement in the residential care system is assumed, whereas for others natural families have hopes of bringing their relatives back home. In either case, on-going contact with natural families is possible and can be an important contributor to the quality of life of the person with mental retardation.

Previous research suggests that most parents whose handicapped children live at home are very involved in their child's lives until the time of placement (Baker & Blacher, 1988). However, few studies have cited information regarding parental contact with children who have been placed in community residential settings. Baker and Blacher (1988) suggested that placement should not mean a severing of family ties, although this is frequently what happens. Bruininks, Hill, and Thorsheim (1980), for example, reported that only 36 percent of the residents in their family care study were visited by their parents at least annually. Willer and Intagliata (1980) found that 60 percent of the clients in their study were visited annually and that 21 percent of their sample had been visited within a month of their survey.

Similarly, Hill, Rotegard, & Bruininks (1984) reported from a large study of clients in a mix of community residential setting types that 60 percent of the clients were visited by family members from one to three times a year, and 20 percent were visited more frequently than that. The latter two studies are of particular interest because the Hill et al. study included a range of community residence types and yet found rates similar to those among families of relatives living only in family foster care homes. Using "increased contact with natural families" as a justification for family care placement was not supported in this comparison, although a British study demonstrated considerably higher rates of family contacts in small family homes than in larger community environments (Felce, 1988). Baker and Blacher (1988) concluded from their review of the literature that individuals with mental retardation who live in the community are frequently isolated from their natural families.

Clearly, annual or even monthly visits do not assure a quality relationship, although it can provide a crude assessment of family contact. Baker and Blacher (1988) pointed out that counting visits tells little about the quality of the relationship between the family and their relative with mental retardation. Still, it would be safe to assume that children who are visited less than annually are unlikely to have close relationships with their natural families.

Numerous reasons have been cited for lack of contact, including attitudes of caregivers toward parental visits, geographic distance from the parental home, or the extent to which relatives are informed or involved in the placement process. Other reasons cited for lack of parental attachment have been guilt over the initial out-of-home placement, length of time since the child was at home, or inability to cope with having a child with mental retardation.

Baker and Blacher (1988) described several dimensions that might affect family involvement, including the child's status as a child or adult, the level of handicap, placement history, and perceived permanence of the placement. Whatever the reasons accounting for the frequency and quality of visits, an individual's relationship with his natural family can be an important indicator of his or her quality of life.

Relationships with non-family members. Willer and Intagliata (1980) studied friendships among people with mental retardation who live in family care settings. Friendship was defined as relationships with people with whom they enjoyed getting together and on whom they felt they could depend. The family care residents they interviewed frequently mentioned mentally retarded peers living in the same home, however, it was obvious that their social networks also extended outside the family care homes to retarded peers they had met in other settings as well as to non-retarded neighbors.

Romer and Heller (1983) and Romer and Berkson (1980) distinguished between: 1) significant peer relationships; 2) less intense degrees of affiliation, and; 3) aggregation, which involves proximity to others without interaction. "Intensity" and "extensity" of affiliation referred to the frequency of interaction with the same person and the number of people interacted with, respectively. Nearly 80 percent of the people studied by Romer and Berkson were found to have significant relationships with at least one person and maintained some degree of stability of friendships over a three-month period. Hill et al. (1984) reported that only a small percentage (15.8 percent) of the residents of community settings had regular contact with non-handicapped peers, and that friends outside the residence were rare.

There has been some question regarding whether a positive correlation exists between levels of sociability and IQ. Romer and Heller (1983) concluded that the majority of the evidence supports the notion that individuals over a wide range of intelligence are equally likely to be involved in interpersonal relationship networks. It is also possible that the type of residence and support provided within the home or by outside "helpers" is more important than the characteristics of the people themselves. McDevitt et al. (1978) found, for instance, that the majority of deinstitutionalized people with mental retardation they studied appeared to be asocial, isolated, and lonely in their independent living situations.

Willer and Intagliata (1984) found that, among the more severely handicapped people they studied, meaningful relationships with non-retarded neighbors had often been initiated by the family care parents, because the caregivers were viewed as integral parts of the neighborhood. The data reported by Crapps and Stoneman (1989) present a more positive outlook: only 6.4 percent of the family care clients they studied had no friends with handicaps and 14.7 percent had no non-handicapped friends. By contrast, 51.1 percent had more than four non-handicapped friends, and 62.1 percent had more than four handicapped friends. However, a high percentage of residents did not visit their friends, either in their own homes or the home of the friends. These data reflect definite progress in recent years with regard to the establishment of friendships with non-family members, although this should still be an area of concern for careproviders and professionals.

DIMENSION 3: COMMUNITY INVOLVEMENT

Prior Research and Theory

The process of deinstitutionalization has become almost synonomous with the notion of community integration. In fact, an assumption of the community living movement has been that people with mental retardation will be able to participate to a greater degree in the "mainstream of community life" (Felce, 1988). The research literature, however, continues to restate the fact that simply moving an individual from a rural or institutional setting to a residential placement that is physically located in an active community does not promise community integration in the true sense of the term (Butler & Bjaanes, 1978, Willer & Intagliata, 1982).

The degree to which people with mental retardation are involved in community activities is dependent on such factors as opportunities for involvement, their acceptance by the non-retarded community, and characteristics of people with mental retardation. Certainly, a person with mental retardation who is geographically isolated from any community is unlikely to achieve a desirable level of community integration. Physical isolation, lack of transportation, and lack of someone to accompany individuals in community activities have been identified in several studies as major barriers to the community integration of people with mental retardation (e.g., Baker et al., 1974; Bjaanes & Butler, 1974; Hill et al., 1984; Schalock & Harper, 1978; Scheerenberger & Felsenthal, 1977). However, the research clearly indicates that physical integration is a necessary but not sufficient means of involving people in the life of a community.

Historically, many people with mental retardation have not been considered an integral part of the community, regardless of their physical presence, because their behavior has been perceived as deviant and undesirable (MacMillan, 1982; Mercer & Richardson, 1975; Stucky & Newbrough, 1983). Before true integration can take place, society must be able to accept willingly individuals with mental retardation into their daily lives and activities. Stucky and Newbrough (1983) discussed this situation:

> Retarded persons can learn to go autonomously about their daily rounds in the community, but their style often does not integrate with middle-class surroundings. They can come to look like other people, but that does not necessarily lead to participation in the lives and activities of their neighbors. They can learn the behavior that corresponds to particular situations, but they have difficulty evaluating the cues of a new situation to determine which is the appropriate behavior. This often leads to mistakes and a sense of failure on their part, and to their rejection by other members of the community (p. 22).

Community integration is also dependent upon the preferences and functioning level of the individual. The majority of the literature on community utilization focuses on lifestyles of high functioning adults with mental retardation who are in independent or semi-independent living situations. Even these individuals, who might be considered to have the best prognosis for community involvement, tend to be isolated and spend the majority of their leisure time either at home or with peers who also have mental retardation.

Seltzer and Seltzer (1987) reported that societal fear of the consequences of people with mental retardation living in their neighborhoods impacts the level of interaction the people with mental retardation have with the broader community. These attitudes of the non-handicapped majority might provide a partial explanation for the findings of McDevitt et al. (1978) who reported that few of the people with mild retardation they interviewed participated in community activities or took advantage of the resources available to them, such as parks or activities at community centers. Even though all people interviewed were adept at using public transportation, most were quite timid when it came to venturing out of their familiar surroundings. In general, leisure time activity tended to be of a solitary nature, with people spending many hours a day watching television.

Bruininks, Rotegard, Lakin, and Hill (1987) also concluded from their review of the literature on leisure activities that a great deal of free time in community residences is spent in activities that do not require interaction (or integration), such as watching television, playing a radio, or doing nothing.

Similarly, Graffam and Turner (1984) found that even the socially active people they interviewed in sheltered workshops were relatively uninvolved in community activities. Schalock et al. (1981) also interviewed adults in independent living and found that although they used community resources (grocery stores, restaurants, church, post office, etc.) frequently, they spent the majority of their non-working hours watching television. In contrast to this rather bleak picture, Felce (1987) reported that small-home residents in Great Britain experienced almost 250 community contacts each year, compared with only seven events per year for residents of institutions and 72 per year for those in large community facilities.

In one study that examined deinstitutionalized people with varying levels of functioning, ability level was the independent variable that was consistently related to aspects of community involvement, with higher functioning people being more active outside the home than lower functioning people (Bell et al., 1981). Some investigators have distinguished between "independent" and "dependent" involvement in community activities. Dependent involvement occurs when the individual with mental retardation is usually accompanied in the community by a non-retarded caregiver or helper.

Several investigators have reported that people in family care and group homes tend to be accompanied by their careproviders or other supervising adults when participating in community activities (e.g., Bjaanes & Butler, 1974; Crapps & Stoneman, 1978; Scheerenberger & Felsenthal, 1976; Willer & Intagliata, 1984). Willer and Intagliata (1984) found that only 22 percent of their foster care sample ventured into the community alone, which is similar to an earlier estimate of 21 percent that had been reported by Scheerenberger and Felsenthal (1976). Moreover, independent community involvement seems to be more prevalent among people in group homes than people in family foster care, who typically have fewer adaptive skills and are generally more dependent on their caregivers (Bjaanes & Butler, 1974). Hence the quality of community involvement is at least partly determined by the ability level of the individual.

Willer and Intagliata (1984) concluded that low levels of independent use of the community by people living in family care was a cause for concern and acknowledged caregiver overprotection, isolated location of homes, and limiting characteristics of the residents (i.e. age extremes and level of functioning) as potential mediating factors.

Conversely, careproviders have also been credited with promoting integration; careproviders who play an important role involving their clients in community activities tend to be younger and have higher levels of psychological well-being (Burchard & Thousand, 1988). It is important to note that in studies conducted by Burchard and her colleagues, the degree of community use has not been found to be related to the severity of the person's handicapping condition nor to the broad residential category.

Measurement of Community Involvement

Community involvement is generally discussed as a single construct, although specific activities are often referred to when citing trends or examples. Semi-structured interviews are commonly used in studies that examine the community involvement of people with mental retardation (e.g., Crapps & Stoneman, 1989; McDevitt et al., 1978; Schalock et al., 1981). In these interviews, as well as checklist surveys, respondents are usually asked to report frequencies of involvement in community activities within a given time period, e.g., how many times has the person been to a movie in the past month? (Bell et al., 1981; Intagliata, Willer, & Wicks, 1981), or how many times have residents in the facility attended sporting events this year (Pratt, et al. 1980)? A notable exception to this restricted measurement has been in the work by Crapps and his colleagues (e.g. Crapps, Langone, & Swaim, 1985; Crapps & Stoneman, 1989), who used multiple methods of measurement to examine the amount, variety, and level of independence of participation in community life.

In the current study, community involvement was measured in terms of the frequency of involvement in a wide range of community activities. The authors acknowledge that this kind of question only scratches the surface of community activity and does not provide information on the quality of the involvement or the integration that actually occurs. However, it does give a crude indication of the individual's life outside the residential facility.

The activities that described types of community involvement in the Family Care Study were contained in three categories: 1) *use of community resources*, such as grocery stores, parks, libraries, restaurants; 2) *social events or activities*, such as movies, sporting events, amusement parks, and; 3) *membership in groups or formal organizations*, such as Boy Scouts, YMCA clubs, or Sunday School. While this is far from a qualitatively meaningful description, this kind of grouping is useful when broadly summarizing an individual's involvement in the community. Figure 5.3 illustrates this domain.

DIMENSION 4: STABILITY

As previously discussed, stability in the lives of non-retarded and high functioning people with mental retardation has been defined in terms of such criteria as occupation, income level, marriage, and residential status. However, meaningful operational definitions of stability for people with more severe degrees of mental retardation and for young people of all levels of mental retardation focus primarily on residential status.

During the 1970s, the "revolving door" clients who were returned from community placement to the institution were considered casualties of the deinstitutionalization movement (Keys, Boroskin, & Ross, 1973), and the quality of their lives was thought to be in jeopardy. In recent years, the focus has shifted to concerns regarding movement within the community, as service systems have tried to avoid some of the pitfalls that have occurred in child welfare foster care programs, i.e., frequent movement from home to home.

As noted previously, the early studies measured placement success by

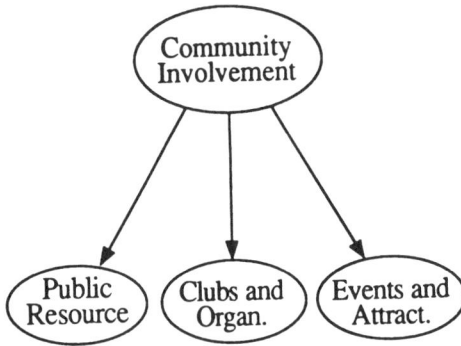

FIGURE 5.3. Proposed measurement structure for the Community Involvement dimension, relating latent variables to their indicators from the Family Care Study.

institutional recidivism rates (Carhill, Rader, & Schonfeld, 1967; Tarjan, Dingman, Eyman, & Brown, 1959; Windle, 1962; Windle, Stewart, & Brown, 1961). Clients who were considered successfully placed had remained in the community. Conversely, a return to the institution was considered a failure in placement (Bishop, 1957; Eagle, 1967; Fernald, 1919; Windle, 1962).

The simple success-failure dichotomy was later criticized for offering a restricted perspective of adjustment or life quality (Aanes & Moen, 1976). Moreover, with restricted eligibility criteria for institutions today (and some states no longer including institutions in their continuum of residential alternatives), individuals who are placed inappropriately may not "return" to this kind of setting. A somewhat refined measure of stability has been referred to as "tenure" in the community, i.e., remaining in a placement for a specified amount of time (Intagliata, Willer, & Wicks, 1981).

Even though perspectives of adjustment have been broadened to include other aspects of life quality, some investigators still find it useful to use the tenure criterion to measure residential placement stability (e.g., Jacobson & Schwartz, 1983; Landesman-Dwyer & Sulzbacher, 1981; Pagel & Whitling, 1978; Schalock, Harper, & Carver, 1981; Sutter, 1980; Willer & Intagliata, 1982). Although community tenure may relate only indirectly to quality of life in other dimensions, the fact that an individual is allowed to become part of a "family," become familiar with his or her surroundings, and feel a sense of belonging and security reflects a degree of stability that is an important aspect of quality of life. However, a simple measure of tenure does not guarantee the presence of the above correlates.

Figure 5.4 portrays the structure of the Stability dimension as it was defined in the Quality of Life Model and was examined for the sample. Although the measurement of stability was limited to a single indicator of tenure, the authors believe that this characteristic is one that is important and meaningful for people of all ages and levels of retardation. This dimension could, of course, be expanded to include measures of occupational stability, income, marital stability, etc., for studies of higher functioning people with mental retardation.

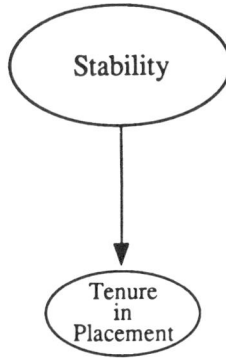

FIGURE 5.4. Proposed measurement structure for the Stability of Placement dimension, relating the latent variable to its single indicator from the Family Care Study.

The foregoing sections have provided the rationale for the proposed structures of the four quality of life dimensions. The complete Quality of Life Model that was conceptualized to represent the life conditions of children and adults with mental retardation who live in family foster care is shown in Figure 5.5.

EVALUATING EMPIRICALLY THE DIMENSIONS OF QUALITY OF LIFE

Confirmatory Factor Analyses of Measurement Models for Quality of Life

It is one matter to propose a theoretical framework for different aspects of life quality. It is quite another to observe hypothesized relationships as they occur in natural settings and then determine whether the aspects of a dimension that are thought to be related are, in fact, correlated in the observed data. The literature abounds with conceptual models that have never been tested empirically. An important objective of the Family Care Study was to propose and test empirically the structure of two of the quality of life dimensions prior to examining their relationships with other variables.

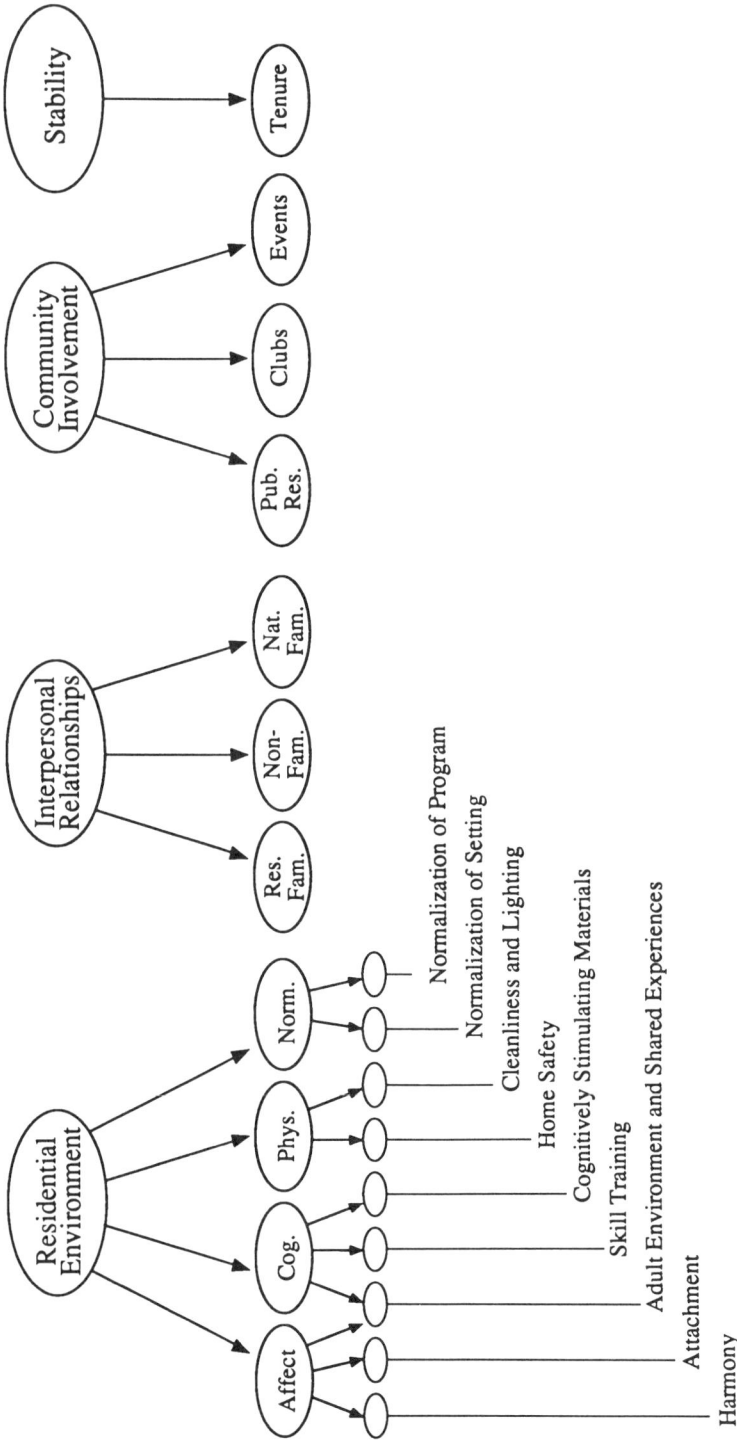

FIGURE 5.5. Final comprehensive measurement structure hypothesized for the Quality of Life Model, relating the latent variables to their indicators from the Family Care Study.

Method

Data used in examination of Quality of Life dimensions. The relational structures of the Residential Environment and Interpersonal Relationship dimensions of the Quality of Life Model were evaluated using data from the complete sample of 333 people who had first-year data. The primary reason for including all subjects in these analyses (rather than using only those who were in the study at all three time points) was that the larger sample increased the likelihood of obtaining more stable estimates of relationships among variables. Year 1 data were also selected because the complete set of environmental measures was completed only in the first year of the study.

Measurement models. Linear structural equation models with latent variables were utilized to test the proposed structure of the Residential Environment and Quality of Interpersonal Relationships dimensions of the Quality of Life Model. Recall that latent variables refer to hypothetical constructs that are not observed, but their effects are expressed in variables that are measured and observed. In a measurement model, observed variables represent multiple indicators of the theoretical constructs under consideration (Bentler & Speckart, 1981). It is possible to conceptualize measurement models as having several levels or orders of latent variables, and the multiple levels (i.e., higher and lower-order factors) of the model can be tested simultaneously. This testing of an hypothesized dimensional structure of relationships among measured variables is referred to as confirmatory factor analysis.

For the Residential Environment and Interpersonal Relationships dimensions, it was important to evaluate the fit of the measurement models that included a single higher-order (general) factor in order to determine whether these relatively complex sets of indicators and latent constructs could be explained by general factors. If so, the general factors would later be used in the causal models that examined relationships among the four quality of life dimensions and other characteristics describing the individual and his or her environment. Separate confirmatory factor analyses were performed to test the proposed dimensional structures of the Residential Environment and the Interpersonal Relationships dimensions of the Quality of Life Model.

The structure of the Community Involvement dimension was not examined, since the method of measurement did not provide data that were appropriate for this kind of evaluation. Moreover, the literature has not suggested what the components of community involvement should be. To use the data obtained at the item level (activity by activity) was not meaningful, i.e., the correlations among items within each type of community involvement (Use of Public Resources, Membership in Clubs and Organizations, Attendance at Special Events) were very low, which was not surprising.

For example, an individual who belongs to an athletic team is not more likely to belong to a Sunday School class or to Boy Scouts (all of which are items in the Clubs/Organization type of involvement) than someone who is not on a team. However, a person who does belong to more than one type of organization is likely to be more involved in community life than one who has fewer such ties. Since the types of involvement focused on: 1) use of public resources; 2) clubs/organizations, and; 3) special events and attractions, summed scores for each type were considered reasonable indicators of community involvement.

The three community involvement sums were moderately correlated (r's=.52, .57, .59), suggesting that individuals who belong to more organizations are also more likely to attend social events and to use more public resources. Thus, the authors concluded that it would be acceptable to utilize a total Community Involvement score in the causal models. The items that were included in each involvement category are available from the first author.

As noted previously, only one measured variable, the length of time in current family care placement, was used to define Stability. Hence, an analysis of the structure of this dimension was also not meaningful. The authors acknowledge that stability is a much broader concept than just knowing how long a person has lived in his/her current home, but measures of stability obtained in the Family Care Study unfortunately were rather restricted.

Procedures. Questionnaire items frequently have low intercorrelations that can be problematic in exploratory and confirmatory factor analyses. A relatively common procedure used to increase the reliability and stability of measured indicators involves the parcelling of survey items. A parcel is a sum of items that measure a particular construct and can be used in combination with other parcels to define a first-order latent variable (Widaman and Kishton, 1992). In the Family Care Study, parcels (containing 2 to 5 items), rather than single item scores, were summed and used as measured indicators for the Residential Environment and Interpersonal Relationships dimensions.

For the Residential Environment dimension, 25 parcels were created by summing items from three data collection instruments. It has been noted that in mental retardation research, method variance tends to dominate substantive variance in quality of life assessment (Heal & Sigelman, 1990). Thus, an attempt was made to integrate items from both the *Foster HOME Inventory* and the *Post Interview Rating Scale* in several parcels in order to reduce the impact of method variance in the measurement model. Only *PASS* items were used to create parcels for the Normalization component since this was the only instrument used to measure normalization. Environment Model parcels are available from the first author. A 25 X 25 covariance matrix that utilized the 25 parcel scores was used as input for this analysis.

To define the Interpersonal Relationship dimension, seven parcels were created from items on the *Individual Client Assessment* and *Natural Parent Questionnaire*. For Parcel 6, part of the Natural Parent component, items from both instruments were combined to reduce the potential impact of method variance on the covariance structure. The contents of these parcels are also available from the first author.

Results

Residential environment. The Residential Environment measurement model in Figure 5.6 reflects the straightforward implementation of the conceptual model described in Figure 5.1, with only slight modifications. In Figure 5.6, the parcels (sums of observed data items) are enclosed in squares, whereas the latent variables are enclosed in circles. The values shown on the directional arrows between the parcels and the nine first-order factors signify factor loadings.

In Figure 5.1 (the hypothesized model) and Figure 5.6 (the best-fitting empirical model), the arrows from higher-order latent variables (constructs, or factors) to lower-order factors indicate the magnitude and direction of causal influence, and the direction of the arrows reflect the level of abstraction of the unmeasured constructs. In other words, the arrows point to the less abstract construct and the lowest level factor is what finally "causes" the obtained scores on the parcels.

Goodness-of-fit refers to how well a proposed causal structure of variables "fits" the data that were actually obtained. The environmental data were skewed to some degree, and the assumption of multivariate normality to justify the more common use of maximum likelihood estimation of model parameters was not met. For this reason, the unweighted least squares (ULS) procedure was used for the Residential Environment factor model. The chi-square statistic, which is used to evaluate the goodness-of-fit of models from data with multivariate normality, is not appropriate for describing the fit of models estimated by ULS.

However, the delta goodness-of-fit index (Bentler & Bonett, 1980) is an acceptable estimate of fit and was calculated for this analysis. The delta index for the Residential Environment measurement model was .974, which indicates an acceptable fit of the data to the model according to guidelines specified by Bentler and Bonett (1980).

Minor modifications to the initially proposed model are shown with bold lines in Figure 5.6 and are discussed more fully in this section. With regard to first-order factors, the two-headed arrow between Educational Materials and Cleanliness/Light denotes a significant negative correlation between the two constructs. This suggests that homes that provide more in the way of cognitively stimulating material may also have more clutter as a result. Parcels 19 and 22 each loaded on two first-order factors.

Some aspects of cleanliness and light are negatively associated with

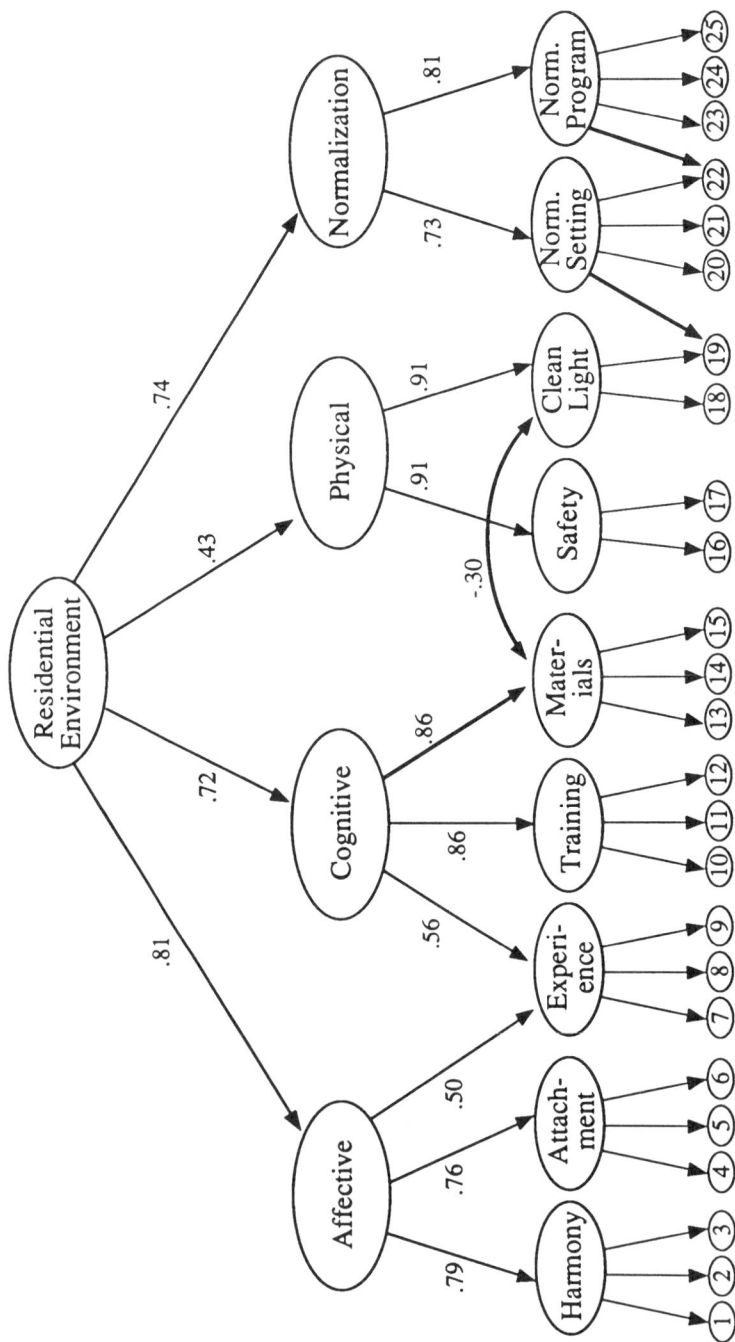

delta = .97

FIGURE 5.6. Results of confirmatory factor analysis for the Residential Environment dimension of quality of life (least squares parameter estimates are listed).

normalization of the residential setting, suggesting that perhaps a more normalized physical environment might also be less tidy and more casual. There was also overlap among components of Setting Normalization and Program Normalization, which was not surprising given the higher-order factor (Normalization) they share in common.

Turning to second-order factors, the authors had hypothesized that adult-shared experiences would be associated only with the Cognitive Stimulation factor, however, the fit of the model was significantly improved when this first-order factor was allowed to be influenced by the Affective factor as well. An examination of the items in the "experience" factor revealed that this was a meaningful modification. For example, the item about the caregiver reading stories to the person with mental retardation has an affective component (personal time shared in close proximity with the resident) as well as a cognitive function (language development, cognitive stimulation, reasoning, etc.). Hence, this factor was renamed "Adult Cognitive Environment and Experiences."

The authors were uncertain when the model was conceptualized whether a single third-order Environment factor would provide an adequate fit of the model to the data. The alternative model would have shown the four second-order factors to be orthogonal (uncorrelated), without evidence of a general environment factor, or as correlated but not amenable to specification of a single third-order factor. As the parameter estimates indicate, there was sufficient evidence to support the presence of a general environment factor. Hence, a single Residential Environment score was used in subsequent analyses that examined causal relationships between the four dimensions in the Quality of Life Model and other characteristics of the individual with mental retardation and his or her careprovider.

The results of the confirmatory factor analysis support earlier conclusions that residential environments must be viewed as multidimensional. It is especially important to recognize that the variability of environmental characteristics within a single placement category resulted in an adequately fitting model. Thus, even within the foster care setting, environments vary considerably according to several components and can be described by three conceptual levels of residential characteristics (a general environment factor, four second-order factors, and nine first-order factors).

Based on information from three sources (*PASS, Foster Home Inventory*, and *Home Quality Rating Scale*), this model presents a mechanism for interpreting and placing in proper context the results of studies that have examined the multiplicity of components of residential living environments. Although the multidimensionality of the environment was supported by the data, the correlations among the factors were sufficiently high to justify the use of a general score in the causal models.

Interpersonal relations. The conceptual model describing the dimensional structure of interpersonal relationships (see Figure 5.2) was evaluated through a series of confirmatory factor analyses in which the presence of a single higher-order (general) factor was considered. The factor loadings of the seven parcels on the three first-order factors were significant, and this portion of the model fit the data adequately. The first model tested allowed correlations among the three factors to be freely estimated. The goodness-of-fit indices for this model (x^2 (11) = 108.03, rho=.87, delta=.93) did not reach the minimum levels recommended by Tucker and Lewis (1973), although the fit was considered to be adequate according to the standard set by Bentler and Bonett (1980).

Other model modifications suggested by the computer program were intuitively difficult to accept and were not made. Moreover, the low correlation between the Residence Family and Natural Family factors made estimation of a single higher-order factor impractical; as a result, the correlated common factor was considered the final model for this domain. The correlated factor model is shown in Figure 5.7.

One explanation for the marginal fit of this model relates to missing data. Inquiries regarding relationships with natural parents were only applicable for 53 percent of the sample; hence, there was considerable missing data in Parcels five, six and seven. The method of handling missing values in computing the covariance matrix was to use all non-missing pairs of values for each pair of variables. Since the covariances among Parcels five, six and seven were based on data from the same group of people (who had natural parent contact), and covariances of Parcels five to seven with Parcels one to four required the omission of people who *did not* have natural parent contact, this could explain why the factor loadings for the Relationships model were reasonable and significant, while the relationships among factors were weak or nonsignificant. Because of this, the authors decided that the correlations among first-order factors for the Interpersonal Relationships domain should not stand in the way of the use of a single summary score across the three types of relationships.

Summary

The results of the analyses just described contributed to the goals of the Family Care Study in two important ways. First, the confirmation of the conceptual structure of the Residential Environment (shown in Figures 5.1 and 5.6) and of Interpersonal Relationships (shown in Figures 5.2 and 5.7) dimensions provides an empirically tested foundation for discussing and further studying these components of quality of life. As noted previously, simply diagramming hypothesized relationships among variables is only the first step in explaining theoretical models.

Second, because of the adequate fit of a model that included a general factor of the Residential Environment, the authors were justified in the use

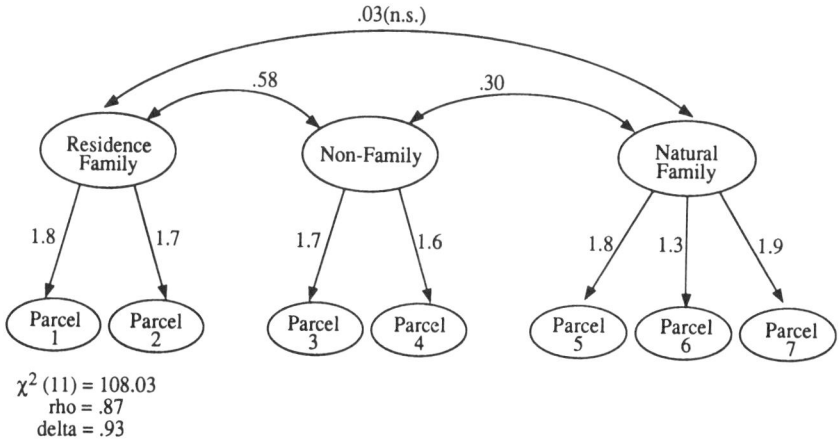

FIGURE 5.7. Results of confirmatory factor analysis for the Quality of Interpersonal Relations dimension of quality of life (maximum likelihood parameter estimates are listed).

of general factor scores in the subsequent analysis of relationships among the quality of life dimensions, careprovider characteristics, and characteristics of the clients studied. The sub-scale scores at each level (i.e., three levels for Environment) have unique descriptive characteristics and yet share enough in common with factors at their same level to support the assumption of a higher-level (general) factor. For example, the affective, cognitive, physical, and normalization aspects of the residential environment provide unique information about environments, and yet family care homes that tend to score high (or low) in one area also score relatively high (or low) in each of the other three areas.

QUALITY OF LIFE DIMENSIONS: RELATIONS WITH OTHER VARIABLES AND STABILITY ACROSS TIMES OF MEASUREMENT

Relations with Client and Careprovider

Mental retardation level. Table 5.1 displays mean scores on quality of life constructs by level of retardation for the Family Care Study sample. The authors had hypothesized that scores on quality of life measures would differ according to the individual's level of functioning and that quality of life should be interpreted only in the context of similar functioning groups of people. This hypothesis was confirmed for Interpersonal Relationships, $F (3,144)=3.95$, $p<.01$, Community Involvement, $F (3,144)=3.27$, $p<.05$, and for the normalization component of the Residential Environment dimension, $F (3,144)=4.43$, $p<.01$.

TABLE 5.1

Quality of Life Scores by Level of Retardation

	LEVEL OF MENTAL RETARDATION								
	MILD		MODERATE		SEVERE		PROFOUND		
	X	SD	X	SD	X	SD	X	SD	F-VALUE
Quality of relationships	2.81	(.57)	2.88	(.60)	3.16	(.50)	2.61	(.70)	3.95**
Foster family	3.06	(.68)	3.16	(.65)	3.21	(.68)	2.89	(.74)	.72
Natural family	1.80	(1.36)	2.04	(1.29)	2.10	(1.61)	1.89	(1.54)	.25
Friend/neighbor	2.62	(.74)	2.73	(.74)	2.94	(.82)	2.13	(1.15)	2.91*
Community involvement	.61	(.13)	.57	(.16)	.51	(.19)	.45	(.22)	3.27*
Events	.72	(.22)	.60	(.27)	.51	(.30)	.43	(.36)	3.77*
Clubs	.23	(.13)	.27	(.18)	.25	(.14)	.25	(.15)	.52
Public resource	.88	(.13)	.84	(.18)	.77	(.26)	.67	(.30)	3.32
Residential environment	3.23	(.30)	3.26	(.33)	3.22	(.29)	3.14	(.43)	.48
Normalization	3.11	(.49)	3.03	(.41)	2.76	(.48)	2.80	(.59)	4.43**
Physical	3.33	(.66)	3.48	(.67)	3.55	(.41)	3.47	(.48)	.73
Cognitive	3.23	(.19)	3.16	(.30)	3.07	(.35)	2.97	(.56)	2.00
Affective	3.12	(.48)	3.15	(.44)	3.04	(.52)	2.96	(.53)	.74
Residential stability	2.52	(1.69)	2.59	(1.71)	3.11	(1.84)	2.14	(1.16)	1.38

*$p < .05$
**$p < .01$

Post hoc comparisons indicated that the means of only those with severe retardation (who had the highest quality relationships) and those with profound retardation (who had the lowest quality relationships) were significantly different from one another. These differences between severe and profound retardation were also present in the comparison of means for the subcategory of the quality of friendships outside the home or family, $F (3,144)=2.91$, $p<.05$.

With regard to community involvement, mean scores decreased with more severe levels of retardation. Those with profound retardation had significantly lower community involvement scores than those with either mild or moderate retardation. In the specific category of attending community events, clients with mild retardation participated significantly more than those with severe or profound retardation, $F (3,329)=3.77$, $p<.05$.

A linear trend was present for scores on normalization, with homes of clients with mild retardation being characterized as significantly more normalized than homes of people with either severe or profound retardation. There were no differences between mental retardation levels with regard to the length of time clients had been in the family care homes.

Correlations with other variables. As part of the challenge to identify characteristics of clients, homes, and careproviders that are associated with positive outcomes, researchers have begun to study the associations among these variables. For example, Crapps and Stoneman (1989) found that careprovider characteristics were related more to client levels of community integration than to friendship variables. Significant correlations were reported between the frequency of community activities and careprovider age, education, tenure as a provider, and income. The only significant correlation they found that related to friendships was a negative relationship between careprovider income and the number of handicapped friends the clients had.

With regard to client variables and quality of life outcomes, the Crapps and Stoneman (1989) data suggested that clients who were younger and/or had been in their homes a shorter period of time tended to be integrated in community activities more frequently than those who were older or had a longer tenure in their homes. A negative relationship was found between level of maladaptive behavior and the frequency of community integration. This is consistent with views of caregivers surveyed by Hill and Bruininks (1984), who felt that clients with behavior problems could be integrated to a greater extent if their behavior could be improved. Finally, Crapps and Stoneman (1989) found that client age and length of time in the home were negatively correlated with the number of non-handicapped friends and their visits with them.

In the Family Care Study, relationships similar to those studied by Crapps and Stoneman were examined. Because the outcome variables in the two studies differed in the way they were operationally defined, direct comparisons cannot be made. Nevertheless, the data may be important to study *in conjunction* with the findings of Crapps and Stoneman in order to provide a more complete picture of the important relationships.

Table 5.2 displays correlations among client, careprovider, and quality of life variables at the first time of measurement. Overall, the direction of relationships was consistent within the subcategories of quality of life dimensions and are reflected in correlations with the total scores for the category. Client age was positively associated with participation in events and clubs, but was unrelated to how often clients used public resources. Neither client age nor level of retardation was related to the quality of relationships with other people, although health problems and the quality of relationships with friends and neighbors were negatively correlated.

Moreover, clients with health problems tended to have been in the homes for shorter periods of time. Younger clients were placed in homes that scored higher in all aspects of the environment. Mental retardation level was not related to the quality of the overall environment, but significant correlations were found for level of mental retardation, normalization and the cognitive environment, with more severe retardation being associated with lower environment scores. Mental retardation level and adaptive behavior were both related to levels of community involvement—higher functioning people were more involved in community activities.

TABLE 5.2

Correlations of Client and Careprovider Characteristics
With Quality of Life Measures

	INTERPERSONAL RELATIONSHIPS				COMMUNITY INVOLVEMENT			
	FOSTER FAMILY	NATURAL FAMILY	FRIEND/ NEIGHBOR	TOTAL	EVENTS	CLUBS	PUBLIC RESOURCE	TOTAL
Client								
Age	−.05	−.08	.19*	−.01	.20*	.31*	−.01	.21*
MR level	.01	.04	.01	.11	−.27*	.01	−.25*	−.25*
Health problem	−.13	−.03	−.20*	−.14	.03	.04	.03	.04
Adaptive behaviors	.13	−.03	.27*	.10	.41*	.24*	.21*	.39*
Maladaptive behaviors	−.07	.10	−.08	−.17*	−.02	−.11	−.06	−.07
Careprovider								
Age	−.03	−.06	.07	−.02	−.11	.12	−.08	−.06
Education	.01	−.06	−.14	−.11	.22*	−.23*	−.16*	.11
Experience	.03	−.14	.24*	.20*	−.03	−.16*	−.06	−.09
Training	−.10	−.09	.03	.01	−.11	.01	−.04	−.07
Seriousness of AB problems	.17*	−.04	.02	.02	−.02	−.09	.03	−.03
Seriousness of MAB	.14	−.13	−.09	−.02	−.05	−.24	−.08	−.14

	RESIDENTIAL ENVIRONMENT					RESIDENTIAL STABILITY
	NORMALIZATION	PHYSICAL	COGNITIVE	AFFECTIVE	TOTAL	
Client						
Age	−.39*	−.19*	−.19*	−.27*	−.32*	.33*
MR level	−.26*	.10	−.20*	−.10	−.06	.06
Health problem	.14	.05	.08	.15	.13	−.16*
Adaptive behaviors	.03	−.07	−.02	.02	−.04	.26*
Maladaptive behaviors	−.05	−.07	.15	−.00	.01	.13
Careprovider						
Age	−.37*	−.07	−.08	−.20*	.17*	.17*
Education	.41*	.12	.31*	.28*	.32*	−.16*
Experience	−.21*	.08	.03	−.14	−.01	.53*
Training	−.19*	−.11	.06	−.04	−.06	.19*
Seriousness of AB problems	.01	.27*	.12	.22	.32*	−.19*
Seriousness of MAB	.05	.16	.19*	.33*	.33*	−.14

*$p < .05$

Contrary to this study's hypothesis and to other findings in the literature, maladaptive behavior was not related to levels of community involvement. However, problem behavior did accompany problems in interpersonal relationships. Mental retardation level was not related to the length of
time clients had been in the home, but both age and adaptive behavior were
positively associated with stability, and clients with health problems had
shorter tenure in the homes.

With regard to careprovider characteristics and quality of life outcomes, the correlations at the first time of measurement suggest positive relationships between careprovider education and quality of the environment as well as between careprovider experience and client tenure. This latter relationship may result from a number of clients who had lived with the same experienced careprovider since he or she began providing family care services.

It is interesting to note that careprovider education was positively related to the likelihood of clients attending community events, yet their level of education had a negative association with the likelihood of clients belonging to clubs and organizations. While careprovider age had a negative association with environment scores, careprovider education was positively associated with total environment scores. Finally, careproviders who were more experienced tended to have clients who had better interpersonal relationships.

Longitudinal Relationships Among Quality of Life Dimensions

In Figure 5.5 a conceptual model was presented that provides a basis for conducting quality of life research. The fact that the structures of the two more complex dimensions were empirically evaluated contributes to the explanatory power of the models that were used to examine relationships among all four quality of life dimensions. The longitudinal model with three points of measurement also allowed for: 1) cross-validation of relationships across years, and; 2) quality of life variables to impact each other beyond the first time of measurement.

Interpersonal relationships and community involvement were examined in each of the three study years, whereas Residential Environment and Stability were measured only in the first year. Since the longitudinal analyses were conducted only on individuals who were in the study for all three time points, placement stability was only meaningful at one time point, i.e., in Year 2 the stability score would be stability in Year 1 plus one year; in Year 3 it would be stability in Year 2 plus one year.

Overall, the best-fitting model had adequate levels of fit, $X^2(102)=138.2$, $p<.001$, and rho=.93. Estimates from this model are shown in Figure 5.8. These estimates reveal adequate levels of stability for Interpersonal Relationships and Community Involvement from year to year. Although these two constructs were correlated each year, there were no significant cross-lagged paths to suggest that community involvement in one year influences interpersonal relationships in the next year, or the reverse relationship.

The quality of the Residential Environment in the first year had a marginally significant causal relationship with Quality of Relationships in Year 3, $\beta=.14$ ($se=.08$) suggesting that environmental influences may be cumulative and may take years to show a measurable impact on the quality of relationships. The directed arrow from Quality of Relationships in the

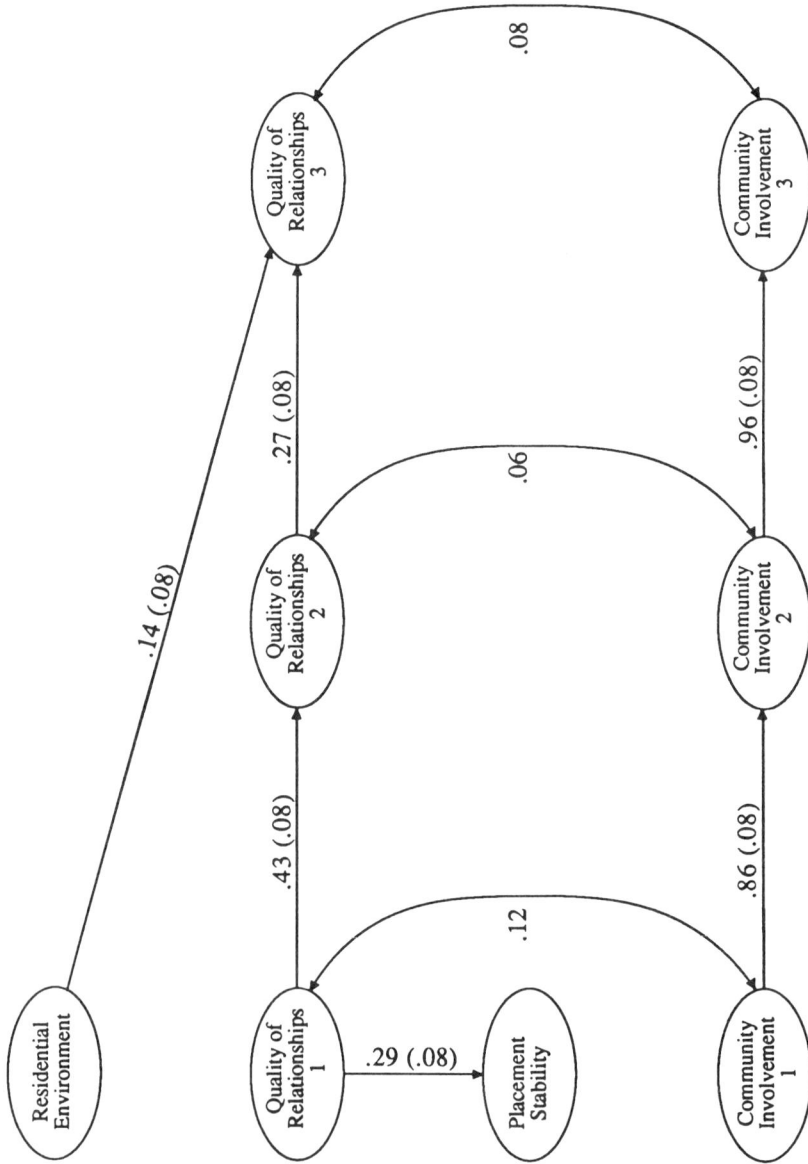

FIGURE 5.8. Structural model representing relations among the quality of life dimensions across the three times of measurement (maximum likelihood parameter estimates are listed, with associated standard errors in parentheses).

first year to Placement Stability, $\beta=.29$ ($se=.08$), suggests that clients who get along well with people in the home and in the neighborhood are those who are likely to remain in the family care home for an extended period of time.

CONCLUSION

The purpose of this chapter was to describe both conceptually and empirically a model for understanding the important aspects of an individual's life. The Quality of Life model incorporates dimensions of the Residential Environment, Quality of Relationships, Community Involvement, and residential stability. As predicted, a person's measured "score" on the quality of life factors is likely to differ according to the characteristics of the individual, including age, level of retardation, health status, levels of adaptive and maladaptive behavior.

Each of the quality of life dimensions is likely to be an important outcome in the assessment of residential placement decisions. Although the data suggest that people who have lower abilities are likely to be less involved in community activities, the authors cannot conclude that these people would be better placed in another type of setting. Relative to others in the homes, their quality of life may be viewed as poor. However, the quality of their lives may be better than it would be in another type of placement. Additional research on this kind of comparison is needed to address this issue.

Chapter 6

Longitudinal Modeling of Influences on the Development of Individuals in Family Care Settings

The aim of this chapter is to integrate the structural models developed in Chapters 3, 4, and 5 into final, more comprehensive models of the across-time relations among the various domains of variables identified in those previous chapters. A series of models that attempt to capture the dynamic interplay between personal and setting characteristics that occurred during the three-year span of the Family Care Study will be presented. As a preview of the findings to be presented in the remainder of this chapter, the authors expected that there would be a somewhat complex interplay of influences across time, with certain behavioral characteristics of the people with mental retardation affecting both their caregivers and aspects of their quality of life and with careproviders and the quality of life of the family care homes influencing the behavioral characteristics of the people with mental retardation.

The focus of this chapter is on developmental outcomes. In Chapter 3, the authors provided a backdrop for these analyses by characterizing changes in the adaptive and maladaptive behaviors of the children and adolescents with mental retardation in the Family Care Study. In Chapters 4 and 5, potential influences on development in the form of careprovider characteristics and the quality of life dimensions of residential environment, interpersonal relations, community involvement, and stability of placement were introduced. As previously mentioned, many of these potential "influences" on development should also be recognized as important outcomes in and of themselves. In this chapter, however, only those relationships among variables that represent direct impacts on, or direct effects of, adaptive and maladaptive behaviors of the persons with mental retardation will be highlighted.

In each of the three major sections of this chapter, the results of the modeling of the interplay of influences involving a major aspect of the behavior of persons with mental retardation are presented. The three major sections present models for adaptive behavior, social maladaption, and personal maladaption, respectively. At the beginning of each section, the set of variables included in each model is described and basic information on model fit is given.

Then, for ease of presentation, figural representations of causal effects in each section are provided separately for careprovider variables and for quality of life indices. Also, to simplify the graphical presentation of results, certain latent variables were deleted from figures if the latent variables had no effect on, and were not affected by, the focal behavior (i.e., adaptive behavior, social maladaption, or personal maladaption) of the people with mental retardation. To ensure that readers understood the results of the modeling, the latent variables deleted from each figure were always carefully noted.

Modeling Influences on, and Effects of, Adaptive Behavior

The first model to be described contained, as focal variables, the adaptive behavior and health at each of the three times of measurement for the persons with mental retardation who were the primary subjects in the Family Care Study. To this core set of variables were added: a) the person's chronological age and level of mental retardation; b) the careprovider variables of experience, education, age, involvement, and rated seriousness of problems in adaptive behaviors, and; c) the quality of life measures related to quality of relationships, stability of placement, community involvement, and residential environment. Placing all of these variables within a single model enables the estimation of relations among the three domains of variables—person variables, careprovider variables, and quality of life indices.

The initial, measurement model for adaptive behavior, described in more detail in the Appendix, had a quite reasonable level of practical fit, ρ = .90, but this model was rejectable statistically. Moreover, there were indications that improvements could easily be made to the model, improvements that included the deletion of almost 200 parameter estimates from the model. The resulting final model for adaptive behavior was far more parsimonious than the measurement model; this final model had an improved level of practical fit, ρ = .91, although the final model was still rejectable statistically, $\chi^2(833) = 1157.1$, $p < .001$.

For ease of figural presentation, the chronological age and level of retardation of the person with mental retardation are not shown in Figures 6.1 and 6.2. Interestingly, the addition of the careprovider and quality of life variables into the model in Figure 3.1 of Chapter 3 had little effect on the path coefficients relating the chronological age and level of retardation of the person with mental retardation with the person's levels of adaptive behavior and health.

Thus, the path coefficients from Client Age to Adaptive Behavior and Health Problems at Time 1 were β = .67 (se = .12) and β = -.42 (se = .10), respectively; and the path coefficients from Level of Mental Retardation to Adaptive Behavior at Time 1 and to Health Problems at Time 3 were

β = -.45 (se = .09) and β = -.16 (se = .06), respectively. Aside from the relations between the age and level of retardation of the person with mental retardation and careprovider and quality of life variables that were described in the preceding section of this chapter, the chronological age and level of retardation of the person with mental retardation did not have any additional effects on any additional variables added at Times 2 and 3.

Influences involving careprovider variables. The first submodel to be discussed here includes the careprovider variables, along with the adaptive behavior and health of the person with mental retardation; this submodel is shown in Figure 6.1. Three significant path coefficients were found among the variables of Careprovider Experience, Careprovider Training, and Careprovider Seriousness of Adaptive Problems. Careprovider Experience was a significant predictor of both Careprovider Training, β = .38 (se = .09), and Careprovider Seriousness of Adaptive Problems, β = -.26 (se = .09). These two paths indicate that careproviders with longer terms of service, or experience, in caring for individuals with mental retardation had higher levels of additional training and had lower ratings of seriousness for problems in adaptive behavior. The third significant path related Careprovider Training and Careprovider Seriousness of Adaptive Problems, β = -.24 (se = .09), suggesting that increases in careprovider training led to lower rated seriousness of client needs and dependencies (i.e., adaptive behavior problems).

Three constructs were represented at each of the three times of measurement—Careprovider Seriousness of Adaptive Problems, Client Adaptive Behavior, and Client Health Problems. The first and third of these deviated from a strict first-order autoregressive pattern of relations, as the Time 3 latent variable for each construct was influenced by both the Time 1 and the Time 2 latent variables for the construct, rather than being influenced by the Time 2 latent variable alone. These departures from a first-order autoregressive pattern are of unknown importance; the unmediated paths from Time 1 latent variables to Time 3 latent variables were added into the structural model because they had significant modification indices and therefore would unbias the estimates of other parameters in the model. Whether these additional direct paths represent crucial phenomena that require explanation cannot be addressed in this study, but could be the focus of future research.

Of central concern is the presence of any causal regression paths among the three constructs across time, as well as whether any of the other careprovider variables influenced the remaining constructs in the model. Here, there appear to be two major patterns. The first pattern involved the Careprovider Seriousness of Adaptive Problems at Time 1, which had a negative path to Adaptive Behavior at Time 2, β = -.12 (se = .04), and a positive path to Adaptive Behavior at Time 3, β = .17 (se = .06).

The first of these paths suggests that as the careprovider's perceived

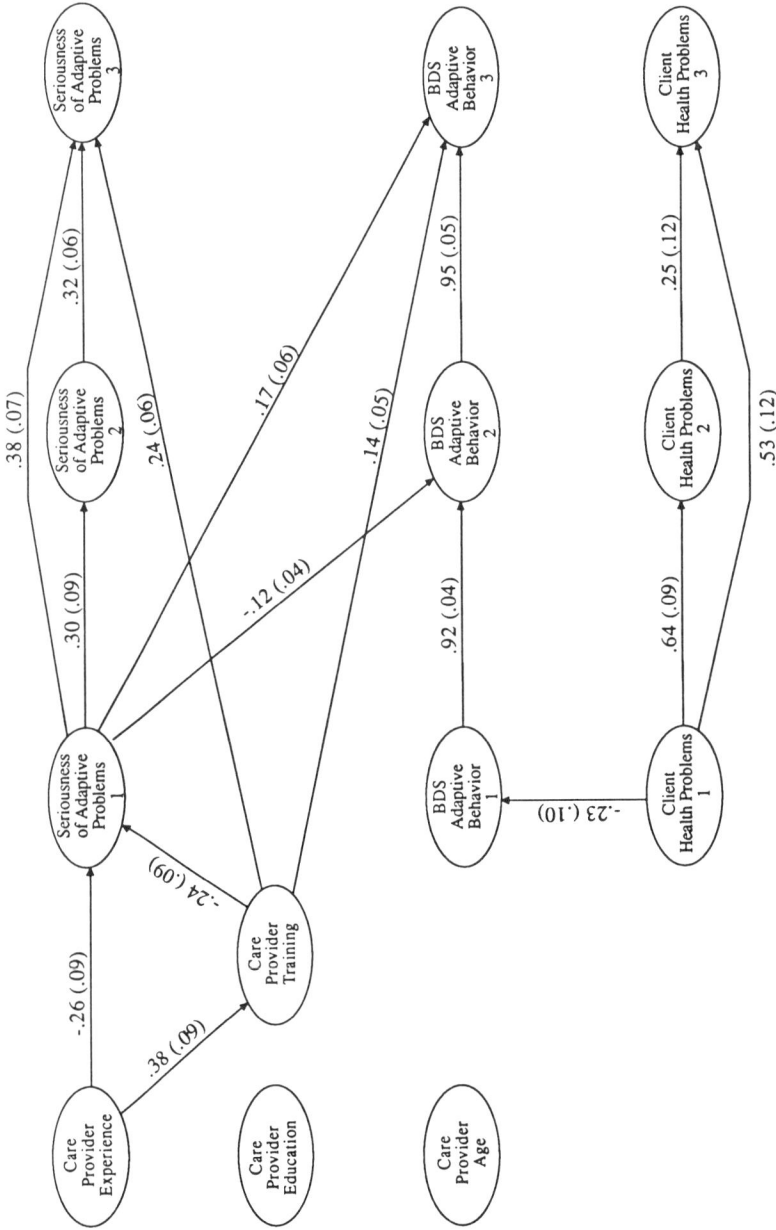

FIGURE 6.1. Structural model relating the adaptive behavior and health problems of the person with mental retardation and careprovider variables across the three times of measurement (maximum likelihood parameter estimates are listed, with associated standard errors in parentheses).

seriousness of problems in adaptive behavior increased at Time 1, *lower* levels of adaptive behavior were exhibited at Time 2. However, the second path implies a reversed relationship, with greater perceived seriousness leading to higher levels of adaptive behavior at Time 3. These two path coefficients may signal a complex relationship of perceived seriousness of adaptive problems with later adaptive behavior, a relationship that has opposing influence at different causal lags.

On the other hand, the differing signs of these two paths, taken together with the lack of relationship of Careprovider Seriousness at Times 2 or 3 with Adaptive Behavior at Time 3, suggests that the estimated relationships may represent statistically significant, but temporally unstable phenomena. The results suggest at least the direction of the causal relationship, with careprovider perceptions of seriousness of behaviors affecting later adaptive behavior by the person with mental retardation, rather than the reverse. That is, paths from the Adaptive Behavior latent variables at Times 1 and 2 to Careprovider Seriousness at Times 2 and 3 were near zero and nonsignificant. Future research could be undertaken to investigate whether the Careprovider Seriousness to later Adaptive Behavior paths represent replicable phenomena.

The second major pattern surrounded Careprovider Training, which had positive paths to two latent variables at Time 3, Careprovider Seriousness of Adaptive Problems, $\beta = .24$ ($se = .06$), and Adaptive Behavior, $\beta = .14$ ($se = .05$). The former path implies that careproviders who continued to be involved in training had higher levels of later perceived seriousness of adaptive problems. The latter path reflects another careprovider effect on later adaptive behavior: the greater the training the careprovider had experienced, the higher the level of adaptive behavior at Time 3.

As with the above effects of Careprovider Seriousness on later Adaptive Behavior, future research should provide answers regarding the strength and stability of these two paths from Careprovider Training to other variables at Time 3.

The only remaining significant path coefficient of interest was the negative path from Health Problems at Time 1 to Adaptive Behavior at Time 1, $\beta = -.23$ ($se = .10$), reflecting the depressing effect that health problems may have on the perceived adaptive behavioral competencies of people with mental retardation. Of greater interest were the other potential paths involving the Health Problems latent variables at Times 1, 2, and 3; Health Problems were largely unrelated to levels of adaptive behavior or to careprovider variables of any sort, whether at the same point in time or at a later point in time.

An interesting observation on the modeling of measures across the three times of measurement occurred for the Adaptive Behavior latent variable. In Chapter 3 (see Figure 3.1), Adaptive Behavior at Time 3 was influenced by Adaptive Behavior at both Times 1 and 2. This deviation from a first-order autoregressive pattern was downplayed in Chapter 3, as it was not clear if this result was some complex pattern that required further substantive explanation or was due to the failure to include important variables in the model. The latter explanation now appears to be more consistent with the data, as the need to specify a path from Adaptive Behavior at Time 1 to Adaptive Behavior at Time 3 was no longer necessary once careprovider and quality of life variables were included in the model.

This outcome underscores the need to achieve the correct specification of a structural model in order for the estimated paths to correspond to proper, simple patterns of influence, presuming that such patterns characterize the causal processes underlying the data.

Influences involving quality of life measures. Next, the relations among quality of life measures and the adaptive behavioral competencies of the individuals with mental retardation are examined. The submodel containing these constructs is shown in Figure 6.2. The longitudinal paths for the Adaptive Behavior and Client Health Problems latent variables were discussed above, as was the path from Client Health Problems to Adaptive Behavior at Time 1; therefore, these paths will not be discussed further here. The latent variables for Community Involvement at the three points of measurement fit well a first-order autoregressive pattern, with a high level of stability in this characteristic of residences across time.

The most striking and consistent effect in the model in Figure 6.2 is the cross-lagged path from Community Involvement at one time of measurement to Adaptive Behavior at the next time of measurement. That is, after controlling statistically for prior levels of adaptive behavior, Community Involvement at Time 1 influenced Adaptive Behavior at Time 2, $\beta = .14$ (se $= .04$), and Community Involvement at Time 2 influenced Adaptive Behavior at Time 3, $\beta = .12$ (se $= .05$).

These paths suggest that higher levels of community involvement lead to higher subsequent levels of adaptive behavior. Presumably, higher levels of community involvement provide the person with mental retardation a larger and wider array of experiences that require ever more advanced, mature responses. These experiences thus provide situations for learning new behaviors. The result is higher levels of later adaptive behavioral competence as the challenges represented by these situations are surmounted.

In addition to the preceding pattern of results, two other path coefficients reached statistical significance. These paths reflected a positive effect of Adaptive Behavior at Time 1 on Residential Environment, $\beta = .29$ (se $= .11$), and a negative effect of Client Health Problems at Time 2 on Community Involvement at Time 2, $\beta = -.27$ (se $= .07$). The former path, from Adaptive Behavior at Time 1 to Residential Environment, embodies the positive effects of adaptive behavior on the quality of the residential environment—as adaptive behavior increases, the quality of the residential

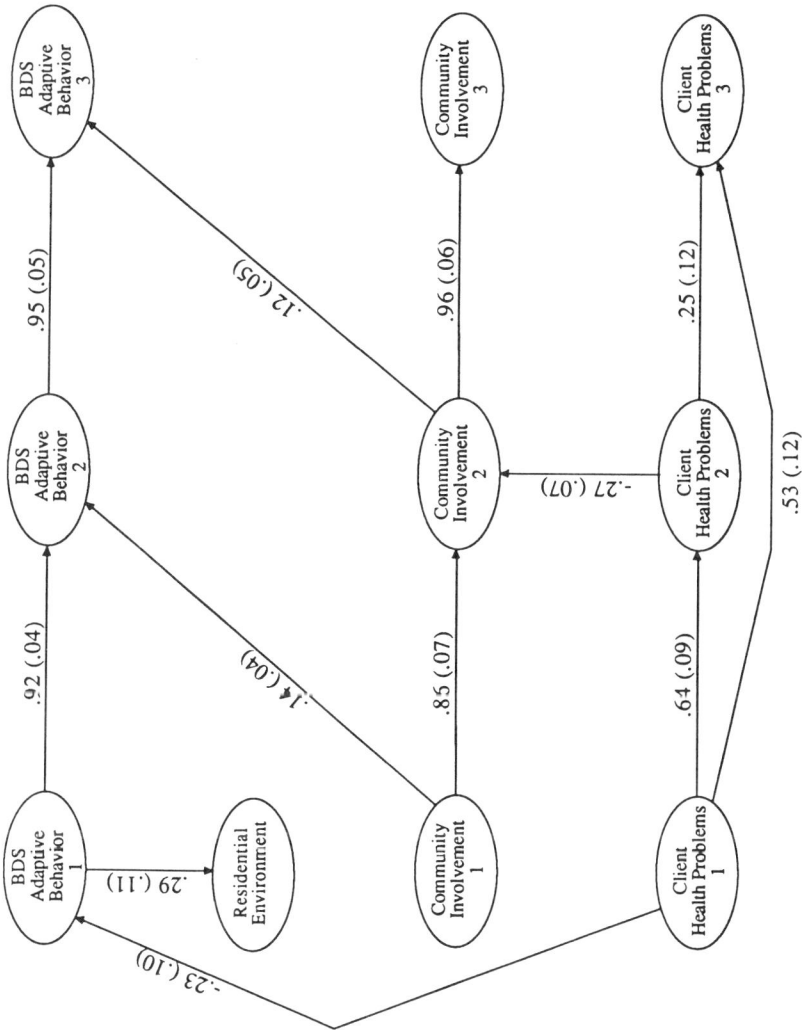

FIGURE 6.2. Structural model relating the adaptive behavior and health problems of the person with mental retardation and quality of life indices across the three times of measurement (maximum likelihood parameter estimates are listed, with associated standard errors in parentheses).

environment shows a concomitant rise. That is, as people with higher levels of adaptive behavior live in a given residential environment, the forms of personal interaction that may be exhibited and sustained is higher. The latter path, from Client Health Problems to Community Involvement, simply shows that caring for a person with health problems leads to lowered opportunities to involve that person in events and activities in the community.

Two latent variables associated with quality of life, Placement Stability and Quality of Relationship, had no effects on adaptive behavior, nor were they affected by adaptive behavior, so these latent variables were excluded from Figure 6.2

Modeling Influences on, and Effects of, Social Maladaption

The second model in this chapter substituted indicators of Social Maladaption by the individuals with mental retardation at each of the three times of measurement in place of the measures of Adaptive Behavior; the indicators of Health Problems were retained in this model. To this core set of variables were added: a) the person's chronological age and level of mental retardation; b) the careprovider variables of experience, education, age, involvement, and rated seriousness of socially maladaptive behaviors, and; c) the quality of life measures related to quality of relationships, stability of placement, community involvement, and residential environment. Placing all of these variables within a single model enables the estimation of causes and effects of socially maladaptive behaviors.

The initial measurement model for socially maladaptive behaviors, discussed in more detail in the Appendix, had an adequate level of practical fit, $\rho = .91$. But, respecification of this model, leading to a final model with 200 fewer parameter estimates, led to an improvement in the degree to which the model represented the data, especially considering the much greater parsimony of the final model. The resulting final model for socially maladaptive behaviors had a slightly higher and quite acceptable level of practical fit, $\rho = .92$, although the model was still rejectable statistically, $\chi^2(635) = 793.7$, $p < .001$.

Consistent with the figures for adaptive behavior, the chronological age and level of retardation of the person with mental retardation are not shown in Figures 6.3 and 6.4. Once again, the addition of the careprovider and quality of life variables had little effect on the path coefficients involving the Client Age and Level of Retardation latent variables. Thus, the path coefficient from Client Age to Health Problems at Time 1 was $\beta = -.43$ ($se = .10$), and the path coefficient from Level of Mental Retardation to Health Problems at Time 3 was $\beta = -.15$ ($se = .06$). The chronological age and level of retardation of the person with mental retardation did not have any other effects on the additional variables added at Times 2 and 3.

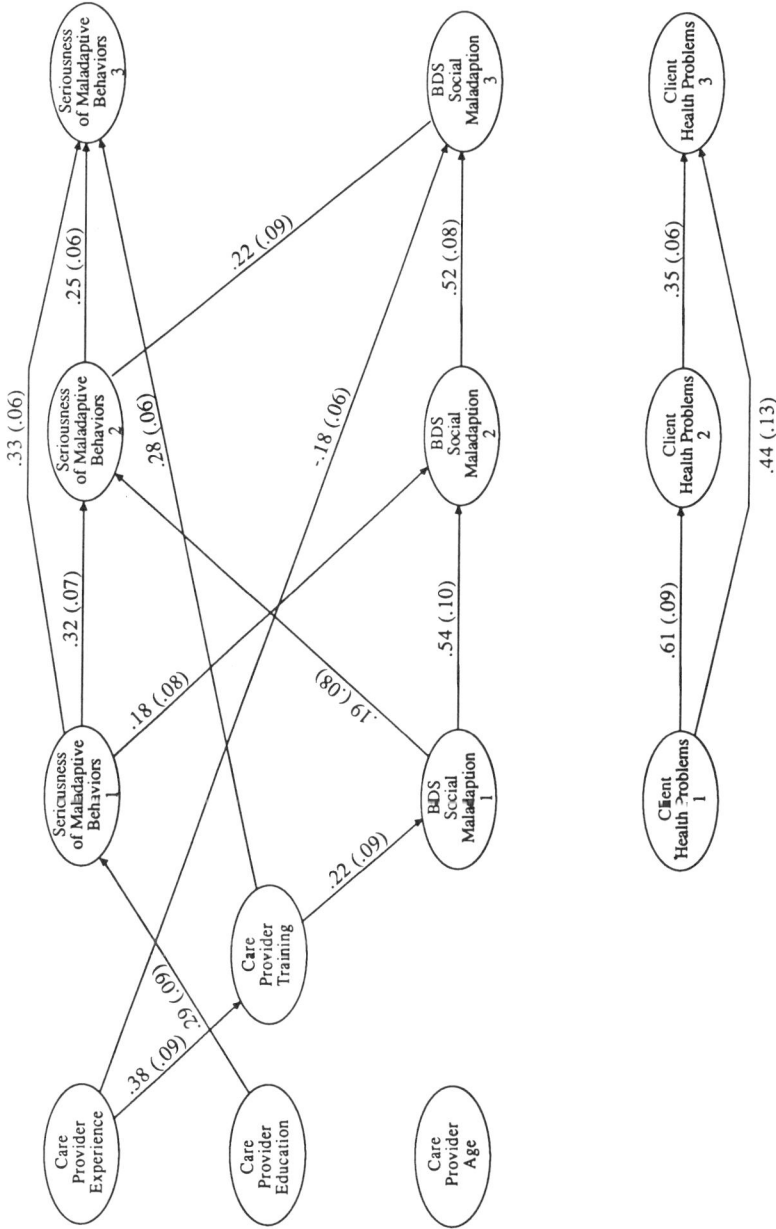

FIGURE 6.3. Structural model relating the social maladaption and health problems of the person with mental retardation and careprovider variables across the three times of measurement (maximum likelihood parameter estimates are listed, with associated standard errors in parentheses).

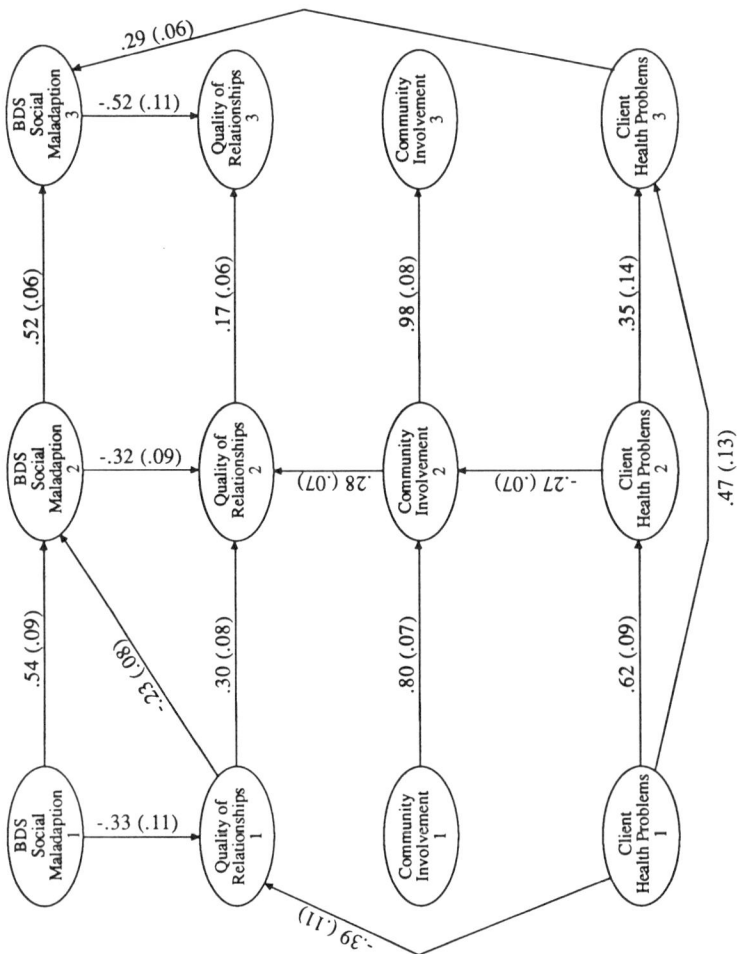

FIGURE 6.4. Structural model relating the social maladaption and health problems of the person with mental retardation and quality of life variables across the three times of measurement (maximum likelihood parameter estimates are listed, with associated standard errors in parentheses).

Influences involving careprovider variables. The relations among careprovider variables and the social maladaption and health problems of the person with mental retardation are shown in Figure 6.3. Several path coefficients from careprovider background variables on other variables in the model were statistically significant. The path from Careprovider Experience to Careprovider Training, $\beta = .38$ ($se = .09$) was discussed in a previous section of this chapter and therefore will not be discussed further.

One significant path led to Social Maladaption at Time 1 from Careprovider Training, $\beta = .22$ ($se = .09$), a path coefficient that probably reflects a selection or assignment effect. That is, careproviders with higher levels of training may tend to allow the placement into their homes of people with higher levels of social maladaption. The final path extended from Careprovider Education to Careprovider Seriousness of Maladaptive Behaviors at Time 1, $\beta = .29$ ($se = .09$). This path suggests that higher levels of education on the part of careproviders are associated with somewhat higher levels of rated seriousness of maladaptive behaviors, perhaps because such careproviders have greater knowledge of problems in the residential home caused by maladaptive behaviors.

One important and consistent pattern of influences involved careproviders' rated seriousness of maladaptive behaviors and the socially maladaptive behaviors of the person with mental retardation. The results showed a consistent causal influence of careprovider seriousness on later levels of social maladaption. That is, Careprovider Seriousness of Maladaptive Behaviors at Time 1 influenced Social Maladaption at Time 2, $\beta = .18$ ($se = .08$), and Careprovider Seriousness at Time 2 affected Social Maladaption at Time 3, $\beta = .22$ ($se = .09$).

These results reflect an interesting pattern of influence: controlling statistically for previous levels of social maladaption, the more serious a careprovider views socially maladaptive behaviors, the *higher* the subsequent levels of social maladaption by the person with mental retardation. This is an unexpected and, on the surface, somewhat paradoxical finding. However, at least two explanations could account for these results.

One explanation involves the unintended worsening of the child-careprovider situation, due to reactions by the person with mental retardation to the attempts by the careprovider to modify his/her socially maladaptive behaviors. That is, the higher the perceived seriousness of socially maladaptive behaviors by the careprovider, the more the careprovider might attempt to modify the behavior of the person with mental retardation. However, these attempts to modify the behavior might exacerbate the situation, leading to higher subsequent levels of socially maladaptive behavior. If the careprovider's attempts to modify behavior were frustrating to the person with mental retardation, then attempts to lower the level of socially maladaptive behavior might have the reverse, unintended effect.

A second potential explanation may be constructed along the line of unintended positive reinforcement of behavior. The more serious a careprovider perceives maladaptive behaviors, the more the careprovider might respond when the person with mental retardation exhibits maladaptive behaviors. But, this response by the careprovider might be positively reinforcing to the person with mental retardation. Thus, the careprovider's attention and behavior are focused on the person with mental retardation contingent on the latter's exhibition of socially maladaptive behaviors, and the person with mental retardation may begin to exhibit higher levels of socially maladaptive behaviors in order to gain the attention of the careprovider, once again leading to unintended effects of perceived seriousness of maladaptive behaviors.

Of course, other potential explanations could be offered for these findings. Here, the authors note that the consistency of the cross-lagged effects (i.e., the same relationships being replicated across time periods) argues for the importance of these effects for research and theory on maladaptive behaviors. Future research should be undertaken to replicate the direction of effects reported in Figure 6.3 and to design tests among competing structural models that could offer differential support for the competing explanations for the findings.

The other side of this relation between perceived seriousness and socially maladaptive behaviors was also shown, as Social Maladaption at Time 1 affected Careprovider Seriousness at Time 2, $\beta = .19$ ($se = .08$). The most direct interpretation of this finding is that experiencing socially maladaptive behaviors by people with mental retardation and the effects that these behaviors had on the home environment led careproviders to regard maladaptive behaviors as a more serious problem. Given the preceding findings of perceived seriousness leading to higher subsequent levels of socially maladaptive behavior, we have the possibility of an escalating spiral of potentially troubling effects—with higher levels of socially maladaptive behavior related to higher levels of subsequent perceived seriousness of those behaviors, which in turn leads to higher levels of subsequent socially maladaptive behaviors. The one finding that mitigates against the spiral hypothesis is the instability of the effect of socially maladaptive behavior on subsequent perceived seriousness of those behaviors, an effect that appeared only for one of the two potential cross-lagged time periods.

Two additional path coefficients were statistically significant. The first was a positive path from Careprovider Training to Careprovider Seriousness at Time 3, $\beta = .28$ ($se = .06$), which implies that the higher the careprovider training, the higher the later perceived seriousness of maladaptive behaviors in subsequent years. As this effect held only at a single point in time, the importance of this path is questionable.

The second significant path is potentially more interesting, revealing a negative relationship between Careprovider Experience and Social Maladaption at Time 3, $\beta = -.18$ ($se = .06$). The direction of this path coefficient suggests that more experienced careproviders may have learned how to react to socially maladaptive behaviors in a manner that leads to lower subsequent levels of the troubling maladaptive behaviors. This finding suggests that a fruitful avenue for future research would be to study the behavioral repertoires of careproviders with varying lengths of experience with persons with mental retardation, as the more experienced careproviders may deal in a more constructive manner with socially maladaptive behaviors than do careproviders with less experience.

Interestingly, Client Health Problems had no relation with socially maladaptive behaviors of the person with mental retardation or with any of the careprovider variables in the model. Thus, poor health on the part of the person with mental retardation does not appear to result in heightened levels of socially maladaptive behaviors or to affect careproviders' perceptions of the seriousness of socially maladaptive behaviors.

Influences involving quality of life measures. The relations of quality of life variables with socially maladaptive behaviors and health problems of the person with mental retardation are shown in Figure 6.4. The most consistent and important finding in this figure is the relation between socially maladaptive behaviors and quality of the person's interpersonal relationships. Specifically, Social Maladaption at each point in time had a negative influence on the Quality of Relationships at the same point in time; the path coefficients were β = -.33, -.32, and -.52, at Times 1, 2, and 3, respectively.

Interestingly, when paths were estimated in the reverse direction, from Quality of Relationships to Social Maladaption, the estimated path coefficients were smaller and nonsignificant. This pattern of findings suggests that Social Maladaption is causally predominant over Quality of Relationships, rather than the reverse. That is, socially maladaptive behavior by the person with mental retardation leads to lowered quality of the relationships the person has with others in his/her circle of friends and acquaintances.

However, because the path coefficients involved constructs assessed at the same point in time, rather than being cross-lagged (i.e., across time) effects, the effects of socially maladaptive behaviors on the quality of the person's interpersonal relationships are short-lived in nature, not affecting directly the long-term relationships experienced by the person.

The reversed causal direction between the quality of relationships and socially maladaptive behavior was also shown, except that this was a cross-lagged path. Specifically, Quality of Relationships at Time 1 had a negative lagged path to Social Maladaption at Time 2, β = -.23 (se = .08). This path suggests that, controlling statistically for prior level of social maladaption, the higher the quality of the interpersonal relationships experienced by the person with mental retardation, the lower the subsequent level of socially maladaptive behavior shown by the person. This is a potentially important result, reflecting another way in which the level of social maladaption on the part of people with mental retardation may be lessened by aspects of the residential environment.

Another set of significant relations shown in Figure 6.4 involved the health of the person with mental retardation, which influenced other variables in the model. These findings reflected significant, but intermittent effects of Client Health Problems at each time of measurement. That is, Client Health Problems at Time 1 had a negative effect on Quality of Relationship at Time 1, $\beta = -.39$ ($se = .11$); Client Health Problems at Time 2 had an inverse relationship on Community Involvement at Time 2, $\beta = -.27$ ($se = .07$); and Client Health Problems at Time 3 had a positive relationship with Social Maladaption at Time 3, $\beta = .29$ ($se = .06$).

Each of these path coefficients represents an easily interpretable relationship, with Health Problems having a negative impact on Quality of Relationship with the careprovider, a lowered level of Community Involvement, and worsened levels of Social Maladaption. Although these effects seem easy to interpret, the findings should be replicated on other samples to ensure the stability and importance of these outcomes of the health status of the person with mental retardation.

Finally, looking at relations among the quality of life constructs, Community Involvement at Time 2 had a positive path to Quality of Relationships at Time 2, $\beta = .28$ ($se = .07$). Thus, the higher the level of involvement in activities in the community by the person with mental retardation, the higher the quality of the person's relationships with other people. As this path was significant only at a single point in time, replication on another sample should be attempted before much interpretive weight is tied to this outcome. As a final note, Stability of Placement and Residential Environment do not appear in Figure 6.4, as neither of these variables influenced the level of social maladaptive behavior by the person with mental retardation, nor were either influenced by the social maladaption of the person.

Modeling Influences on, and Effects of, Personal Maladaption

The third and final longitudinal model to be presented in this chapter contained, as core variables, the personally maladaptive behavior and health at each of the three times of measurement of the individuals with mental retardation living in family care homes. As with the previous models, the following variables were included in this model: a) the person's chronological age and level of mental retardation; b) the careprovider variables of experience, education, age, involvement, and rated seriousness of personally maladaptive behaviors, and; c) the quality of life measures related to quality of relationships, stability of placement, community involvement, and residential environment. The aim of this analysis was to determine whether the causal texture of influences on personally maladaptive behaviors was similar to, or different from, those identified for adaptive behaviors and socially maladaptive behaviors.

The initial measurement model for personally maladaptive behaviors (see the Appendix for more details regarding this model) had an adequate level of fit, $\rho = .92$, but substantial improvements in model specification were possible. After deletion of more than 200 parameters from this model, the resulting final model for personally maladaptive behaviors had much greater parsimony and an identical level of practical fit, $\rho = .92$, although the model was still rejectable on a statistical basis, $\chi^2(637) = 778.2$, $p < .001$.

As in the preceding sections, the chronological age and level of retardation of the person with mental retardation are not shown in Figures 6.5 and 6.6. Paralleling both of the preceding models, the path coefficients involving Client Age and Level of Retardation were affected very little by the addition of the careprovider and quality of life variables. Thus, the path coefficient from Client Age to Health Problems at Time 1 was $\beta = -.43$ ($se = .10$); and the path coefficients from Level of Mental Retardation to Personal Maladaption at Time 1 and to Health Problems at Time 3 were $\beta = .44$ ($se = .11$) and $\beta = -.15$ ($se = .06$), respectively. Also, as in the preceding analyses, Client Age and Level of Retardation did not have any effect on other variables in the final model, over and above the relations described in the first part of this chapter.

Influences involving careprovider variables. The relations among careprovider variables and the Personal Maladaption and Health Problems of the person with mental retardation are shown in Figure 6.5. The most striking aspect of the relationships among Personal Maladaption at each of the three times of measurement and all careprovider variables was the absence of statistically significant paths between these sets of variables.

Quite simply, Personal Maladaption was unrelated, either within time points or across time points, with the careprovider variables in the model. The significant relations among careprovider variables were discussed above, during consideration of Social Maladaption models, so will not be discussed further here.

Influences involving quality of life measures. The relations among Personal Maladaption and quality of life variables are shown in Figure 6.6. Personal Maladaption at each of the three times of measurement had negative effects on Quality of Relationships at the same points in time, with path coefficients of $\beta = -.53$, $-.15$, and $-.21$, at Times 1, 2, and 3, respectively.

These paths reflect a worsening of the relationship between the careprovider and the person with mental retardation because of the latter's level of personally maladaptive behavior. This effect was most pronounced at the first time of measurement, but was significant at all three times of measurement. Except for the preceding effects, Personal Maladaption had no other significant effects on quality of life measures, and no quality of life variables had an impact on Personal Maladaption.

There are several additional significant path coefficients in Figure 6.6, such as the path from Client Health Problems at Time 1 to Quality of Relationship at Time 1. Each of these paths was described above, during consideration of the effects of Social Maladaption, depicted in Figure 6.4, so they will not be discussed further. As with Social Maladaption, two quality of life dimensions—Stability of Placement and Residential Environment—are not shown in Figure 6.6, because these had no effects on, nor were they affected by, Personal Maladaption.

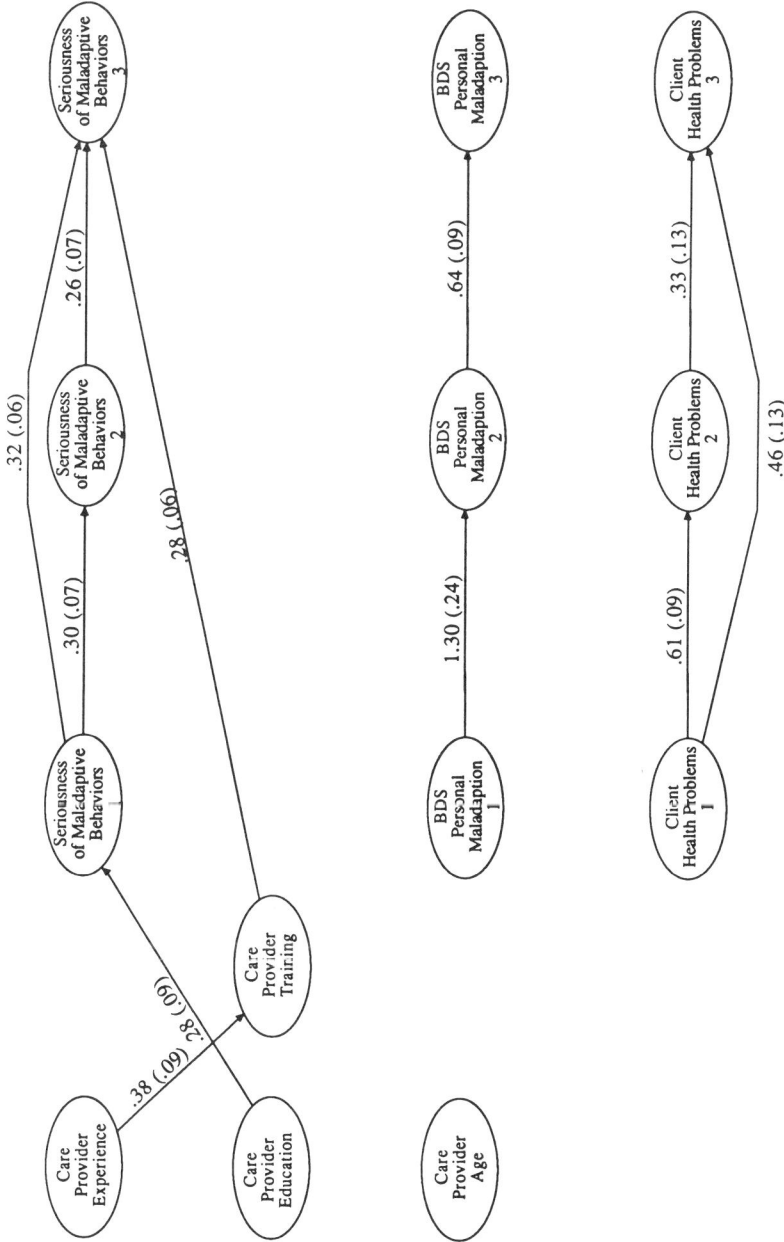

FIGURE 6.5. Structural model relating the personal maladaption and health problems of the person with mental retardation and careprovider variables across the three times of measurement (maximum likelihood parameter estimates are listed, with associated standard errors in parentheses).

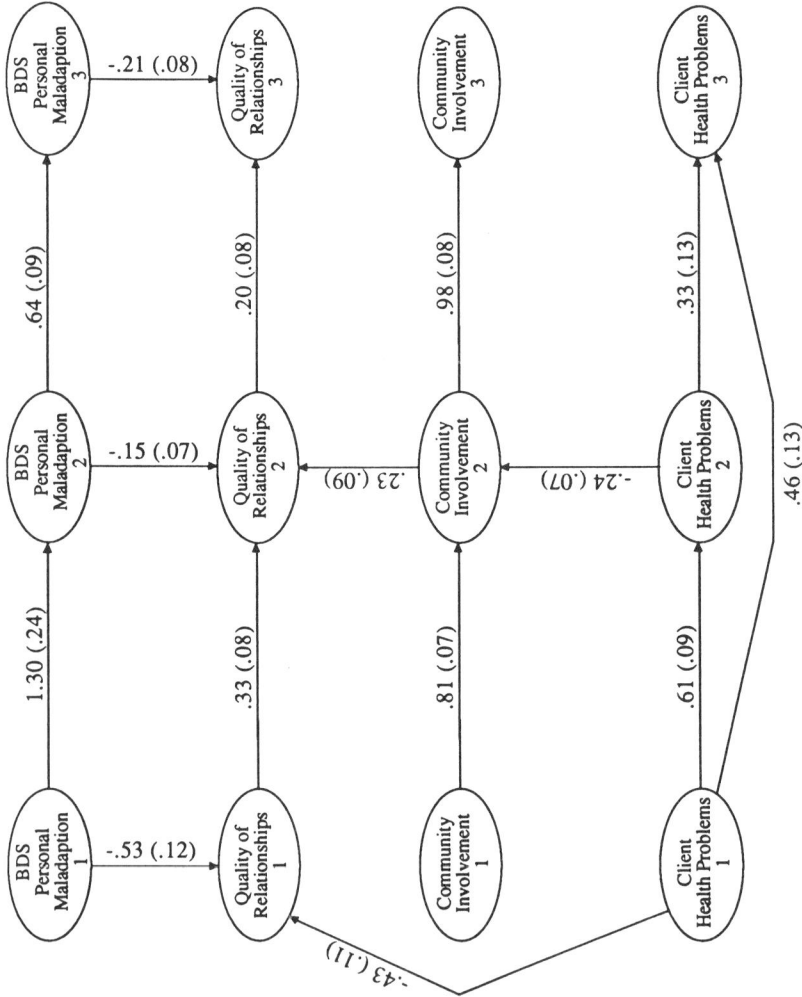

FIGURE 6.6. Structural model relating the personal maladaption and health problems of the person with mental retardation and quality of life variables across the three times of measurement (maximum likelihood parameter estimates are listed, with associated standard errors in parentheses).

Chapter 7

Results of the Family Care Study: Findings And Implications

The general aims of the Family Care Study were to characterize persons with mental retardation living in small family care homes and to describe their careproviders and the family care homes in which they lived. Across three times of measurement, the authors followed the behavior, development, and quality of life of a sample of 148 children and adolescents with mental retardation. Like others before, the authors sought to marshal evidence that would identify factors associated with optimal development and a high quality of life.

During the Family Care Study, information from numerous sources was obtained in order to describe and explain relationships among variables as well as the causal effects of different contextual variables on the outcomes of behavioral development and quality of life. The longitudinal design allowed cross-validation of findings across years within the sample.

Relationships among variables that were replicated across time periods were considered more stable and reliable than those that appeared at only one time in the models; such stable relationships should therefore provide a firmer cornerstone for future research and theory on behavioral development and quality of life of persons with mental retardation.

The broad range of predictor and outcome variables also presented opportunities to view relationships among variables in the context of a larger set of constructs. The structural modeling techniques that were used to characterize relationships among client, careprovider, quality of life, and developmental outcomes allowed the study of the dynamic relationships among variables that did not need to be cast in the traditional form of dependent or independent variables.

FINDINGS FROM THE FOSTER FAMILY CARE STUDY

Persons With Mental Retardation Residing in Foster Family Care Homes

Who were these individuals? One goal of the Family Care Study was to examine people with mental retardation who resided in small family care homes, an examination designed to characterize them. The conclusion that must be drawn from this investigation is that children and adolescents with mental retardation living in small family care homes represent a very mixed array of people, showing a great deal of diversity on virtually every dimension or characteristic that one may wish to identify.

With regard to basic personal characteristics, the children and adolescents who were studied were approximately evenly split on gender, showed approximately the same diversity of ethnic status as shown by state-wide populations, and represented the full range of degrees of mental retardation. Given this diversity on basic variables, it is difficult to characterize the sample in any simple terms. These individuals also showed diversity on dimensions related to their family and placement backgrounds and behavioral competencies. Such diversity is useful when formulating models of individual differences in development, but is an obstacle to simple summary description.

One observation of these individuals with mental retardation residing in family care homes can be made with some degree of certainty: their behavioral characteristics—particularly, their levels of adaptive behavior, social maladaption, and personal maladaption—represented rather stable dimensions of individual difference. Mean levels of a behavior may wax and wane as a function of the age of the individual, and this may occur independently of the degree of stability of individual differences. But, in the focus on the predictors of individual differences in behavioral competence and on changes in competence across time, the authors were interested primarily in factors that influence behavioral status at a given point in time, including factors that affect individuals differentially.

In the Family Care Study, the authors found that individual differences in adaptive behavior at one point in time were strongly related to individual differences on the same latent variable one year later; the same held for individual differences in social maladaption and personal maladaption. This outcome was represented by the fact that the best predictors of levels of adaptive or maladaptive behavior at a given point in time were the individuals' levels of the same behaviors at the previous time of measurement, one year prior. These autoregressive relationships suggest that each individual is on several trajectories of growth and development of particular forms of behavior that may be largely unaffected by environmental or other influences.

Thus, high stability of individual differences in a given form of adaptive or maladaptive behavior is both a boon and a bane. Stability is a boon, reflecting the fact that an important behavioral trait is being measured well and in a reliable fashion. On the other hand, stability is a bane, as the identification of variables that moderate changes across time in the highly stable characteristic may be difficult. That is, high stability implies that other variables likely moderate change across time to only a rather minor degree. The search for such potential moderators of development, despite the difficulty of the undertaking, was pursued in the later chapters of this monograph.

How did these persons come to reside in foster family care homes? Children and adolescents who were placed in foster family care homes came to that setting by a number of routes. For the majority of biological families, placements were made in order to ease problems—psychological, financial, or physical problems—in their own homes. Less often, but still fairly frequently, families from disadvantaged environments sought out-of-home placement in an effort to provide an improved training environment that would facilitate development of the child. Sometimes the placement decision was made as soon as the child was born; more often, however, decisions to place the child occurred later, during times of transition or crisis in the natural home. As with the personal characteristics of the children and adolescents, the reasons for placing these individuals in foster family care homes displayed a good deal of diversity.

The reluctance to place individuals with mental retardation in institutions or other rather restrictive settings may have led to the heterogeneity observed in the individuals with mental retardation living in foster family care homes. That is, rather restrictive settings are considered a last resort for placement, with people being placed in less restrictive settings whenever possible. As a result, regardless of the characteristics of the individuals, some form of community placement—such as foster family care—is usually the first placement option considered and attempted. However, given the time frame of the study, almost one-third of the people with mental retardation were placed in a foster family care home only after a period of residence in a large state institution. Such institutional placements may have been made prior to the current emphasis on placement in the least restrictive environment.

Despite diversity in the reasons for placement, the prevailing philosophy of placing people in less restrictive settings results in a wide array of personal and behavioral characteristics exhibited by those placed in smaller community residences. Thus, the diversity observed in the sample was likely due to the general philosophy regarding placement, and the diversity observed was a useful outcome as the authors attempted to characterize individual differences in the development and quality of life of people with mental retardation living in foster family care settings. Of course, individuals residing in family care settings do not reflect the full potential range of personal and behavioral characteristics of the population of people with mental retardation, because people who are medically fragile or who exhibit severe behavioral problems are often placed in more restrictive settings, such as institutions or skilled nursing facilities. Because of this, the generalizations based on results of the study must be restricted somewhat, to people with mental retardation whose behavioral and personal characteristics are commensurate with placement in the community.

Careproviders in Foster Family Care Homes

Overall, people who provide residential care in their homes for individuals with mental retardation can be characterized as being accepting of the needs, dependencies, and behavior problems displayed by their residents. In the foster family care homes studied, residents appeared to be well-matched with caregivers in terms of the behaviors they displayed (or lacked) and the tolerance by their caregivers of those behaviors or behavioral deficiencies. Behaviors that caregivers exhibited the lowest levels of preference to handle were those that created additional, and possibly avoidable, work for them, as well as those that may have had an element of fear for the safety of the resident or others living in or near the home.

The caregivers in the Family Care Study were similar in terms of age, education, and experience to those described in other studies. In general, they were more than 50 years old, had a high school education, and had been providing care for at least a few years at the time of the study. The majority of providers had attended at least one training program intended to enhance their caregiving skills. Better educated providers were more likely to participate in additional training programs, and the added training seemed to influence their views on the seriousness of problems in behavior. Further, those who were younger and had more formal education viewed maladaptive behavior as more serious than those who were older or had less education.

The Quality of Life in Foster Family Care Homes

A Quality of Life Model was presented in the Family Care Study to provide a basis for studying important dimensions in the lives of people with mental retardation living in family care homes. The association between level of functioning (as measured by mental retardation level or adaptive behavior) and involvement in community activities confirmed the expectation that people with higher levels of ability would be more integrated in their communities. Moreover, it suggests that quality of life should be viewed in the context of individual characteristics (e.g., quality of life scores of people with severe retardation should not be compared with scores of people with mild retardation).

Individuals with profound mental retardation scored lowest on all quality of life measures (except the level of normalization provided in the home, where the scores were not different from those with severe retardation). Although a study of individuals in only one placement type cannot address how these people might fare in other settings, relative life quality of people with varying levels of functioning can be examined. One can conclude that life in foster family care homes is experienced differently by people who bring different levels of ability to the home setting.

The directed causal relationships found among quality of
confirmed the notion that these dimensions may be viewed _
ences on other aspects of life quality and as outcomes (i.e., as independent
variables or as dependent variables). For instance, the quality of the residential environment had a positive influence on interpersonal relationships,
though not until the third year. This suggests the possibility that some
environmental characteristics may have a slow, but important, cumulative
effect on the lives of residents in the home. Not surprisingly, a positive path
was found from quality of relationships to stability in the family care home,
reflecting the importance of interpersonal relationships on the likelihood of
remaining in the home.

At one time, normalization was viewed as a process. That is, it was
thought of as something *done* to existing residential settings, to transform
them into places that maximized the client's right to live a life as normal as
possible within the context of his or her abilities and disabilities. In the Foster
Family Care Study, another side of normalization came to light—as, at least
partially, a product of the people residing in the home, since both client and
careprovider characteristics were related to the level of normalization in the
home. Clients who were older or had more severe forms of retardation were
likely to live in homes that were less normalized.

Moreover, older careproviders and providers with more experience and
training were found to provide less normalized environments. Careproviders
who had more formal education had homes that were more normalized. The
variability in the degree of normalization, as well as the relationships found
between client and careprovider variables, suggests that foster family homes
have not uniformly maximized the level of normalized lifestyles and
programs in their homes.

One explanation for the negative relationships found between the
caregiver characteristics of age, experience and training with normalization
is that older careproviders who had been providing care for many years had
probably established their routines and philosophy of care before the current
emphasis on the principle of normalization. These individuals may have
been less likely to restructure their care practices to conform with normalization than providers who were younger and still shaping their methods of
care provision when normalization became an important philosophy in the
United States. Also, since older clients were in less normalized homes it
could be that the combination of older caregivers with more experience and
their older clients were more resistant to changing their lifestyles.

The negative association between levels of careprovider training and
normalization was puzzling since it would seem that additional training
would have emphasized the importance of providing more homelike care.
However, it is possible that *recent* training, as opposed to *more* training, was
more influential in this instance. Since caregivers are becoming increasingly
more educated, it may also be true that additional, and perhaps more recent,

education may have contributed to the caregiver's knowledge of the importance of normalization in the family care home.

In conclusion, the differences found in the homes studied (from factors
to survey items) confirm the findings of earlier studies that foster family care
is far from being a homogeneous residential classification.

Behavioral Development of Persons with Mental Retardation in Foster Family Care Homes

In the modeling of the relations across time of the personal characteristics and behavioral competencies of the people with mental retardation,
along with careprovider measures and indices of quality of life, the authors
found that rather different models were required to describe these relations
across domains of adaptive and maladaptive behavior. These will be
reviewed briefly, touching on the differences in the patterns of relationships
found.

Causes and effects of adaptive behavior. In general, adaptive behavior
was affected by certain careprovider and quality of life dimensions, but
adaptive behavior failed to influence these other domains of variables. Thus,
adaptive behavior appeared to be affected by both the careprovider's
perceived seriousness of adaptive behavioral needs as well as by careprovider
training, although the magnitudes of these effects were neither large nor
consistent across time.

More importantly, adaptive behavior was affected across time by
involvement in community events and activities experienced by the person
with mental retardation. Whereas community involvement, a core dimension of quality of life, may be proposed as an important end in itself, the
current results suggest that the community involvement of people with
mental retardation may also influence other important outcomes, such as
offering the person the opportunity to improve his or her level of adaptive
behavioral skills.

Although not large in a traditional sense, the magnitude of these effects
must be interpreted within the context of the very high degree of stability
of the adaptive behavior construct. That is, given high stability of a
behavioral characteristic, no outside variable is able to display large patterns
of influence; the magnitude of effects found in the Family Care Study are
probably as large as can be expected in such a situation. Thus, given the
consistency of the pattern of across-time influence, the effects of community
involvement on the development of adaptive behaviors, especially for
higher-functioning clients who have behavioral competencies that enable
them to benefit from these experiences, cannot be underestimated.

Given the possibility of bi-directional relations between variables, the
authors also examined the effects of adaptive behavior on subsequent
measures of careprovider and quality of life measures. In contrast to factors

that influenced change in adaptive behavior, no evidence was found that adaptive behavior has any effects across time on either careprovider or quality of life variables. The only effect found for adaptive behavior was its positive influence on the quality of the residential environment.

Thus, the adaptive behavior of a person with mental retardation may be influenced by characteristics of careproviders and quality of life, yet adaptive behavior has only limited effects on such variables. Of course, this characterization of adaptive behavior must be qualified by referring to the array of variables appearing in the Family Care Study; perhaps adaptive behavior has important effects on other variables that were not included in the study; the search for such variables should be the focus of future research.

Causes and effects of socially maladaptive behaviors. The characterization of change in social maladaption is rather different than that for adaptive behavior. That is, social maladaption was consistently affected by the careprovider's perceived seriousness of maladaptive behaviors, although this was in an unexpected direction, with higher levels of seriousness leading to higher subsequent levels of social maladaption. In other words, when careproviders viewed client maladaptive behavior as more serious, the level of maladaptive behavior was more likely to increase in the following year. One explanation of this finding is that careprovider behavior that results from a lack of tolerance of resident behavior is more likely to escalate than to reduce problem behaviors.

Social maladaption was also influenced by careprovider experience. Interestingly, social maladaption also appeared to lead to changes in careprovider perceptions of seriousness of socially maladaptive behaviors, with higher levels of social maladaption leading to increased levels of perceived seriousness. Thus, there were bi-directional relations between social maladaption and careprovider perceptions of seriousness of socially maladaptive behaviors.

Bi-directional relations between social maladaption and quality of life variables were also observed. Social maladaption had negative simultaneous paths to quality of relationships, with higher levels of social maladaption related to lower quality of interpersonal relations. But, quality of relationships had a significant negative lagged relationship with social maladaption, such that the higher the initial quality of interpersonal relationships, the lower the level of social maladaption at a later point in time. Thus, across both careprovider and quality of life variables, social maladaption was affected by other variables in the models and had a causal influence on other variables in return.

Causes and effects of personally maladaptive behaviors. The causal picture for personal maladaption was different still than those for either adaptive behavior or social maladaption. First and foremost, personal maladaption was unaffected by any of the careprovider or quality of life variables included in our models. Personal maladaption was related to level of retardation, with more profoundly retarded individuals exhibiting higher levels of personally maladaptive behavior. However, there was no indication that levels of personal maladaption changed significantly over time, and individual differences in personal maladaption were uninfluenced by other variables in the structural models.

On the other hand, personal maladaption affected one quality of life dimension, quality of interpersonal relations. People with mental retardation who exhibit higher levels of personal maladaptive behavior tend to have lower quality relations with other persons, which is an understandable, if unfortunate, outcome.

Summary. In the broad picture: a) adaptive behavior is malleable to a certain extent by careprovider and quality of life variables, but does not influence these variables appreciably; b) social maladaption is both influenced by and influences careprovider and quality of life dimensions, and; c) personal maladaption seems relatively impervious to modification by careprovider and quality of life variables, but has some effect on the quality of life experienced by the person with mental retardation. These differing patterns of causal influence on, and influence of, the behavioral characteristics of people with mental retardation underscores the need to evaluate multidimensional representations of behavior. Additionally, the findings support the use of state-of-the-art methods of analyzing and representing data, in order to capture the dynamic interplay of forces in the lives of people with mental retardation.

Finally, the findings do offer some guidelines regarding the care of people with mental retardation. Specifically, it appears that increasing levels of involvement in events and activities in the community may contribute to improvement in levels of adaptive behavior. Also, in general, foster care parents who viewed problems in adaptive and socially maladaptive behaviors as more serious were those whose clients did not improve in these areas. This might reflect problems with the methods used by these providers as they attempt to intervene in the specific areas of need. But, it may also be a possible indicator that caregivers who view client behaviors as more serious are ill-suited to the careprovider role, particularly for clients with higher levels of need or behavior problems.

Before offering these as firm guidelines for the selection of careproviders, additional research should be undertaken to replicate these findings. Research in a form like that of the Family Care Study can yield information that has both practical implications for the care of persons with mental retardation as well as implications for theory and research on mental retardation.

IMPLICATIONS OF THE FAMILY CARE STUDY

Implications for Theory

In a seminal paper, Bell (1968) argued that many studies of purported parental socialization of children's behavior were unconvincing. Rather, children's influence on their parents was an alternative hypothesis for the results observed, an alternative hypothesis that was usually reasonable to entertain and often impossible to rule out. Bell stressed the need for research that would allow researchers to determine whether the direction of influence was truly from parents to children, or whether children were potent causal agents of their own socialization.

More recently, and 20 years after the article by Bell, Clarke-Stewart (1988) reviewed 10 years of research on parenting effects in five domains of child behavior, including cognitive development. Although applauding the widely ranging forms of research being pursued, Clarke-Stewart found few studies that met all requirements for unambiguous attribution of causal influence of parents on children or the reverse. She stated that crucial studies of parent-child effects should have three attributes: a) be longitudinal; b) use multivariate data and analyses, and; c) be oriented to the processes that lead to the parental or child effects.

The first two of these attributes—longitudinal designs with multivariate data and analyses—are needed to disentangle the bi-directional effects between parents and children that likely reflect the manner in which parent and child behavior become structured over time. An orientation to the processes by which such influences between parents and children may be affected would provide valuable information—representing the behavioral capacities that bring about the effects, rather than attributing causal effects to more static personal attributes or characteristics.

The Family Care Study embodied well the first two of the three characteristics recommended by Clarke-Stewart (1988)—longitudinal design and utilization of multivariate data and analyses. In fact, the forms of multivariate analyses of longitudinal data that were used are commonly considered to be state-of-the-art techniques for the analysis of social science data, among the techniques most applicable for investigating causal influences across time.

Using these techniques, the Family Care Study identified bi-directional influences between people with mental retardation, their caregivers, and the characteristics of the homes in which they lived. Certain aspects of the behavior of the people with mental retardation were affected by caregiver or home characteristics, other aspects of their behavior affected caregiver behavior or home characteristics, and still other aspects of the individuals' behavior both affected and were affected by caregiver behavior and characteristics of the home.

If the authors had approached the analyses using traditional correlational or analysis of variance procedures, they likely would have found that individual differences in the behavioral characteristics of the people with mental retardation were related to, or correlated with, various characteristics of the caregivers and their homes. Commonly, such findings are translated into conclusions that the caregivers and/or their homes influenced the children and adolescents living there, that the direction of causal influence is from caregiver or home to the child or adolescent; it was precisely this form of conclusion that prompted the paper by Bell (1968).

But, using covariance structure modeling, the authors found that models with bi-directional patterns of causal influence provided better levels of fit to the data than did models containing only uni-directional paths from caregivers or characteristics of their homes to the children and adolescents living in these homes. The best fit models from this study underscore the thrust of the Bell critique—that studies of socialization must utilize data and statistical methods that uncover the bi-directional nature of the influences between children and adolescents and their caregivers.

The one aspect of the Family Care Study that, in retrospect, may be perceived as a shortcoming is the relative dearth of process-oriented measures. Of course, some of the measures used in the models were more process-oriented than others, but none were direct indices of the caregiving processes that may bring about behavioral changes in the people living in the family homes in the study.

In recent work, researchers have begun collecting process-oriented measures at rather molecular levels, such as counts of certain types of behavior based on home observations, or at more molar levels, such as ratings of caregivers' styles of parenting. At the time at which the Family Foster Care Study was designed and data collection began, such process-oriented measures were less commonly used than at present.

In research designed to replicate and extend aspects of this study, the authors have begun to include measures that are more process-oriented in nature. Such research should provide a more complete picture of the manner in which caregivers' effects on children and the children's effects on the caregivers occur.

Turning away from general issues toward more particular substantive matters, the results of the Family Care Study have implications for the manner in which researchers and practitioners conceive of the behavior and quality of life of people with mental retardation. Supporting certain distinctions among dimensions of adaptive and maladaptive behavior (cf. Widaman et al., 1987), the structural models of patterns of causal influence across the three times of measurement in the study were decidedly rather different for adaptive behavior, social maladaption, and personal maladaption. The different patterns of influence over time for these different forms of behavior have been discussed in detail earlier in this chapter.

Here the differential models for these domains of behavior support the notion that the behavior of individuals with mental retardation is complex and multiply determined. Moreover, the variables that influence or are influenced by certain forms of personal behavior differ as a function of the form of behavior studied. Rather than reducing too swiftly and too greatly the theoretical and nomological networks used to characterize the behavior of people with mental retardation, researchers must remain vigilant to the possibility of differential influences over time as a function of types of behavior exhibited by the individuals of interest.

The presence of various structural models for different forms of behavior should be a signal to researchers that they are dealing with a natural division of behavioral phenomena for which different laws of influence must be developed and evaluated. Coupled with research on the structure of behaviors in the domain of adaptive and maladaptive forms of behavior (e.g., Widaman et al., 1987), research on the causal structure of behavior across time provides additional impetus to the utility of distinctions among forms of behavior exhibited by persons with mental retardation.

A second major accomplishment of this study was the formulation and evaluation of testable models that included dimensions of the quality of life of people with mental retardation. For too long, research on the lives of these individuals has been narrowly focused on the growth and development of adaptive behaviors and on methods for accelerating it. Certainly, research of this sort has great importance for theory and for the optimal use of the behavioral competencies of the individuals under study. However, focusing exclusively on the growth and development of adaptive competencies is unfortunate, as other important aspects of life are ignored. Regardless of their levels of behavioral competencies, these people can have interesting and fulfilling relationships with other people and can influence the quality of their residential environment. Even if behavioral competencies have ceased to exhibit noticeable change, people with mental retardation may have satisfying and enjoyable life experiences. These aspects are the forms of experience subsumed in the measures of quality of life.

In Chapter 5, the authors evaluated the measurement models for two dimensions of quality of life, confirming *a priori* hypotheses about the indicators of these dimensions. Then, in Chapter 6, the dimensions of quality of life were included in the final structural models of the bi-directional relations among characteristics of people with mental retardation, their caregivers, and the homes in which they resided. Certain dimensions of quality of life had significant influences on the people with mental retardation, such as the influence of community involvement on later levels of adaptive behavior. Other dimensions of quality of life were influenced by the individuals with mental retardation, such as the negative effects of personal maladaption on the quality of the personal relationships the person experienced. These findings provide a richer, fuller understanding of the lives of people with mental retardation, offering views into aspects of their experiences that are largely unrelated to the restricted forms of behavioral competence that may characterize other parts of their lives.

Implications for Practice and for Care of Persons with Mental Retardation

The complexity of integrating theoretical and empirically based knowledge with current practices related to the care of people with mental retardation has been articulated, and even debated, in recent literature (e.g., Bruininks, 1990; Gottlieb, 1990; Heal, 1990; Krauss, 1990; Menolascino & Stark, 1990; Ramey, 1990; Zigler, Hodapp, & Edison, 1990). Thus, the often asked questions "Who should provide foster family care for persons with mental retardation?" and "Which individuals are best suited to foster family care placement?" are not easily answered, even by studies like this, that examine causal relationships among the relevant characteristics of clients, careproviders, and living environments.

The reason the above questions are difficult to address is related, in part, to the lack of agreement on what constitutes appropriate evaluation criteria (Landesman, 1988). Whereas developmental progress was one of the first outcomes to be emphasized after the professional field moved away from considering only the success-failure dichotomy of community placement, development of adaptive behavior is not the only aspect of an individual's life that should determine placement.

If one assumes that improved adaptive and maladaptive behavior are always associated with increased independence and greater opportunities for normalized living, then perhaps positive changes in these domains should be viewed as very important measurable outcomes. However, the results reported in this monograph suggest that improved adaptive behavior does not always lead to improvements in other aspects of quality of life.

It might also be true that, for some clients, their developmental progress may represent a secondary priority in relation to other aspects of their lives that can be influenced by different characteristics of the residential environment. Thus, the emphasis today extends beyond evaluating a person's attained levels of abilities and socially appropriate behavior, to include other dimensions of their lives, such as interpersonal relationships, affective and normalization aspects of the home, and meaningful involvement in activities outside the home.

Moreover, although measurement of such constructs presents a major challenge to researchers, overall estimates of the happiness and general well-being of the person with mental retardation (in relation to his or her happiness in other settings) may also take precedence over measurable developmental progress.

Science will "never provide us with perfect or all-encompassing answers" to questions regarding residential placement (Zigler et al., 1990b, p. 31). Still, the authors agree with Zigler that data-based arguments must play an important role in decisions regarding the placement and care of individuals with mental retardation. It is in this spirit that the authors suggest ways in which the findings can contribute to discussions about the policies and practices that affect the lives of people with mental retardation.

Selection of caregivers. In general, caregivers with greater amounts of training and education provide a better quality of care to their clients. Indeed, our results revealed that both training and education level of caregivers had significant positive influences on levels of adaptive behavior, and on reduced levels of perceived seriousness of problems in adaptive behavior. As a result, selection of caregivers could well be made on the basis of personal and behavioral/psychological characteristics like those listed above as well as others represented in the structural models in Chapter 6.

On the other hand, at least three considerations may mitigate against recommending absolute criteria for the selection of caregivers based on the results of the Family Care Study. First, and an obvious concern, the results of the study should be first replicated to determine whether they represent the patterns of influence in other samples of people from this population. It should be noted that clear recommendations on a topic as important as selection of caregivers should be based on a strong, extensive basis of research evidence. At present, such a research basis does not exist; the importance of the topic should be sufficient to ensure its development.

Second, it may not always be possible to make caregiver selections according to specific psychosocial characteristics or demographic variables of the potential provider. In many geographic areas, family care homes are in such great demand that decisions to place clients may be made on a "space available" basis, rather than by selecting providers who have optimal characteristics.

Individuals who wish to become careproviders are licensed according to minimal standards that apply in large measure to the physical characteristics of the home. However, these practical considerations should not overshadow findings that certain personal and psychological characteristics of careproviders are associated with optimal development and high quality of life for people placed in their homes. For example, careproviders with more training were found to perceive adaptive behavior deficiencies as less serious, which in turn is related to greater improvements in these behaviors. This suggests that supervising agencies should encourage, and perhaps even require, ongoing training, as many already do. Furthermore, definitive evidence, based on well-designed and replicated studies, may lead to more specific guidelines for service agencies who are able to select careproviders from a large pool of applicants.

Third, and perhaps most importantly, future research should investigate the possibility that there may be a "goodness-of-fit" between caregiver and the individual with mental retardation that provides the optimal environment for maximizing the person's development on a variety of fronts. In this vein, Lerner (1989) described a "goodness-of-fit" model, in which the personal and behavioral characteristics of the child or adolescent influence and are influenced by characteristics of the caregiver, with feedback loops in the system over time.

The results of the current study suggest that the notion of a goodness-of-fit between caregiver and the person with mental retardation may lead to optimal development of certain forms of behavior. Consider the following findings: there were negative influences of the perceived seriousness of problems with adaptive and maladaptive behaviors on the part of caregivers on later levels of adaptive and maladaptive behaviors of the persons with mental retardation, and the reverse pattern of influence did not occur.

These findings suggest that the behavioral competencies of people with mental retardation be matched with the levels of perceived seriousness of caregivers regarding problems in adaptive and maladaptive behavior for optimal development to occur. They also suggest that people with high levels of problems in adaptive or maladaptive behavior should only be placed with caregivers who are willing to deal with such problems, as an unwillingness to handle such problems led to an exacerbation of the behaviors involved.

Additional research should be pursued on the goodness-of-fit of personal and caregiver characteristics to determine whether these are replicable findings and to determine whether the goodness-of-fit notion represents as powerful an influence on the behavior of children and adolescents with mental retardation as it appears to be on the behavior of non-retarded children (cf. Lerner, 1989).

The goodness-of-fit of careproviders and clients should take into account the outcomes that are deemed to be most important for the individuals involved. For example, the preceding discussion of optimal careprovider characteristics focused on the outcome of behavioral development. However, depending on the evaluation criteria, different characteristics of caregivers may emerge as being important predictors of other outcomes.

In Chapter 5 the authors noted characteristics of careproviders that were associated with different levels of community involvement, interpersonal relationships, and characteristics of the residential environment. Stability is another dimension of quality of life that seems to be affected by the caregiver-client match. One encouraging finding from the Family Care Study was that clients and careproviders seemed to be well matched in terms of careprovider tolerance of their needs for assistance and their problem behaviors.

The importance of this match was illustrated in a study by Sutter and Mayeda (1981), who used the same instruments for evaluating careprovider tolerance of behaviors and levels of adaptive behavior as were used in the Family Care Study. They found that reinstitutionalized clients were more likely to have been mismatched in terms of their behaviors and the willingness of their caregivers to deal with those behaviors.

The second study of employee/employer matches also found that clients who were unsuccessful in their job placements were also more likely to be mismatched with their employers in terms of behaviors and tolerances. Thus, a practical implication of these findings would be to ask caregivers to respond to a survey like the one used for this study, in order to provide useful information to those making placement decisions for individual clients (i.e., maximize chances for the best match).

Placement of persons with mental retardation. One point should be clear from the results of this study. The Family Care Study confirmed that an individual's developmental status at any point in time is determined primarily by his or her status at the previous time of measurement. This is not to say that environments and caregiving have no effect on development. However, it does suggest that foster family care placement, per se, is unlikely to result in dramatic changes in an individual's trajectory of growth. This is particularly true for people with profound levels of retardation.

Eyman and Widaman (1987) reported relatively flat life-span developmental curves for people with profound retardation, regardless of placement, in a study of 30,749 people in different residential settings. Some may believe that moving people with severe and profound levels of retardation to less restrictive, more normalized environments will cause them to exhibit larger improvements in behavior, or to "blossom." Indeed, some natural parents in the study indicated that they had placed their children outside their homes in order to optimize their development. However, the data do not support the optimistic belief that family care homes will produce dramatic departures from developmental expectations. Even though the way these individuals might have fared in other setting types can not be compared, it can be said that changes in levels of adaptive and maladaptive behavior were not large for the people with severe and profound levels of retardation living in the family care homes that were studied.

The preceding conclusions were drawn from the study of intra-individual differences in adaptive and maladaptive behavior levels over the two-year span of the study, which investigated the potential for within-setting type (family care) variability to influence change. Eyman and Widaman (1987) approached the question of environmental effects on development differently, by examining cross-sectional and semi-longitudinal life-span developmental curves for individuals in different residential placements. In the study, only modest differences in life-span curves were found when different residence types were compared for people of similar retardation levels.

This suggests that, for clients of the same level of retardation, residence type does not appear to affect life-span developmental curves to a marked degree. If different curves had been found across broad residential categories (e.g., institutions vs. community care), this would support the popular notion that institutions inhibit or slow down, rather than promote, development among their residents (in contrast to placement in smaller community facilities, such as foster family care, that presumably impact developmental change positively). The fact that life-span curves were not dramatically different across residential setting types is yet another indication that smaller settings, averaging across the variability of care within setting types, do not necessarily enhance or inhibit developmental progress relative to larger settings.

Unfortunately, the examination of clients in a single type of residential setting—foster family care—does not allow comparative evaluations of how well these individuals might have fared in other placements during the same time period. However, the various outcome measures for different subgroups of the sample were examined, enabling the drawing of conclusions about relative differences in developmental change and quality of life.

The associations found between level of mental retardation and quality of life variables were not surprising. People with more severe forms of retardation (and possibly other concomitant handicapping conditions) were found to be less involved in community life, had lower-quality interpersonal relationships, and were less stable in their placements. Their minimal levels of developmental progress have already been discussed. Does this mean that foster family care is not the best placement for these people? As already noted, this determination can not be made since there is no way of knowing what would have occurred in other setting types. From an administrative standpoint, however, one might view family foster care as a limited resource and wish to reserve it for those who would appear to benefit most from this residential model, in which case within-setting comparisons are appropriate.

The data suggest that higher functioning individuals are those whose development is more rapid and who enjoy a higher quality of life. It might also be said that these are the people who are most likely to contribute maximally to the positive experiences of careproviders by showing visible gains in skills and abilities, providing more interpretable affective feedback, and placing fewer demands on careproviders to help meet their daily living needs than their lower-functioning counterparts. From this perspective, it could be predicted that placement of higher functioning individuals in foster family care would reduce the likelihood of "careprovider burnout."

On the other hand, if foster family care represents the setting in which lower functioning individuals are most likely to experience *their own* highest levels of quality of life and adaptive behavior, given the physical and cognitive barriers they face, then it might be unfair to deny them access to this residential placement option. It is at this point that the data fall short of providing definitive evidence for the determination of "best-practice." This data as well as the work of others, provide simply the foundation for more informed discussion among practitioners, scholars, and advocates.

Directions for Future Research

The outcomes of the Family Care Study have several important implications for future research on people with mental retardation. Perhaps the most important and immediate implication is the need to replicate the causes and effects identified in the models for adaptive behavior, social maladaption, and personal maladaption. As noted in earlier chapters, there was a good deal of *a priori* specification of the structural equation models that were presented. Of course, certain model modifications were made that were more exploratory in nature. Given current concerns regarding the replicability of results of exploratory forms of analysis, attempts to replicate and improve the models should have research priority. The authors view the models as simply a first statement of potential relations among the sets of variables represented in the study.

It is expected that the models, under the pressure of future, well-designed empirical studies, will require modification in order to represent well the relations between the domains of variables included in models from the Family Care Study. Even if, after years of research, the commonly accepted models of relations among these sets of variables look rather different than those presented in the monograph, the authors would consider these efforts to have been worthwhile, by providing an impetus to the field to engage in further and more detailed investigation of the development of people with mental retardation. The ultimate goal is an empirically validated and theoretically adequate theory of the behavioral development and quality of life of persons with mental retardation; attempts to replicate the models in this monograph would contribute to the goal.

A second focus for future research, presuming that useful models are well replicated, should be to provide more detail on the causal sequences found, to identify how the influences of the causal agents are effected. That is, when using structural modeling, it is common to draw paths representing causal influences and to offer explanations for those influences. But, the explanations offered may be incorrect or incomplete and should be evaluated in future research. For example, certain outcomes related to careprovider training were found in the Family Care Study.

It was assumed that careproviders with greater amounts of training would behave differently with clients, interact differently with them than would careproviders with lesser amounts of training, and that this would lead to positive changes in the clients' behavior. That is, if a careprovider receives training, this should not be expected to influence a client's behavior directly. Rather, the training would likely alter the way in which the careprovider interacts with the person with mental retardation, and this altered form of interaction might well represent the causal link between careprovider training and change in client behavior.

However, this inference, regardless of its cogency, is still simply an inference, which should be verified in future research in which measures of relevant careprovider behaviors are collected along with measures of careprovider training and the behavior of the person with mental retardation. Only in such a fashion will the causal influences between careproviders and people with mental retardation be more adequately understood and represented. In pursuing such research, investigators would be attempting to explicate the processes that might bring about behavioral change, a goal stressed by Zigler et al. (1990a, 1990b).

Yet another avenue for further research on the development of people with mental retardation should be to widen the causal network in various ways. After completing data collection on any project, one commonly wishes that additional data had been collected. This is an almost universal reaction in any longitudinal study, because it is difficult to foresee, at early stages in the collection of data, the range of variables that will be important explanatory constructs once the collection of data is completed.

There were some notable omissions of domains of variables in the Foster Family Care Study, including, but not limited to, more detailed information on community involvement and stability, the parenting behaviors exhibited by the careproviders, careprovider attitudes toward aspects of child development, and careprovider reports of their behaviors in a variety of situations. A major task for future research is the integration of such additional domains of variables into structural models of influences on the development and quality of life of individuals with mental retardation.

The authors acknowledge, with little trepidation, certain deficiencies in the sets of variables employed in the Family Care Study. The net was cast broadly, collecting a wide array of data, and the failure to include certain domains of potentially important variables, or to omit detail in the description of some constructs, is easy to identify in retrospect.

Moreover, measurement in some domains continues to become more refined and reliable. Other researchers will help cast a still broader net in research in the future, integrating other domains of constructs into models of development and quality of life for people with mental retardation.

A fourth way of using the results of the Family Care Study to improve future research is to use the study as a backdrop for posing important questions that go beyond the data from this particular study. One important question is whether structural models such as those in the Family Care Study hold for all people with mental retardation or whether models must be modified to characterize accurately the data from subgroups of individuals.

In the Family Care Study, the models fit across all people with mental retardation, regardless of level of retardation and other personal character-istics. Some previous research (e.g., Eyman & Widaman, 1987) has found differences across levels of retardation in changes during childhood and adolescence in levels of adaptive behavior. Such differences were not confirmed in the Family Care Study, perhaps due to relatively low power of the statistical tests (small sample sizes for subgroups), but level of retarda-tion is one easily identifiable characteristic that may moderate the form of models of developmental processes.

Moreover, analyzing data from only a single type of placement—family care homes—restricts certain conclusions one might wish to draw. For example, it is interesting to speculate about the development of certain types of individuals with mental retardation in different settings. That is, for some people, foster family care homes might offer optimal environments for their personal and behavioral development, whereas other types of placement might prove optimal for other types of people.

Once again, these sorts of questions are outside the reach of data from the Family Care study, but consideration of the study may lead interested researchers to formulate more interesting questions for future research than they would otherwise have entertained.

In summary, the authors feel that the Family Care Study has offered an important and interesting opportunity for the investigation of the behavioral development and quality of life for people with mental retardation living in small foster family homes. This type of study should further the ultimate goal, the development and testing of an adequate theory of the behavioral development and quality of life of people with mental retardation in any and all settings in which they may reside.

The statistical analytic methods used provided most useful ways of representing and structuring the data from the Family Care Study and, in the process, helped structure thinking about the development of behaviors by individuals with mental retardation. Although the Family Care Study may be considered only an initial step down a path to understanding of the development of people with mental retardation, the authors hope that others will use this study as a springboard, surpassing these efforts by formulating and testing ever better structural models for this domain of research. Only then will the field of mental retardation have a fuller, more complete, and more adequate understanding of the lives of persons with mental retardation.

Appendix

Structural Modeling of Longitudinal Relations in the Family Care Study

To investigate the longitudinal relations among constructs assessed during the Family Care Study, the authors employed structural equation modeling, using the LISREL 7 program (Jöreskog & Sörbom, 1988). Using structural equation modeling with latent variables, it is possible to combine the latent variable representations of factor analysis with the linear relations between predictors and criteria estimated by regression analysis to arrive at a useful representation of the patterns of causal relations among a set of latent variables or factors. In the remaining parts of this appendix, the way in which the analyses were performed and results reported from the structural modeling of the data from the Family Foster Care Study will be discussed.

GENERAL ISSUES IN MODELING DATA

Model Specification

Measurement model. In structural equation modeling, it is common to distinguish two aspects of a model, the measurement model and the structural model. The measurement model consists of two parts: a) the specified relations linking the unmeasured, latent variables and the measured variables that serve as their indicators, and; b) the residual variances and covariances of the measured variables. Figural portrayals of the relations between measured, or observed, variables and latent variables are presented in Figure A.1, along with the residual variance of the measured variables, which represents variance in the measured variables that is unrelated to the latent variables.

In Figure A.1(a), a single-indicator latent variable is shown. The latent variable is labeled η_1; this latent variable is enclosed in a circle, and its variance ψ_1 is represented as a curved, double-headed arrow from η_1 to itself. The measured variable that is the single indicator of η_1 is variable X_1, denoted by the square. The linear relationship between latent variable η_1 and its indicator X_1 is shown by the straight, single-headed arrow from η_1 to X_1. The path coefficient λ_1 is analogous to a raw score regression weight for predicting X_1 from η_1; residual variance in X_1 that is linearly unrelated to η_1

is reflected in the parameter ε_1, associated with the curved, double-headed arrow from X_1 to itself. The relations shown in Figure A.1(a) are therefore equivalent to the linear equation:

[A.1] $X_1 = \lambda_1 \eta_1 + \varepsilon_1$,

where all terms are as defined above. In Equation A.1, ε_1 refers to the residual variable, the residual in X_1 that is linearly unrelated to η_1; in Figure A.1, ε_1 stands for the variance of the residual variable. This slight duplicity of meaning for the term ε_1 is of no particular concern: although one may signify the residual variable in an equation, such as Equation A.1, this residual variable cannot be determined directly—only the variance of the residual variable can be estimated.

a)

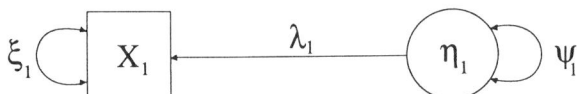

b)

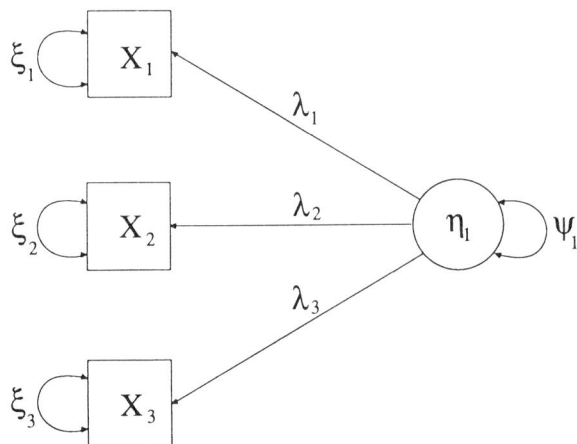

FIGURE A.1. Parameters of the measurement model for (a) a latent variable with a single indicator, and (b) a latent variable with three indicators.

In the Family Foster Care Study, a number of constructs were represented in the models as single-indicator latent variables, constructs such as client age and level of mental retardation. When specifying a single-indicator latent variable, it is necessary to set the scale for the latent variable by fixing two of the three parameters associated with the latent variable—λ_1, ψ_1, and ε_1—and then estimating the third parameter. The authors chose to fix the measured variable residual variance ε_1 at zero and to fix the latent variable variance ψ_1 at unity, and then to estimate the path coefficient λ_1.

This way of setting the scale for a latent variable implicitly invokes two important assumptions: a) that the latent variable is perfectly commensurate with the measured variable (i.e., there is no error when predicting scores on the observed variable from scores on the latent variable), and; b) that scores on the latent variable have unit variance (i.e., that scores on the latent variable are in standard score form). Neither of these assumptions was particularly problematic in this study, as the single-indicator latent variables used (e.g., chronological age) were measurable with great precision. Moreover, the manner in which the scale of measurement is fixed does not affect the statistical significance of any path coefficients in a model, simply resulting in a particular scaling of both path coefficients and their standard errors.

The structural relations embodied in the measurement model for a multiple-indicator latent variable are shown in Figure A.1(b). Once again, there is a single latent variable η_1, which has a variance ψ_1. However, the latent variable η_1 in Figure A.1(b) has three measured variables or indicators. The three indicators of η_1 are labeled X_1 through X_3. The linear relationship between the latent variable η_1 and each indicator X_j is reflected in the magnitude of the path coefficient, or factor loading, λ_j. The variance of the indicator X_j that is linearly unrelated to the latent variable is estimated as the variance of the corresponding unique factor ε_j. Thus, the measurement model for a three-indicator latent variable is shown graphically in Figure A.1(b), and the linear relations shown there can be represented equivalently by the following three equations:

[A.2(a)] $X_1 - \lambda_1 \eta_1 + \varepsilon_1$

[A.2(b)] $X_2 = \lambda_2 \eta_1 + \varepsilon_2$

[A.2(c)] $X_3 = \lambda_3 \eta_1 + \varepsilon_3$,

where all symbols are as defined above. Following the convention introduced in consideration of the single-indicator model (discussed above), ε_j refers to the residual variable in observed variable X_j in the preceding equations, whereas ε_j refers to the variance of the residual variable in Figure A.1(b). Once again, this is not a matter of particular concern, as only the variance of the residual variable is estimable.

When specifying a multiple-indicator latent variable, it is necessary to set the scale for the latent variable by fixing only one of the parameters associated with the latent variable to a nonzero value and then estimating the remaining parameters. For the three-indicator latent variable shown in Figure A.1(b), there are seven parameters: three path coefficients from the latent variable to measured variables—λ_1, λ_2, and λ_3; three unique factor variances—the variances of ε_1, ε_2, and ε_3, and; one latent variable variance—ψ_1. In the modeling, latent variable variances were frequently fixed to some nonzero value, such as unity, and then all factor loadings and unique variances were estimated.

Structural model. The second part of a latent variable model is the structural model, which comprises the specification of linear relations among the latent variables. In general, with r latent variables, there are $r (r-1)/2$ possible linear relations among the latent variables that may be specified. A restricted structural model is one in which fewer than $r (r-1)/2$ relations are estimated among the r latent variables.

If all possible linear relations are estimated among a set of latent variables, the resulting model is uninteresting from a structural point of view, as there are a very large number of competing models making the same number of estimates that would fit the data equally well. Moreover, these competing statistical models with equal levels of fit would be consistent with very different theoretical models of the way in which the data were produced. Such a situation is problematic for theory building in any given domain, as competing models representing incompatible theoretical propositions have identical fit to the data. In contrast, there is great value associated with the use of restricted structural models, as a restricted model constrains the set of theoretical propositions that are consistent with the representation.

In Figure A.2, a restricted structural model is presented for the relations among four latent variables, η_1 through η_4. With four latent variables, a total of six linear relations could be specified among the variables. As shown in Figure A.2, only four linear relations are specified among the variables. Specifically, one covariance was specified, between η_1 and η_2, and three direct relations were specified. The three direct relations were the effects of η_1 on η_3, of η_2 on η_3, and of η_3 on η_4. The magnitudes of the various effects are represented by the estimates of the various parameters, ψ_{21} for the covariance between the first two latent variables, and β_{31}, β_{32}, and β_{43} for the three direct relations in the model.

The structural relations portrayed in Figure A.2 can be represented equivalently by two linear equations of the following form:

[A.3(a)] $\quad \eta_3 = \beta_{31}\, \eta_1 + \beta_{32}\, \eta_2 + \zeta_3$

[A.3(b)] $\quad \eta_4 = \beta_{43}\, \eta_3 + \zeta_4 \, ,$

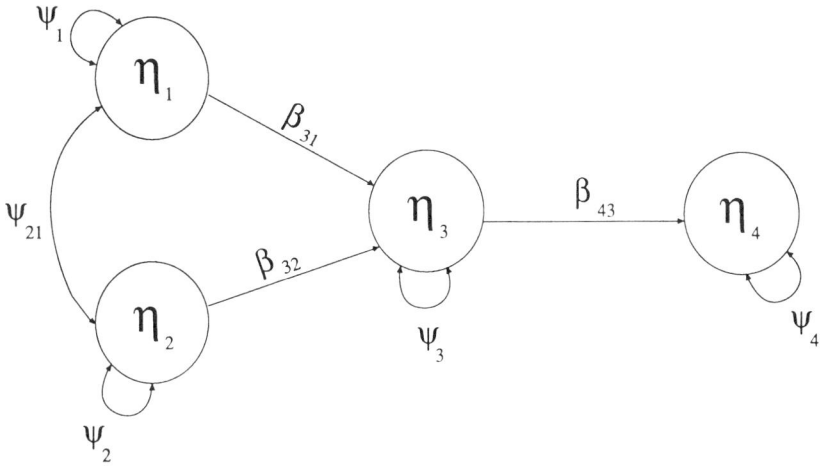

FIGURE A.2. Parameters of the structural model for a model exhibiting a restricted pattern of relations among four latent variables.

where ζ_3 and ζ_4 represent the residual variables for η_3 and η_4, respectively, and all other parameters are defined above. Paralleling the way in which measurement model parameters were portrayed, the variances (i.e., ψ_3 and ψ_4) of the residual variables (i.e., ζ_3 and ζ_4, respectively) are shown in Figure A.2, whereas the residual variables themselves (ζ_3 and ζ_4) are given in Equations A.3(a) and A.3(b).

The figural presentations of basic parts of a structural equation model that are presented in Figures A.1 and A.2 may provide additional acquaintance with the parameters of a structural equation model. That is, the parameters of a structural equation model consist of various classes of parameters, specifically: a) directed relations between latent variables and their indicators; b) residual variances of the indicators, or measured variables; c) variances of latent variables; d) directed relations among latent variables; e) covariances among latent variables, and; f) residual variances of latent variables. Parameter classes (a)-(c) were depicted in Figure A.1; parameter classes (d)-(f) were shown in Figure A.2. Given a matrix of covariances among the indicators for latent variables in a model, it is possible to estimate the parameters of a structural equation model, given the fixing of certain of the parameters to define the scale for each of the latent variables (described above).

Parameter Estimation

Technical details regarding parameter estimation go far beyond the level of discussion that may be provided in this Appendix. Interested readers are referred to more technical sources such as Jöreskog and Sörbom (1988) and primary sources cited therein. However, some general comments on estimation may be offered here to provide acquaintance with the issues involved. Each particular method of estimation (e.g., maximum likelihood, unweighted least squares) is associated with a given fitting function, F; parameters of a structural model are modified in a series of iterative re-estimation steps in order to minimize the value of the fitting function.

Minimizing the fitting function leads to a minimization of the difference between the original data (i.e., the observed covariances among the measured variables, or indicators) and the reproduced data (i.e., the covariances among indicators that are reproduced by the structural model). To use maximum likelihood estimation, data must be assumed to follow a multivariate normal distribution, in order to place confidence in parameter estimates and their standard errors. If data depart from multivariate normality, then unweighted least squares is a more easily justified method of estimation.

Evaluation of Model Fit

Statistical fit. As noted in the body of this monograph, a likelihood ratio test statistic accompanies the use of maximum likelihood estimation of parameters. This test statistic is distributed as a chi-squared variate, with degrees of freedom equal to $[(n(n + 1)/2) - q]$, where n is the number of observed variables in a model, and q is the number of parameters estimated in a given substantive model. The chi-square value is a direct multiplicative function of the fitting function value F and sample size. Hence, the smaller the value of the fitting function, the smaller the chi-square associated with the model. If the chi-square value is statistically significant, this is an indication of a significant degree of lack of fit of the model to the observed data. That is, there is a statistical basis for rejecting the given model in favor of a model with at least one additional parameter estimate.

Practical fit. To aid in the evaluation of model fit, indices of practical fit were used, which is a common practice in structural equation modeling. Indices of practical fit are used in structural equation modeling, supplementing indices of statistical fit, because indices of statistical fit are frequently too powerful, suggesting rejection of a model that has fairly trivial levels of lack of fit. With maximum likelihood estimation of parameters, the Tucker-Lewis coefficient ρ was used (Tucker & Lewis, 1973), which is calculated as:

$$\rho = \frac{(\chi^2_n / df_n) - (\chi^2_s / df_s)}{(\chi^2_n / df_n) - 1},$$

where χ^2_n and df_n are the chi-square and degrees of freedom for a null model,

χ^2_s and df_s are the chi-square and degrees of freedom for a substantive model of interest. The null model employed in the current study had the standard form, embodying the assumption that all measured variables were mutually uncorrelated. In this form of null model, the variance of each of the measured variables is estimated, but all structural relations between latent and observed variables and among latent variables are constrained to be zero.

Unweighted least squares estimation was used for quality of life models in Chapter 5, because the data departed importantly from multivariate normality. With unweighted least squares estimation, the ρ coefficient could not be computed, because a likelihood ratio chi-square statistic cannot be justified under this method of estimation. So, the Bentler-Bonett coefficient Δ was employed (Bentler & Bonett, 1980), which is calculated as:

$$\Delta = \frac{F_n - F_s}{F_n},$$

Where F_n and F_s are the minimums of the least squares fitting function for the null model and a substantive model of interest, respectively.

Firm standards for interpreting ρ and Δ coefficients have not yet been developed. However, Bentler and Bonett (1980) suggested that a model having a ρ and/or value less than .90 should not be accepted as a final representation of the data, as such models can often be easily modified to improve the level of fit of the model to the data. By implication, ρ and Δ values over .90 indicate adequate representation of the observed data.

Model Respecification

As noted in the body of the monograph, the structural models were respecified based on LISREL modification indices and the substantive meaningfulness of the parameters to be added. At no time did this represent a serious problem to model fitting, as the parameter estimates and their standard errors for all directed relations among latent variables were essentially unaffected by the model respecifications. That is, the respecifications that were made served only to improve the overall fit of models to data and did not influence the statistical significance of specific paths in any model.

SPECIFIC ASPECTS OF THE SPECIFICATION OF MODELS IN THE FAMILY FOSTER CARE STUDY

Model Specification

The measurement model. The measurement model for each of the models presented in the body of the monograph reflected the predicted pattern of relations between the latent variables hypothesized and the observed variables that served as their indicators. As an initial specification, each of the indicators for a given latent variable was allowed to load only on the single latent factor for which it was hypothesized to be an indicator. This *a priori* specification of the factor pattern coefficients was relaxed in a few situations to improve model fit, but only if the additional paths reflected interpretable influences of the given latent variable on the particular observed measure.

One issue regarding structural modeling that must be described is the manner in which the scale for each latent variable was determined. Consider first the latent variables that were represented only at the first time of measurement. Eight latent variables were measured at the first time of measurement alone, and seven of these were single-indicator constructs. For example, the chronological age of the person with mental retardation was the single measured variable used as an indicator of the construct of Client Age. This construct, as well as the remaining six single-indicator constructs, was identified by fixing the error variance of the measured variable (i.e., client age) at 0 and the latent variable variance at 1.0, and then estimating the direct relation between the latent variable and the observed variable.

This specification allows all of the variance in the observed variable of client age to be reflected at the latent variable level, which was appropriate given the high reliability with which most of these variables were measured. The eighth latent variable represented at the first time of measurement alone was Quality of the Environment. Quality of Environment was a two-indicator construct, identified by fixing the factor variance at 1.0 and estimating the remaining parameters (i.e., direct relations between latent and observed variables, residual variances of observed variables).

For each of the latent variables appearing at all three times of measurement (e.g., Adaptive Behavior), the latent variable variance was fixed at 1.0 at the first time of measurement to establish the scale of measurement for the latent variable. The variance of the latent variable was then estimated freely at the second and third times of measurement. These latter variances were identified mathematically because the authors invoked metric stationarity of the factor pattern across times of measurement. Metric stationarity across times of measurement means that the path coefficients (or factor loadings) relating a latent variable to its indicators remain identical, or invariant, across times of measurement.

For example, metric stationarity for the Health Problems latent variable exists if the factor loading of the health index at the first time of measurement is identical to the factor loadings of the health index at the second and third times of measurement, *and* the factor loadings for the other indicator(s) of the latent variable (i.e., the health rating, in this case) are also invariant across times of measurement. Given the constraint of metric stationarity, identifying a latent variable at a single time of measurement (e.g., by fixing the latent variable variance at 1.0 at the first time of measurement) is sufficient to identify the latent variable at all subsequent times of measurement.

One additional aspect of the measurement model for all measured variables appearing at more than a single time of measurement must be mentioned. Specifically, covariances among the residuals for a particular measured variable across times of measurement were allowed. The logic of this type of specification is this: The residual variance of an indicator represents a combination of two sources of variance, a) random error variance, and b) reliable variance of the indicator that is unrelated to the latent variables in the model. As this latter source of variance of an indicator is present at each time of measurement, it is reasonable to assume that this variance may be stable across time, resulting in covariances across time among residuals for the same observed variable (e.g., the health rating at each of the three times of measurement). This is a common form of specification that is frequently used in structural equation modeling of longitudinal data.

The structural model. When fitting the structural equation models, a two-step procedure initially described by Bentler and Speckart (1981) and formulated as a general strategy by Anderson and Gerbing (1988) was followed. First, what was termed an *unrestricted structural model* was fit, in which there are no constraints in the structural model. [Note: Anderson and Gerbing (1988) termed this model the "measurement model," but for this study have employed the term "measurement model" to refer to the relations between latent and observed variables. Therefore, to avoid confusion, the term "unrestricted structural model" will be used to denote the initial model pursued under the Anderson and Gerbing two-step procedure]. That is, all latent variables are freely correlated in the "unrestricted structural model." The reasons for fitting this form of model are these: a) specification of additional parameters (e.g., additional factor loadings or correlated residuals) can be performed with an unrestricted structural model, model respecifications that are not influenced by improperly specified, restricted patterns of relations among latent variables; b) any remaining lack of fit is due to lack of fit of measurement model parameters (e.g., relations between latent and observed variables, etc.), and; c) the "unrestricted structural model" serves as a basis of comparison for models with restricted patterns of relations among latent variables.

The second step was to arrive at a *final restricted structural model* with an interpretable, restricted pattern of relations among the latent variables. To do so, an initial, *a priori* structural model was specified that allowed: a) covariances among latent variables that were not predicted by any other latent variables; b) paths from the preceding variables to other, longitudinal latent variables measured at Time 1, and; c) first-order autoregressive paths for latent variables measured at each time of measurement. That is, Adaptive Behavior at Time 1 was presumed to influence Adaptive Behavior at Time 2, which in turn was assumed to influence Adaptive Behavior at Time 3.

Second-order autoregressive paths (i.e., from Time 1 to Time 3) were also allowed if suggested by modification indices. Each *a priori* model was respecified to a minor degree, based on LISREL modification indices and the substantive interpretability of paths, to arrive at the final models presented in Chapters 3 through 6. Ideally, the difference in fit between the "unre-

TABLE A.1

Summary of Fit Statistics for Structural Models
In Chapters 3–6

STRUCTURAL MODEL	χ^2	df	PROB	ρ
Chapter 3				
0. Null	3542.9	406	<.001	—
1. Measurement model	461.0	277	<.001	.91
2. Final model	530.0	340	<.001	.93
Difference between Models 1 and 2	69.0	63	>.28	.02
Chapter 4				
0. Null	2101.9	210	<.001	—
1. Measurement model	202.9	112	<.001	.91
2. Final model	271.0	159	<.001	.92
Difference between Models 1 and 2	68.1	47	<.02	.01
Chapter 5				
0. Null	822.9	136	<.001	—
1. Measurement model	108.5	76	.009	.92
2. Final model	138.2	102	.010	.93
Difference between Models 1 and 2	29.8	26	.276	.01
Chapter 6				
Adaptive behavior				
0. Null	5427.2	990	<.001	—
1. Measurement model	908.8	634	<.001	.90
2. Final model	1157.1	833	<.001	.91
Difference between Models 1 and 2	248.3	199	<.01	.01
Social maladaption				
0. Null	3138.2	741	<.001	—
1. Measurement model	559.1	435	<.001	.91
2. Final model	793.7	635	<.001	.92
Difference between Models 1 and 2	234.6	200	<.05	.01
Personal maladaption				
0. Null	2907.9	741	<.001	—
1. Measurement model	534.9	431	<.001	.92
2. Final model	778.2	637	<.001	.92
Difference between Models 1 and 2	243.3	206	<.04	.00

stricted structural model" and the "final restricted structural model" would be negligible, implying that the constraints invoked in moving from the "unrestricted structural model" to the final model did not worsen the fit of the model to the data.

Evaluation of Model Fit

Overall model fit. In Table A.1, the fit statistics for each of the models in Chapters 3, 4, 5, and 6 of the monograph are presented. In the table, the chi-square and degrees of freedom for the model are listed as well as the probability associated with this chi-square. Also listed in the table is the practical fit index ρ for each model. The null model listed is the standard form of null model, which embodies the hypothesis that the observed variables are uncorrelated with one another. The forms of the measurement model and final model were described above. In Table A.1, indices of difference in fit between the measurement model and the final model for each chapter are presented, listing the difference in both statistical and practical indices of fit.

As shown in Table A.1, the measurement model for each chapter was statistically rejectable (all $ps < .01$), although the measurement model always had a minimally acceptable level of practical fit (all ρ values $\geq .90$). The final model for each chapter was also rejectable on a statistical basis (all $ps \leq .01$), but each final model also had acceptable levels of practical fit (all ρ values $\geq .91$).

The final model for a given data set must fit the data worse (i.e., have a chi-square value equal to or larger) relative to the measurement model, because the final model represents restrictions on the measurement model. However, as noted above, the worsening of fit when moving from the measurement model to the final model may be nonsignificant or fairly

TABLE A.2

**Residual and Explained Variance for Latent Variables
In Models Presented in Chapter 6**

LATENT FACTOR	RESIDUAL VARIANCE TIME OF MEASUREMENT	ESTIMATE	Se	EXPLAINED VARIANCE, OR R^2
Adaptive behavior model				
Client age	1	1.000	0.000	0.000
Level of retardation	1	1.000	0.000	0.000
Careprovider age	1	1.000	0.000	0.000
Careprovider education	1	1.000	0.000	0.044
Careprovider experience	1	1.000	0.000	0.032
Careprovider training	1	1.000	0.000	0.126
Health problems	1	1.000	0.000	0.147
Seriousness of adaption problems	1	1.000	0.000	0.155
BDS adaptive behavior	1	1.000	0.000	0.439
Community involvement	1	1.000	0.000	0.208
Relationships	1	1.000	0.000	0.176
Stability	1	1.000	0.000	0.335
Environment	1	1.000	0.000	0.536

(continued on next page)

TABLE A.2 *(continued)*

Residual and Explained Variance for Latent Variables
In Models Presented in Chapter 6

LATENT FACTOR	TIME OF MEASUREMENT	RESIDUAL VARIANCE ESTIMATE	Se	EXPLAINED VARIANCE, OR R^2
Health problems	2	0.457	0.137	0.515
Seriousness of adaption problems	2	1.234	0.219	0.076
BDS adaptive behavior	2	0.096	0.030	0.947
Community involvement	2	0.087	0.067	0.932
Relationships	2	1.000	0.000	0.225
Health problems	3	0.244	0.107	0.719
Seriousness of adaption problems	3	0.325	0.073	0.557
BDS adaptive behavior	3	0.212	0.045	0.894
Community involvement	3	0.420	0.138	0.734
Relationships	3	1.000	0.000	0.136
Social maladaption model				
Client age	1	1.000	0.000	0.000
Client MR level	1	1.000	0.000	0.000
Careprovider age	1	1.000	0.000	0.000
Careprovider education	1	1.000	0.000	0.039
Careprovider experience	1	1.000	0.000	0.035
Careprovider training	1	1.000	0.000	0.128
Health problems	1	1.000	0.000	0.153
Seriousness of maladaptive behaviors	1	1.000	0.000	0.094
BDS social maladaption	1	1.000	0.000	0.051
Community involvement	1	1.000	0.000	0.192
Relationships	1	1.000	0.000	0.221
Stability	1	1.000	0.000	0.336
Environment	1	1.000	0.000	0.658
Health problems	2	0.458	0.137	0.492
Seriousness of maladaptive problems	2	0.610	0.112	0.234
BDS social maladaption	2	0.879	0.193	0.359
Community involvement	2	0.135	0.063	0.882
Relationships	2	1.000	0.000	0.311
Health problems	3	0.221	0.111	0.726
Seriousness of maladaptive behaviors	3	0.297	0.066	0.480
BDS social maladaption	3	0.787	0.170	0.381
Community involvement	3	0.265	0.112	0.805
Relationships	3	1.000	0.000	0.401
Personal maladaption model				
Client age	1	1.000	0.000	0.000
Client MR level	1	1.000	0.000	0.000
Careprovider age	1	1.000	0.000	0.000
Careprovider education	1	1.000	0.000	0.039
Careprovider experience	1	1.000	0.000	0.034
Careprovider training	1	1.000	0.000	0.128
Health problems	1	1.000	0.000	0.155
Seriousness of maladaptive behaviors	1	1.000	0.000	0.088
BDS personal maladaption	1	1.000	0.000	0.160
Community involvement	1	1.000	0.000	0.189
Relationships	1	1.000	0.000	0.338
Stability	1	1.000	0.000	0.333
Environment	1	1.000	0.000	0.607

(continued on next page)

TABLE A.2 *(continued)*

**Residual and Explained Variance for Latent Variables
In Models Presented in Chapter 6**

LATENT FACTOR	RESIDUAL VARIANCE			EXPLAINED VARIANCE, OR R^2
	TIME OF MEASUREMENT	ESTIMATE	Se	
Health problems	2	0.480	0.143	0.481
Seriousness of maladaptive behaviors	2	0.651	0.118	0.202
BDS personal maladaption	2	0.486	0.415	0.805
Community involvement	2	0.136	0.062	0.881
Relationships	2	1.000	0.000	0.255
Health problems	3	0.236	0.113	0.716
Seriousness of maladaptive behaviors	3	0.271	0.062	0.505
BDS personal maladaption	3	1.557	0.567	0.394
Community involvement	3	0.243	0.108	0.818
Relationships	3	1.000	0.000	0.231

trivial. Inspection of Table A.1 reveals that the difference in statistical fit between the measurement and final models was not large, only once reaching the $p < .01$ level. Of the remaining five difference tests, three were of borderline significance, between the .05 and .01 levels, and two were nonsignificant.

More importantly, the ρ value for the restricted final model was always equal to or higher than the ρ value for the associated measurement model, suggesting that the final model was a more efficient representation of the data. These findings, taken together with the relative parsimony of the final models, suggests strongly that the final model for each data set is the preferred representation of each set of data.

Parameters of the structural model. The structural relations among latent variables, the core of the structural model, were given in figures presented in Chapters 3 through 6. The last table presented in this appendix, Table A.2, provides additional information about each structural model from Chapter 6. This information was presented only for Chapter 6 models due to constraints of space and the similarity of values across Chapters 3 through 6.

In Table A.2, the variances or residual variances of the latent variables in each of the three models from Chapter 6 are presented. Consider first the adaptive behavior model, parameters for which are presented in the first section of Table A.2. Inspection of the table shows that the variance or residual variance for each of the Time 1 constructs was fixed at unity to identify the latent variables, or factors; because each of these parameters was fixed (i.e., not estimated), the standard error for each parameter was zero. The factors appearing at the first time of measurement had little of their variance explained by other variables at Time 1, except for three factors— Adaptive Behavior, Stability of Placement, and Residential Environment.

The client's chronological age and level of retardation were the significant predictors of Adaptive Behavior, $R^2 = .439$; the client's age and the careprovider's experience were the primary predictors of Stability of Placement, $R^2 = .335$; and client's age, careprovider's age, and careprovider's education had significant influences on Residential Environment, $R^2 = .536$.

Five constructs were represented at each of the three times of measurement. Of these, Adaptive Behavior and Community Involvement had high levels of explained variance at Times 2 and 3, $R^2 > .70$, due primarily to the high stability of these constructs across time. Health Problems also had sizeable levels of explained variance at Times 2 and 3, with $R^2 > .50$, again due to the stability of this behavioral characteristic across time. The remaining two constructs—Seriousness of Adaptive Problems and Quality of Relationships—had rather lower levels of explained variance at Times 2 and 3.

The second and third sections of Table A.2 provide the parameter estimates for the Social Maladaption and Personal Maladaption models, respectively. Patterns of results with regard to residual variance are largely similar to those for the Adaptive Behavior model discussed above, with one major exception. This exception is that, at each time of measurement, the Social Maladaption and Personal Maladaption latent variables had rather lower levels of explained variance than did the Adaptive Behavior latent variables. This is not a novel finding, as maladaptive behaviors have frequently been found to be less stable than forms of adaptive behavior. Moreover, the lower levels of explained variance may have stemmed from the rather restricted scales on which the indicators of maladaptive behavior were scored. Regardless, the levels of explained variance in the two forms of maladaptive behavior seem rather appropriate.

Parameters of the measurement model. The parameters of the measurement models for the three models in Chapter 6 are presented in a series of supplemental tables. Supplemental Table A.3 presents measurement model parameters for the Adaptive Behavior model from Chapter 6, and parallel parameter estimates for the Social Maladaption and Personal Maladaption models are presented in Supplemental Tables A.4 and A.5, respectively. The correlated residuals from the measurement portion of all three models are presented in Supplemental Table A.6. Due to space constraints, these four supplemental tables are not presented here; they are available from the first author on request.

To summarize these parameter estimates briefly, each measured variable loaded significantly and primarily on the factor for which it was hypothesized to be an indicator. Of course, a variety of additional, secondary loadings were also allowed, because it was unreasonable to assume on an *a priori* basis that all variables in the models would be factorially simple in nature. Regarding levels of common variance (or communality), the level of communality ranged between .50 and .95 for approximately 80 percent of the measured variables, suggesting that more than half of their variance was related to the latent variables (or factors) in the model. Such levels of communality are fairly high and quite acceptable for covariance structure modeling. Of the remaining 20 percent of the measured variables, their levels of communality fell almost uniformly between .30 and .50, which reflect adequate levels of common variance.

In summary, the tables presented here indicate that the final models presented throughout the monograph: a) showed acceptable levels of overall fit; b) explained well the relations among the measured variables, and; c) explained well the relations among the latent constructs. These results provide added support for the authors' contention that the structural models presented in this monograph are appropriate representations of the data from the Family Care Study and should serve as a theoretical context for further research on the contextual influences on the development of adaptive and maladaptive behaviors by children and adolescents with mental retardation.

References

Aanes, D. & Haagenson, L. (1978). Normalization: Attention to a conceptual disaster. *Mental Retardation, 16,* 55-56.

Aanes, D. & Moen, M. (1976). Adaptive behavior changes of group home residents. *Mental Retardation, 14*(4), 36-40.

Adams, M. (1970). Foster care for mentally retarded children: How does child welfare meet this challenge? *Child Welfare, 49,* 260-269.

Adams, M. (1975). Foster family care for the intellectually disadvantaged child: The current state of proactive and some research perspectives. In M. Begab & S. Richardson (Eds.), *The mentally retarded and society: A social science perspective* (pp. 267-285). New York: University Park Press.

Anderson, J. C. & Gerbing, D. W. (1988). Structural equation modeling in practice: A review and recommended two-step approach. *Psychological Bulletin, 103,* 411-423.

Arndt, S. (1981). A general measure of adaptive behavior. *American Journal of Mental Deficiency, 85,* 554-556.

Bachrach, L. L. (1985). Deinstitutionalization: The meaning of the least restrictive environment. In R. H. Bruininks & K. C. Lakin (Eds.), *Living and learning in the least restrictive environment* (pp. 23-36). Baltimore: Paul H. Brookes Publishing Co..

Baker, B. L. & Blacher, J. (1988). Family involvement with community residential programs. In M. P. Janicki, M. W. Krauss, & M. M. Seltzer (Eds.), *Community residences for persons with developmental disabilities* (pp. 173-188). Baltimore: Paul H. Brookes Publishing Co.

Baker, B. L., Seltzer, G. B., & Seltzer, M. M. (1974). *As close as possible: Community residences for retarded adults.* Boston: Little Brown & Co.

Balla, D. A. (1976). Relationship of institution size to quality of care: A review of the literature. *American Journal of Mental Deficiency, 81,* 117-124.

Balla, D. A., Butterfield, E. C., & Zigler, E. (1974). Effects of institutionalization on retarded children: A longitudinal cross-institutional investigation. *American Journal of Mental Deficiency, 78,* 530-549.

Bank-Mikkelson, N. E. (1980). Denmark. In R. J. Flynn & K. E. Nitsch (Eds.), *Normalization, social integration, and community services.* Baltimore: University Park Press.

Bartnik, E. & Winkler, R. C. (1981). Discrepant judgments of community adjustment of mentally retarded adults: The contribution of personal responsibility. *American Journal of Mental Deficiency, 86,* 260-266.

Bauer, J. E. & Heinke, W. (1976). Treatment family care homes for disturbed foster children. *Child Welfare, 55*(7), 478-490.

Bell, R. Q. (1968). A reinterpretation of the direction of effects in studies of socialization. *Psychological Review, 75,* 81-95.

Bell, N. J., Schoenrock, C. J., & Bensberg, G. J. (1981). Change over time in the community: Findings of a longitudinal study. In R. H. Bruininks, C. E. Meyers, B. B. Sigford, & K. C. Lakin (Eds.), *Deinstitutionalization and community adjustment of mentally retarded people* (pp. 195-206). Washington, DC: American Association on Mental Deficiency.

Bentler, P. M. (1980). Multivariate analysis with latent variables: Causal modeling. *Annual Review of Psychology, 31,* 419-456.

Bentler, P. M. (1985). *Theory and implementation of EQS: A structural equations program.* Los Angeles: BMDP Statistical Software.

Bentler, P. M. & Bonett, D. G. (1980). Significance tests and goodness of fit in the analysis of covariance structures. *Psychological Bulletin, 88,* 588-606.

Bentler, P. M. & Speckart, G. (1981). Attitudes "cause" behaviors: A structural equation analysis. *Journal of Personality and Social Psychology, 40,* 226-238.

Berkson, G. & Landesman-Dwyer, S. (1977). Behavioral research on severe and profound mental retardation (1955-1974). *American Journal of Mental Deficiency, 81,* 428-454.

Best-Sigford, B., Bruininks, R. H., Lakin, K. C., Hill, B. K., & Heal, L. W. (1982). Resident release patterns in a national sample of public residential facilities. *American Journal of Mental Deficiency, 87,* 130-140.

Bishop, E. B. (1957). Family care: The patients. *American Journal of Mental Deficiency, 61,* 583-591.

Bishop, E. B. (1959). Family care boarding homes. *American Journal of Mental Deficiency, 63,* 703-706.

Bjaanes, A. T. & Butler, E. W. (1974). Environmental variation in community care facilities for mentally retarded persons. *American Journal of Mental Deficiency, 78,* 429-439.

Blunden, R. (1988). Programmatic features of quality services. In M. P. Janicki, M. W. Krauss, & M. M. Seltzer (Eds.), *Community residences for persons with developmental disabilities* (pp. 117-121). Baltimore: Paul H. Brookes Publishing Co.

Borthwick-Duffy, S. A. (1992). Quality of life and quality of care in mental retardation. In L. Rowitz (Ed.), *Mental retardation in the year 2000* (pp. 52-66). New York: Springer-Verlag.

Borthwick, S. A., Meyers, C. E., & Eyman, R. K. (1981). Comparative adaptive and maladaptive behavior of mentally retarded clients of five residential settings in three western states. In R. H. Bruininks, C. E. Meyers, B. B. Sigford, & K. C. Lakin (Eds.), *Deinstitutionalization and community adjustment of mentally retarded people* (pp. 351-359). Washington, DC: American Association on Mental Deficiency.

Borthwick-Duffy, S. A., Eyman, R. K., & White, J. F. (1987). Client characteristics and residential placement patterns. *American Journal of Mental Deficiency, 92,* 24-30.

Boyle, G. J. & Comer, P. G. (1990). Demographic characteristics of direct-service personnel in community residential units. *Australia and New Zealand Journal of Developmental Disabilities, 16,* 33-37.

Bradley, R. (1986). *The importance of home environment on the education of children.* Lecture given to University of California Education Graduate Students, Riverside, CA.

Bradley, R. H. & Caldwell, B. M. (1979). Home observation for measurement of the environment: A revision of the preschool scale. *American Journal of Mental Deficiency, 84,* 235-244.

Browder, J. A., Ellis, L., & Neal, J. (1974). Foster homes: Alternatives to institutions? *American Journal of Mental Deficiency, 12,* 33-36.

Brown, S., Windle, C., & Stewart, E. (1959). Statistics on a family care program. *American Journal of Mental Deficiency*, 64, 535-542.

Bruininks, R. (1986, May). *The implications of deinstitutionalization for community adjustment.* Paper presented at the Annual Meeting of the American Association on Mental Deficiency, Denver, CO.

Bruininks, R. H. (1990). There is more than a zip code to changes in services. *American Journal on Mental Retardation*, 95, 13-15.

Bruininks, R. H., Hauber, F. A., & Kudla, M. J. (1980). National survey of community residential facilities: A profile of facilities and residents in 1977. *American Journal of Mental Deficiency*, 84, 470-478.

Bruininks, R. H., Hill, B. K., & Thorsheim, M. J. (1980). *A profile of specially licensed foster homes for mentally retarded people in 1977.* Minneapolis, MN: University of Minnesota, Department of Psycho-educational Studies.

Bruininks, R. H., Kudla, M. J., Hauber, F. A., Hill, B. K., & Wieck, C. A. (1981). Recent growth and status of community-based residential alternatives. In R. H. Bruininks, C. E. Meyers, B. B. Sigford, & K. C. Lakin (Eds.), *Deinstitutionalization and community adjustment of mentally retarded people* (pp. 14-27). Washington, DC: American Association on Mental Deficiency.

Bruininks, R. H. & Lakin, K. C. (Eds.). (1985). *Living and learning in the least restrictive environment.* Baltimore: Paul H. Brookes Publishing Co.

Bruininks, R. H., Rotegard, L. L., Lakin, K. C., & Hill, B. K. (1987). Epidemiology of mental retardation and trends in residential services in the United States. In S. Landesman & P. Vietze (Eds.), *Living environments and mental retardation* (pp. 17-42). Washington, DC: American Association on Mental Retardation.

Burchard, S. N. & Thousand, J. (1988). Staff and manager competencies. In M. P. Janicki, M. W. Krauss, & M. M. Seltzer (Eds.), *Community residences for persons with developmental disabilities* (pp. 251-266). Baltimore: Paul H. Brookes Publishing Co.

Butler, E. W. & Bjaanes, A. T. (1978). Activities and the use of time by retarded persons living in community care facilities. In G. P. Sackett (Ed.), *Observing behavior (Vol. I): Theory and applications in mental retardation* (pp. 379-399). Baltimore: University Park Press.

Butler, E. W. & Bjaanes, A. T. (1980, May). *Deinstitutionalization, environmental normalization, and client normalization.* Paper presented at the Annual Meeting of the American Association on Mental Deficiency, San Francisco, CA.

Butterfield, E. C. (1985). The consequences of bias in studies of living arrangements for the mentally retarded adult. In D. Bricker & J. Filler (Eds.), *Severe mental retardation: From theory to practice* (pp. 245-263). Lancaster, PA: Lancaster Press.

Butterfield, E. C. & Zigler E. (1965). The influence of differing institutional social climates on the effectiveness of social reinforcement in the mentally retarded. *American Journal of Mental Deficiency*, 70, 48-56.

Caldwell, B. (1968). *Instruction manual: Home observation for measurement of the environment.* Unpublished manuscript.

Carhill, K. G., Rader, L. C., & Schonfeld, H. (1967). Level of retardation as a factor in the successful family care placement of mentally retarded children. *Psychiatric Social Work Review*, 1, 9.

Clarke-Stewart, K. A. (1988). Parent's effects on children's development: A decade of progress? *Journal of Applied Developmental Psychology*, 9, 41-84.

Coates, D. L. & Vietze, P. M. (1987). Design of research on families. In S. Landesman & P. Vietze (Eds.), *Living environments and mental retardation* (pp. 61-76). Washington, DC: American Association on Mental Retardation.

Conroy, J. Efthimiau, J. & Lemanowicz, J. (1982). A matched comparison of the developmental growth of insitutionalized and deinstitutionalized mentally retarded adults. *American Journal of Mental Deficiency, 86,* 581-587.

Craig, E. M. & McCarver, R. B. (1984). Community placement and adjustment of deinstitutionalized clients: Issues and findings. In N. R. Ellis & N. W. Bray (Eds.), *International review of research in mental retardation* (Vol. 12, pp. 95-122). Orlando: Academic Press.

Crapps, J. M., Langone, J., & Swaim, S. (1985). Quantity and quality of participation in community environments by mentally retarded adults. *Education and Training of the Mentally Retarded, 20,* 123-129.

Crapps, J. M. & Stoneman, Z. (1989). Friendship patterns and community integration of family care residents. *Research in Developmental Disabilities, 10,* 153-169.

Crawford, J. L., Aiello, J. R., & Thompson, P. E. (1979). Deinstitutionalization and community placement: Clinical and environmental factors. *Mental Retardation, 17,* 59-63.

Damon, A. (1965). Discrepancies between findings of longitudinal and cross-sectional studies in adult life: Physique and physiology. *Human Development, 8,* 16-22.

Eagle, E. (1967). Prognosis and outcome and community placement of institutionalized retardates. *American Journal of Mental Deficiency, 72,* 232-243.

Edgerton, R. (1967). *The cloak of competence.* Los Angeles: University of California Press.

Edgerton, R. B. (1990). Quality of life from a longitudinal research perspective. In R. L. Schalock (Ed.), *Quality of life: Perspectives and issues* (pp. 149-160). Washington, DC: American Association on Mental Retardation.

Elardo, R. & Bradley, R. H. (1981). The Home Observation for Measurement of the Environment (HOME) Scale: A review of research. *Developmental Review, 1,* 113-145.

Emerson, E. B. (1985). Evaluating the impact of deinstitutionalization on the lives of mentally retarded people. *American Journal of Mental Retardation, 90,* 277-288.

Encyclopedia of social work. (1977). (Vol. 1, 17th ed). Washington, DC: National Association of Social Workers.

Encyclopedia of social work. (1987). (Vol. 1, 18th ed.). Silver Spring, MD: National Association of Social Workers.

Evans, D. P. (1983). *The lives of mentally retarded people.* Boulder, CO: Westview Press.

Eyman, R. K. (1981). *Study of the Impact of Foster Care Family in the Development and Behavior of Mentally Retarded Children.* NICHD Grant No. CRMC-77-13, Final Project Report.

Eyman, R. K. & Borthwick, S. A. (1980). Patterns of care for mentally retarded persons. *Mental Retardation, 18,* 63-66.

Eyman, R. K., Borthwick, S. A., & Tarjan, G. (1984). Current trends and changes in institutions for the mentally retarded. In N. R. Ellis & N. W. Bray (Eds.), *International review of research in mental retardation* (Vol. 12, pp. 178-203). New York: Academic Press.

Eyman, R. K. & Call, T. (1977). Maladaptive behavior and community placement of the mentally retarded. *American Journal of Mental Deficiency, 82,* 137-144.

Eyman, R. K., Demaine, G. C., & Lei, T. (1979). Relationship between community environments and resident changes in adaptive behavior: A path model. *American Journal of Mental Deficiency, 83,* 330-338.

Eyman, R. K. & Widaman, K. F. (1987). Life-span of institutionalized and community-based mentally retarded persons, revisited. *American Journal of Mental Deficiency, 91,* 559-569.

Fanschel, D. (1976). Status changes of children in foster care. *Child Welfare, 55,* 143-171.

Felce, D. (1987). The planning and evaluation of community-based residences for individuals with severe and profound mental retardation. In S. Landesman & P. Vietze (Eds.), *Living environments and mental retardation* (pp. 127-149). Washington, DC: American Association on Mental Retardation.

Felce, D. (1988). Behavioral and social climate in community group residences. In M. P. Janicki, M. W. Krauss, & M. M. Seltzer (Eds.), *Community residences for persons with developmental disabilities* (pp. 133-147). Baltimore: Paul H. Brookes Publishing Co.

Fernald, W. E. (1919). After-care study of the patients discharged from Waverly for a period of twenty-five years. *Ungraded, 5,* 25-31.

Flanagan, J. C. (1982). Measurement of quality of life: Current state of the art. *Archives of Physical and Medical Rehabilitation, 63,* 56-59.

Flynn, R. J. (1980). Normalization, PASS, and service quality assessment. In R. J. Flynn & K. E. Nitsch (Eds.), *Normalization, social integration, and community services* (pp. 323-359). Baltimore: University Park Press.

Futterman, A. D. & Arndt, S. (1983). The construct and predictive validity of adaptive behavior. *American Journal of Mental Deficiency, 87,* 546-550.

Gollay, E., Freedman, R., Wyngaarden, M., & Kurtz, N. (1978). *Coming back: The community experiences of deinstitutionalized mentally retarded people.* Cambridge, MA: Abt Associates.

Goode, D. A. (1990). Thinking about and discussing quality of life. In R. L. Schalock (Ed.), *Quality of life: Perspectives and issues* (pp. 41-57). Washington, DC: American Association on Mental Retardation.

Gottlieb, J. (1990). Mainstreaming and quality education. *American Journal on Mental Retardation, 95,* 16-17.

Graffam, J. & Turner, J. L. (1984). Escape from boredom: The meaning of eventfulness in the lives of clients at a sheltered workshop. In R. B. Edgerton (Ed.), *Lives in process: Mildly retarded adults in a large city* (pp. 121-144). Washington, DC: American Association on Mental Deficiency.

Groner, N. E. (1988). Fire safety practices. In M. P. Janicki, M. W. Krauss, & M. M. Seltzer (Eds.), *Community residences for persons with developmental disabilities* (pp. 313-325). Baltimore: Paul H. Brookes Publishing Co.

Grossman, H. J. (Ed.). (1983). *Classification in mental retardation.* Washington, DC: American Association on Mental Deficiency.

Halpern, A. S., Nave, G., Close, D. W., & Nelson, D. (1986). An empirical analysis of the dimensions of community adjustment for adults with mental retardation in semi-independent living programs. *Australia and New Zealand Journal of Developmental Disabilities, 12,* 147-157.

Hayduk, L. A. (1987). *Structural equation modeling with LISREL.* Baltimore: The Johns Hopkins University Press.

Haywood, H. C. & Newbrough, J. R. (Eds.). (1981). *Living environments for developmentally retarded persons.* Baltimore: University Park Press.

Heal, L. W. (1985). Methodology for community integration research. In R. H. Bruininks, C. E. Meyers, B. B. Sigford, & K. C. Lakin (Eds.), *Deinstitutionalization and community adjustment of mentally retarded people* (pp. 199-224). Washington, DC: American Association on Mental Deficiency.

Heal, L. W. (1990). Bold relief or bold re-leaf? *American Journal on Mental Retardation, 95,* 17-19.

Heal, L. W. & Fujiura, G. T. (1984). Methodological consideration in research on residential alternatives for developmentally disabled persons. In N. R. Ellis & N. W. Bray (Eds.), *International review of research in mental retardation* (Vol. 12, pp. 206-244). Orlando: Academic Press.

Heal, L. W. & Sigelman, C. K. (1990). Methodological issues in measuring the quality of life of individuals with mental retardation. In R. L. Schalock (Ed.), *Quality of life: Perspectives and issues* (pp. 161-176). Washington, DC: American Association on Mental Retardation.

Heal, L., Sigelman, C. K., & Switzky, H. N. (1978). Research on community residential alternatives for the mentally retarded. In N. R. Ellis (Ed.), *International review of research in mental retardation* (Vol.. 9, pp. 210-249). Orlando: Academic Press Inc.

Hill, B. K. & Bruininks, R. H. (1984). Maladaptive behavior of mentally retarded individuals in residential facilities. *American Journal of Mental Deficiency, 88,* 380-387.

Hill, B. K., Rotegard, L. L., & Bruininks, R. H. (1984). The quality of life of mentally retarded people in residential care. *Social Work, 29,* 275-281.

Intagliata, J., Crosby, N., & Neider, L. (1981). Foster family care for mentally retarded people: A qualitative review. In R. H. Bruininks, C. E. Meyers, B. B. Sigford, & K. C. Lakin (Eds.), *Deinstitutionalization and community adjustment of mentally retarded people* (pp. 233-259). Washington, DC: American Association on Mental Deficiency.

Intagliata, J., Willer, B., & Wicks, N. (1981). Factors related to the quality of community adjustment in family care homes. In R. H. Bruininks, C. E. Meyers, B. B. Sigford, & K. C. Lakin (Eds.), *Deinstitutionalization and community adjustment of mentally retarded people* (pp. 217-230). Washington, DC: American Association on Mental Deficiency.

Ittleson, W. H. (1978). Environmental perception and urban experience. *Environment and Behavior, 10,* 193-213.

Jacobson, J. W. & Schwartz, A. A. (1983). Personal and service characteristics affecting group home placement success: A prospective analysis. *Mental Retardation, 21,* 1-17.

Janicki, M. P., Jacobson, J. W., Zigman, W. B., & Gordon, N. H. (1984). Characteristics of employees of community residences for retarded persons. *Education and Training of the Mentally Retarded, 19,* 35-44.

Janicki, M. P., Jacobson, J. W., Zigman, W. B., & Lubin, R. A. (1987). In S. Landesman & P. Vietze (Eds.), *Living environments and mental retardation* (pp. 173-194). Washington, DC: American Association on Mental Retardation.

Janicki, M. P., Krauss, M. W., & Seltzer, M. M. (1988). Context, models, and issues for community residences. In M. P. Janicki, M. W. Krauss, & M. M. Seltzer (Eds.), *Community residences for persons with developmental disabilities* (pp. 3-14). Baltimore: Paul H. Brookes Publishing Co.

Jöreskog, K. G. & Sörbom, D. (1988). *LISREL 7: A guide to the program and applications.* Chicago: SPSS.

Justice, R. S., Bradley, J., & O'Connor, G. (1971). Foster family care for the retarded: Management concerns of the caretaker. *Mental Retardation, 9*(4), 12-15.

Kanner, L. (1964). *A history of the care and study of the mentally retarded.* Springfield, IL: Charles C. Thomas.

Kastner, L. S., Reppuci, N. D., & Pezzoli, J. J. (1979). Assessing community attitudes toward mentally retarded persons. *American Journal of Mental Deficiency, 84,* 137-144.

Kernan, K. T., Begab, M. J., & Edgerton, R. B. (Eds.). (1983). *Environments and behavior: The adaptation of mentally retarded persons.* Baltimore: University Park Press.

Keys, V., Boroskin, A., & Ross, R. (1973). The revolving door in an MR hospital: A study of returns from leave. *Mental Retardation, 11,* 55-56.

King, R. D., Raynes, N. V., & Tizard, J. (1971). *Patterns of residential care.* London: Routledge & Kegan Paul.

Krauss, M. W. (1990). In defense of common sense. *American Journal on Mental Retardation, 95,* 19-21.

Kuhlen, R. G. (1963). Age and intelligence: The significance of cultural change in longitudinal vs. cross-sectional findings. *Vita Humana, 6,* 113-124.

Labouvie, E. W., Bartsch, T. W., Nesselroade, J. R., & Baltes, P. B. (1974). On the internal and external validity of simple longitudinal designs. *Child Development, 45,* 282-290.

Lakin, K. C., Bruininks, R. H., & Sigford, B. B. (1981). Early perspectives on the community adjustment of mentally retarded people. In R. H. Bruininks, C. E. Meyers, B. B. Sigford, & K. C. Lakin (Eds.), *Deinstitutionalization and community adjustment of mentally retarded people* (pp. 28-50). Washington, DC: American Association on Mental Deficiency.

Lakin, K. C., Hill, B. K., & Bruininks, R. H. (1988). Trends and issues in the growth of community residential services. In M. P. Janicki, M. W. Krauss, & M. M. Seltzer (Eds.), *Community residences for persons with developmental disabilities* (pp. 25-42). Baltimore: Paul H. Brookes Publishing Co.

Lambert, N. M. & Nicholl, R. C. (1976). Dimensions of adaptive behavior of retarded and nonretarded public-school children. *American Journal of Mental Deficiency, 81,* 135-146.

Landesman, S. (1986). Quality of life and personal life satisfaction: Definition and measurement issues. *Mental Retardation, 24,* 141-145.

Landesman, S. (1987). The changing structure and function of institutions: A search for optimal group care environments. In S. Landesman & P. Vietze (Eds.), *Living environments and mental retardation* (pp. 79-126). Washington, DC: American Association on Mental Retardation.

Landesman, S. (1988). Preventing "institutionalization" in the community. In M. P. Janicki, M. W. Krauss, & M. M. Seltzer (Eds.), *Community residences for persons with developmental disabilities* (pp. 105-116). Baltimore: Paul H. Brookes Publishing Co.

Landesman, S. & Vietze, P. (Eds). (1987). *Living environments and mental retardation.* Washington, DC: American Association on Mental Retardation.

Landesman-Dwyer, S. (1983). Residential environments and the social behavior of handicapped individuals. In M. Lewis (Ed.), *Beyond the dyad.* New York: Plenum Publishing.

Landesman-Dwyer, S. (1985). Describing and evaluating residential environments. In R. H. Bruininks & K. C. Lakin (Eds.), *Living and learning in the least restrictive environment* (pp. 185-196). Baltimore: Paul H. Brookes Publishing Co.

Landesman-Dwyer, S. & Sackett, G. P. (1978). Behavioral changes in nonambulatory, profoundly retarded individuals. In C. E. Meyers (Ed.), *Quality of life in severely and profoundly mentally retarded people: Research foundations for improvement* (pp. 55-144). Washington, DC: American Association on Mental Deficiency.

Landesman-Dwyer, S. & Sulzbacher, F. (1981). Residential placement and adaptation of severely and profoundly retarded individuals. In R. H. Bruininks, C. E.

Meyers, B. B. Sigford, & K. C. Lakin (Eds.), *Deinstitutionalization and community adjustment of mentally retarded people* (pp. 182-194). Washington, DC: American Association on Mental Deficiency.

Lazerson, M. (1975). Educational institutions and mental subnormality: Notes on writing a history. In M. J. Begab & S. A. Richardson (Eds.), *The mentally retarded and society: A social science perspective* (pp. 33-52). Baltimore: University Park Press.

Lei, T. & Eyman, R. K. (1979). Characteristics of individuals referred to services for the developmentally disabled. *Mental Retardation, 17,* 196-198.

Lei, T. J., Nihira, L., Sheehy, N., & Meyers, C. E. (1981). A study of small family care for mentally retarded people. In R. H. Bruininks, C. E. Meyers, B. B. Sigford, & K. C. Lakin (Eds.), *Deinstitutionalization and community adjustment of mentally retarded people* (pp. 265-281). Washington, DC: American Association on Mental Deficiency.

Lei, T. J., Sheehy, N., & Wilson, S. (1980, April). *Who provides small family care for mentally retarded children?* Paper presented at the annual meeting of the Pacific Sociological Association, San Francisco, CA.

Lerner, R. M. (1989). Individual development and the family system: A life-span perspective. In K. Kreppner & R. M. Lerner (Eds.), *Family systems and life-span development* (pp. 15-31). Hillsdale, NJ: Erlbaum.

Lewis, M., Feiring, C., & Brooks-Gunn, J. (1987). The social networks of children with and without handicaps: A developmental perspective. In S. Landesman & P. Vietze (Eds.), *Living environments and mental retardation* (pp. 377-400). Washington, DC: American Association on Mental Retardation.

Maas, H. S. (1969). Children in long-term foster care. *Child Welfare, 18(6),* 321-333.

MacCallum, R. C., Roznowski, M., & Necowitz, L. B. (in press). Model modifications in covariance structure analysis: The problem of capitalization on chance. *Psychological Bulletin.*

MacMillan, D. L. (1982). *Mental retardation in school and society.* Boston: Little, Brown, and Company.

Maloney, M. P. & Ward, M. P. (1979). *Mental retardation and modern society.* New York: Oxford University Press.

Marsh, H. W., Balla, J. R., & McDonald, R. P. (1988). Goodness-of-fit indexes in confirmatory factor analysis: The effect of sample size. *Psychological Bulletin, 103,* 391-410.

McCall, R. B. & Appelbaum, M. (1973). Bias in the analysis of repeated measures designs: Some alternative approaches. *Child Development, 44,* 401-415.

McCarver, R. B. & Craig, E. M. (1974). Placement of the retarded in the community: Prognosis and outcome. In N. R. Ellis (Ed.), *International review of research in mental retardation* (Vol. 7). New York: Academic Press.

McCord, W. T. (1982). From theory to reality: Obstacles to the implementation of the normalization principle in human services. *Mental Retardation, 20,* 247-253.

McCormick, M., Balla, D., & Zigler, E. (1975). Resident-care practices in institutions for mentally retarded persons: A cross-institutional, cross-cultural study. *American Journal of Mental Deficiency, 80,* 1-17.

McDevitt, S. C., Smith, P. M., Schmidt, D. W., & Rosen, M. (1978). The deinstitutionalized citizen: Adjustment and quality of life. *Mental Retardation, 16,* 22-24.

McGrew, K. & Bruininks, R. (1989). The factor structure of adaptive behavior. *School Psychology Review, 18,* 64-81.

Menolascino, F. J. & Stark, J. A. (1990). Research versus advocacy in the allocation of resources: Problems, causes, solutions. *American Journal on Mental Retardation, 95,* 21-25.

Mercer, J. R. & Richardson, J. G. (1975). Mental retardation as a social problem. In N. Hobbs (Ed.), *Issues in the classification of children* (pp. 463-496). San Francisco: Jossey-Bass Publishers.

Meyers, C. E. & Blacher, J. (1987). Historical determinants of residential care. In S. Landesman & P. Vietze (Eds.), *Living environments and mental retardation* (pp. 3-16). Washington, DC: American Association on Mental Retardation.

Meyers, C. E., Mink, I. T., & Nihira, K. (1981). *Home Quality Rating Scale: User's manual.* Los Angeles: University of California, Neuropsychiatric Institute.

Mink, I. T. & Nihira, K. (1986). Family life styles and child behaviors: A study of direction of effects. *Developmental Psychology, 22,* 610-616.

Mink, I. T. & Nihira, K. (1987). Direction of effects: Family life-styles and behavior of TMR children. *American Journal of Mental Deficiency, 92,* 57-64.

Morrisey, J. A. (1966). Status of a foster care program. *Mental Retardation, 4*(2), 8-11.

Nesselroade, J. R. & Baltes, P. B. (1974). Adolescent personality development and historical change: 1970-1972. *Monographs of the Society for Research in Child Development, 39*(1, Serial No. 154).

Neuropsychiatric Institute Research Group (1979). *Behavior Development Survey user's manual.* Pomona, CA: University of California at Los Angeles Research Group, Lanterman State Hospital.

Nihira, K. (1969a). Factorial dimensions of adaptive behavior in adult retardates. *American Journal of Mental Deficiency, 73,* 868-878.

Nihira, K. (1969b). Factorial dimensions of adaptive behavior in mentally retarded children and adolescents. *American Journal of Mental Deficiency, 74,* 130-141.

Nihira, K. (1976). Dimensions of adaptive behavior in institutionalized mentally retarded children and adults: Developmental perspective. *American Journal of Mental Deficiency, 81,* 215-226.

Nihira, K. (1977). Development of adaptive behavior in the mentally retarded. In P. Mittler (Ed.), *Research to practice in mental retardation: Vol. II.* Baltimore: University Park Press.

Nihira, K., Foster, R., Shellhaas, M., & Leland, H. (1975). *AAMD adaptive behavior scale manual.* Washington, DC: American Association on Mental Deficiency.

Nihira, K., Mink, I. T., & Meyers, C. E. (1984). Salient dimensions of home environment relevant to child development. In N. R. Ellis & N. W. Bray (Eds.), *International review of research in mental retardation* (Vol. 12, pp. 149-175). Orlando: Academic Press.

Nihira, L. & Nihira, K. (1975). Jeopardy in community placement. *American Journal of Mental Deficiency, 79,* 538-544.

Nirje, B. (1980). The normalization principle. In R. J. Flynn and K. E. Nitsch (Eds.), *Normalization, social integration, and community services.* Baltimore: University Park Press.

Novak, A. A. & Berkeley, T. R. (1984). A systems theory approach to deinstitutionalization policies and research. In N. R. Ellis & N. W. Bray (Eds.), *International review of research in mental retardation* (Vol. 12, pp. 245-283). Orlando: Academic Press Inc.

O'Connor, G. (1976). *Home is a good place.* (AAMD Monograph No. 2). Washington, DC: American Association on Mental Deficiency.

Pagel, S. E. & Whitling, C. A. (1978). Readmissions to a state hospital for mentally retarded persons: Reasons for community placement failure. *Mental Retardation, 16,* 164-166.

Pratt, M. W., Luszcz, M. A., & Brown, M. E. (1980). Measuring dimensions of the quality of care in small community residences. *American Journal of Mental Deficiency, 85,* 188-194.

Ramey, S. L. (1990). Staging (and re-staging) the trio of services, evaluation, and research. *American Journal on Mental Retardation, 95,* 26-29.

Raynes, N., Pratt, M., & Roses, S. (1979). *Organisational structure and the care of the mentally retarded.* London: Croom-Helm.

Riegel, K. F., Riegel, R. M., & Meyer, G. (1968). The prediction of retest resisters in research on aging. *Journal of Gerontology, 23,* 370-374.

Robinson, J. W. (1988). Design features and architectural considerations. In M. P. Janicki, M. W. Krauss, & M. M. Seltzer (Eds.), *Community residences for persons with developmental disabilities* (pp. 327-346). Baltimore: Paul H. Brookes Publishing Co.

Romer, D. & Berkson, G. (1980). Social ecology of supervised communal facilities for mentally disabled adults: II. Predictors of affiliation. *American Journal of Mental Deficiency, 85,* 229-242.

Romer, D. & Heller, T. (1983). Social adaptation of mentally retarded adults in community settings: A social-ecological approach. *Applied Research in Mental Retardation, 4,* 303-314.

Rotegard, L. L., Bruininks, R. H., Holman, J. G., & Lakin, K. C. (1985). Environmental aspects of deinstitutionalization. In R. H. Bruininks & K. C. Lakin (Eds.), *Living and learning in the least restrictive environment* (pp. 155-184). Baltimore: Paul H. Brookes Publishing Co.

Rothschild, A. M. (1974). An agency evaluates its foster home service. *Child Welfare, 53*(1), 42-50.

Saetermoe, C. L., Widaman, K. F., & Borthwick-Duffy, S. (1991). Validation of the parenting style survey for parents of children with mental retardation. *Mental Retardation, 29,* 149-157.

Sanderson, H. W. & Crawley, M. (1982). Characteristics of successful family-care parents. *American Journal of Mental Deficiency, 86,* 519-525.

SAS Institute, Inc. (1985). *Statistical Analysis System Version V.* Cary, NC: SAS Institute, Inc.

Schaie, K. W. (1983). The Seattle longitudinal study: A 21-year exploration of psychometric intelligence in adulthood. In K. W. Schaie (Ed.), *Longitudinal studies of adult psychological development* (pp. 64-135). New York: Guilford.

Schalock, R. L. (1986, May). *Current approaches to quality of life assessment.* Paper presented at the Annual Meeting of the American Association on Mental Deficiency, Denver, CO.

Schalock, R. L. (1990). Attempts to conceptualize and measure quality of life. In R. L. Schalock (Ed.), *Quality of life: Perspectives and issues* (pp. 141-148). Washington, DC: American Association on Mental Retardation.

Schalock, R. L. & Harper, R. S. (1978). Placement from community-based mental retardation programs: How well do clients do? *American Journal of Mental Deficiency, 83,* 240-247.

Schalock, R. L., Harper, R. S., & Carver, G. (1981). Independent living placement: Five years later. *American Journal of Mental Deficiency, 2,* 170-177.

Schalock, R. L. & Keith, K. D. (1984). *DD client and staff variables influencing outcome of service delivery: Present and future models.* Lincoln NE: Nebraska Department of Health/Division of Developmental Disabilities.

Schalock, R. L., Keith, K. D., & Hoffman, K. (1990). *1990 quality of life questionnaire standardization manual.* Hastings, NE: Mid-Nebraska Mental Retardation Services, Inc.

Scheerenberger, R. C. (1980). *Deinstitutionalization and institutional reform.* Springfield, IL: Charles C. Thomas.

Scheerenberger, R. C. (1982). *Public residential services for the mentally retarded, 1981.* Minneapolis: University of Minnesota, Department of Psychoeducational Studies.

Scheerenberger, R. C. (1983). *Public residential services for the mentally retarded: 1982.* Madison, WI: National Association of Superintendents of Public Residential Facilities for the Mentally Retarded.

Scheerenberger, R. C. & Felsenthal, D. (1976). *A study of alternative community placements.* Madison, WI: Research Institute of the Wisconsin Association of Retarded Citizens.

Scheerenberger, R. C. & Felsenthal, D. (1977). Community settings for MR persons: Satisfaction and activities. *Mental Retardation, 15*(4), 3-7.

Seligman, M. (Ed.). (1983). *The family with a handicapped child.* Orlando, FL: Grune & Stratton.

Seltzer, G. B. (1981). Community residential adjustment: The relationship among environment, performance, and satisfaction. *American Journal of Mental Deficiency, 85,* 624-630.

Seltzer, M. M. & Seltzer, G. B. (1987). Community responses to community residences for persons who have mental retardation. In S. Landesman & P. Vietze (Eds.), *Living environments and mental retardation* (pp. 195-210). Washington, DC: American Association on Mental Retardation.

Seltzer, M. M., Sherwood, C. C., Seltzer, G. B., & Sherwood, S. (1981). Community adaptation and the impact of deinstitutionalization. In R. H. Bruininks, C. E. Meyers, B. B. Sigford, & K. C. Lakin (Eds.), *Deinstitutionalization and community adjustment of mentally retarded people* (pp. 82-88). Washington, DC: American Association on Mental Deficiency.

Sigelman, C. K., Schoenrock, C. J., Winer, J. L., Spanhel, C. L., Hromas, S. G., Martin, P. W., Budd, E. C., & Bensberg, G. J. (1981). In R. H. Bruininks, C. E. Meyers, B. B. Sigford, & K. C. Lakin (Eds.), *Deinstitutionalization and community adjustment of mentally retarded people* (pp. 114-129). Washington, DC: American Association on Mental Deficiency.

Stark, J. A. & Goldsbury, T. (1990). Quality of life from childhood to adulthood. In R. L. Schalock (Ed.), *Quality of life: Perspectives and issues* (pp. 71-83). Washington, DC: American Association on Mental Retardation.

Sternlicht, M. (1978). Variables affecting foster care placement of institutionalized retarded residents. *Mental Retardation, 16*(1), 25-28.

Stoneman, Z. & Crapps, J. M. (1988). Correlates of stress, perceived competence, and depression among family care providers. *American Journal on Mental Retardation, 93,* 166-173.

Stucky, P. E. & Newbrough, J. R. (1983). Mentally retarded persons in the community. In K. T. Kernan, M. J. Begab, & R. B. Edgerton (Eds.), *Environments and behavior: The adaptation of mentally retarded persons* (pp. 21-36). Baltimore: University Park Press.

Sutter, P. (1980). Environmental variables related to community placement failure in mentally retarded adults. *Mental Retardation, 18,* 189-191.

Sutter, P. & Mayeda, T. (1981). Matching developmentally disabled client characteristics to careprovider and employer preferences. In R. H. Bruininks, C. E. Meyers, B. B. Sigford, & K. C. Lakin (Eds.), *Deinstitutionalization and community adjustment of mentally retarded people* (pp. 260-264). Washington, DC: American Association on Mental Deficiency.

Sutton, M., Sutter, P., Long, K., & Kelley, D. (1983). *Barriers to community placement for the institutionalized mentally retarded.* Paper presented at the Western Psychological Association Convention, San Francisco, CA.

Switzky, H. N. & Haywood, H. C. (1985). Perspectives on methodological and research issues concerning severely mentally retarded persons. In D. Bricker & J. Filler (Eds.), *Severe mental retardation: From theory to practice* (pp. 264-284). Lancaster, PA: Lancaster Press.

Tarjan, G., Dingman, H. F., Eyman, R., & Brown, S. (1959). Effectiveness of hospital release programs. *American Journal of Mental Deficiency, 64,* 609-617.

Taylor, S. & Bogdan, R. (1981). A qualitative approach to the study of community adjustment. In R. H. Bruininks, C. E. Meyers, B. B. Sigford, & K. C. Lakin (Eds.), *Deinstitutionalization and community adjustment of mentally retarded people* (pp. 71-81). Washington, DC: American Association on Mental Deficiency.

Thorndike, E. L. (1939). *Your city.* New York: Harcourt, Brace.

Tucker, L. R. & Lewis, C. (1973). A reliability coefficient for maximum likelihood factor analysis. *Psychometrika, 38,* 1-10.

Vaux, C. L. (1935). Family care of mental defectives. *American Association of Mental Deficiency Proceedings, 40,* 168-189.

Widaman, K. F., Borthwick-Duffy, S. A., & Little, T. D. (1991). The structure and development of adaptive behaviors. In N. W. Bray (Ed.), *International review of research in mental retardation* (Vol. 17, pp. 1-54). New York: Academic Press.

Widaman, K. F., Gibbs, K. W., & Geary, D. C. (1987). Structure of adaptive behavior: I. Replication across fourteen samples of nonprofoundly mentally retarded people. *American Journal of Mental Deficiency, 91,* 348-360.

Widaman, K. F. & Kishton, J. (1992). *Alternative bases for parcelling items for confirmatory analyses.* Manuscript submitted for publication.

Willer, B. & Intagliata, J. (1980). *Deinstitutionalization of mentally retarded persons in New York State* (Final Report). New York: Office of Human Development, U. S. Department of Health and Human Service, Region II.

Willer, B. & Intagliata, J. (1982). Comparison of family care and group homes as alternatives to institutions. *American Journal of Mental Deficiency, 86,* 588-595.

Willer, B. & Intagliata, J. (1984). *Promises and realities for mentally retarded persons: Life in the community.* Baltimore: University Park Press.

Windle, C. (1962). Prognosis of mental subnormals. *American Journal of Mental Deficiency, 66* (Monograph Supplement), 8-25.

Windle, C. D., Sabagh, G., Brown, S. J., & Dingman, H. F. (1961). Caretaker characteristics and placement success. *American Journal of Mental Deficiency, 65*(6), 739-743.

Windle, C., Stewart, E., & Brown, S. J. (1961). Reasons for community failure of released patients. *American Journal of Mental Deficiency, 66,* 213-217.

Wolfensberger, W. (1972). *The principle of normalization in human services.* Toronto: National Institute on Mental Retardation.

Wolfensberger, W. (1980a). A brief overview of the principle of normalization. In R. J. Flynn & K. E. Nitsch (Eds.), *Normalization, social integration, and community services.* Baltimore: University Park Press.

Wolfensberger, W. (1980b). Research, empiricism, and the principle of normalization. In R. J. Flynn & K. E. Nitsch (Eds.), *Normalization, social integration, and community services.* Baltimore: University Park Press.

Wolfensberger, W. & Glenn, L. (1975). *PASS 3: A method for qualitative evaluation of human services.* Toronto: National Institute on Mental Retardation.

Wyngaarden, M. (1981). Interviewing mentally retarded persons: Issues and strategies. In R. H. Bruininks, C. E. Meyers, B. B. Sigford, & K. C. Lakin (Eds.), *Deinstitutionalization and community adjustment of mentally retarded people* (pp. 351-359). Washington, DC: American Association on Mental Deficiency.

Zautra, A. (1983). The measurement of quality in community life: Introduction to the special issue. *Journal of Community Psychology, 11,* 83-87.

Zigler, E. & Balla, D. (1976). Motivational factors in the performance of the retarded. In R. Koch & J. C. Dobson (Eds.), *The mentally retarded child and his family: A multi-disciplinary handbook* (2nd ed.). New York: Brunner/Mazel.

Zigler, E. & Balla, D. (1977). Impact of institutional experience on the behavior and development of retarded persons. *American Journal of Mental Deficiency, 82,* 1-11.

Zigler, E., Balla, D., & Hodapp, R. (1984). On the definition and classification of mental retardation. *American Journal of Mental Deficiency, 89,* 215-230.

Zigler, E., Hodapp, R. M., & Edison, M. R. (1990a). From theory to practice in the care and education of mentally retarded individuals. *American Journal on Mental Retardation, 95,* 1-12.

Zigler, E., Hodapp, R. M., & Edison, M. R. (1990b). Themes in the debate about normalization: Rejoinder. *American Journal on Mental Retardation, 95,* 30-31.

About the Authors

Sharon A. Borthwick-Duffy has been affiliated since 1973 with the UCLA/MRRC and UC Riverside Research Groups at Lanterman Developmental Center in Pomona, California. Her research focuses on residential placement issues, quality of life, dual diagnosis, life expectancy, and influences on the development of adaptive behavior among persons with mental retardation. She is currently an Associate Professor of Special Education in the School of Education at the University of California at Riverside.

Keith F. Widaman is currently a Professor of Developmental Psychology in the Department of Psychology at the University of California at Riverside. His primary research interests are the structure and life-span development of adaptive behaviors by persons with mental retardation, familial and caregiving influences on the development of adaptive behaviors, life expectancy, and issues in quantitative psychology, including the modeling of longitudinal data.

Todd D. Little was a post-doctoral researcher at the University of California at Riverside during data analysis and the writing of this monograph. He is currently a Research Scientist at the Max Planck Institute for Human Development and Education in Berlin, Germany. An important focus of his research is the application of structural modeling to developmental data.

Richard K. Eyman is currently a Professor of Education in the School of Education at the University of California at Riverside. His primary research interests are the life expectancy and life-span development of adaptive behaviors of people with mental retardation. Dr. Eyman has also been associated for more than 30 years with the research group at Lanterman Developmental Center, formerly Pacific State Hospital.